Learning and Knowledge Management
in the Firm

NEW HORIZONS IN THE ECONOMICS OF INNOVATION

General Editor: Christopher Freeman, *Emeritus Professor of Science Policy, SPRU – Science and Technology Policy Research, University of Sussex, UK*

Technical innovation is vital to the competitive performance of firms and of nations and for the sustained growth of the world economy. The economics of innovation is an area that has expanded dramatically in recent years and this major series, edited by one of the most distinguished scholars in the field, contributes to the debate and advances in research in this most important area.

The main emphasis is on the development and application of new ideas. The series provides a forum for original research in technology, innovation systems and management, industrial organization, technological collaboration, knowledge and innovation, research and development, evolutionary theory and industrial strategy. International in its approach, the series includes some of the best theoretical and empirical work from both well-established researchers and the new generation of scholars.

Titles in the series include:

The Emergence and Growth of Biotechnology
Experiences in Industrialised and Developing Countries
Rohini Acharya

Knowledge and Investment
The Sources of Innovation in Industry
Rinaldo Evangelista

Learning and Innovation in Economic Development
Linsu Kim

The Economics of Knowledge Production
Funding and the Structure of University Research
Aldo Geuna

Innovation and Research Policies
An International Comparative Analysis
Paul Diederen, Paul Stoneman, Otto Toivanen and Arjan Wolters

Learning and Knowledge Management in the Firm
From Knowledge Accumulation to Strategic Capabilities
Gabriela Dutrénit

Knowledge Spillovers and Economic Growth
Regional Growth Differentials across Europe
M.C.J. Caniëls

Successful Innovation
Towards a New Theory for the Management of Small and Medium Sized Enterprises
Jan Cobbenhagen

Firm Size, Innovation and Market Structure
The Evolution of Industry Concentration and Instability
Mariana Mazzucato

Trade Specialisation, Technology and Economic Growth
Theory and Evidence from Advanced Countries
Keld Laursen

Learning and Knowledge Management in the Firm

From Knowledge Accumulation to Strategic Capabilities

Gabriela Dutrénit

Professor of Economics, Economics Department and Master in Economics and Management of Technology, Metropolitan Autonomous University – Xochimilco, Mexico

NEW HORIZONS IN THE ECONOMICS OF INNOVATION

Edward Elgar

Cheltenham, UK • Northampton, MA, USA

Published by
Edward Elgar Publishing Limited
Glensanda House
Montpellier Parade
Cheltenham
Glos GL50 1UA
UK

Edward Elgar Publishing, Inc.
136 West Street
Suite 202
Northampton
Massachusetts 01060
USA

A catalogue record for this book
is available from the British Library

Library of Congress Cataloguing in Publication Data
Dutrénit, Gabriela, 1957–
      Learning and knowledge management in the firm : from knowledge
    accumulation to strategic capabilities / Gabriela Dutrénit.
      (New horizons in the economics of innovation)
      Includes bibliographical references.
      1. Organizational learning. 2. Knowledge management.
    3. Employees—Training of. 4. Employees—Effect of technological
    innovations on. 5. Glass container industry—Employees—Training of
    Case studies.   I. Title. II. Series.
    HD58.82.D87 2000
    658.4'038—dc21   99–41929
                                                                            CIP

ISBN 1 84064 204 1
Printed and bound in Great Britain by Bookcraft (Bath) Ltd.

Contents

v

List of Figures

List of Boxes

List of Tables

List of Abbreviations

AGCC	Anchor Glass Containers Corporation
AST Award	Adrián Sada Trevino Award
CATVE	Centro de Adiestramiento Técnico de Vitro Envases (Center of Technical Training of VGC)
CEO	Chief Executive Officer
DCL	Developing Countries Literature
Dirtec	Dirección de Tecnología (Direction of Technology of VGC)
Ditac	Dirección de Investigación Tecnológica y Ambiental Corporativa (Direction of Technology of the Vitro-Group from 1990)
FIC	Fomento de Industria y Comercio
INEGI	Instituto National de Estadística, Geografía e Informática
ISI	Import Substitution Industrialisation
IS machine	Individual Sections machine
NNPB	Narrow Neck Press Blow
SML	Strategic Management Literature
UIT	Unidad de Investigación Tecnológica (Unit of Technological Research of Fama)
VGC	Vitro-Glass Containers (The Glass Container Division of Vitro-Group, named 'Vitro Envases de Norteamérica')
Vitro-Basic Industries	The Basic Industries Division of Vitro-Group
Vitro-Glassware	The Glassware Division of Vitro-Group
Vitro-Group	Vitro S.A.
Vitro-Tec	R&D unit of Vitro S.A. during 1977–89.

Acknowledgements

This book originated as a Ph.D. thesis written at the Science and Policy Research Unit at the University of Sussex under the supervision of Martin Bell and Keith Pavitt. I sincerely thank my patient supervisors for providing insights, stimulating comments and sharp criticisms. This book has also been made possible by the support provided by different people and institutions.

I would like to acknowledge the contribution of many people at SPRU who helped me to design and carry out the research. In particular, discussions and friendship with Chris Freeman, Nick von Tunzelmann, Giovanni Dosi, Carlota Pérez, Mike Hobday, Pari Patel, as well as Jorge Katz from ECLA, were extremely useful at different stages of the research. Cynthia Little's editing work and friendship were also very helpful. Over the years, I have had the opportunity to share ideas, experiences and difficulties with many colleagues at Sussex; they are too many to mention, however I wish to thank especially Chaisung Lim, Amon Salter, Keith Sequeira, Orietta Marsili, Milady Parejo, Roselina Epifanio, Jeremy Hall, Luciana D'Adderio, Fatima Diniz, Mark Davis, Jonathan Sapsed, Andrea Principe, Carlos Montalvo and Arturo Torres.

In Mexico I would like to thank Kurt Unger and my colleagues of the Master in Economics and Management of Technological Change, in particular Mario Capdevielle, Mario Cimoli, Jaime Aboites, Daniel Villavicencio, Rigas Arvanitis, Juan Manuel Corona and Arturo Lara, with whom I had long disussions about the technological behaviour of Mexican firms. I wish to acknowledge the support received from my colleagues of the Economics and Business Administration Department, in particular Hilda Dávila, Cuauhtémoc Pérez, José Flores and Felipe Campuzano, and from the Social Sciences and Humanities Division of my University, the Autonomous Metropolitan University (campus Xochimilco). I would also like to acknowledge the financial support of the Mexican National Council of Science and Technology (CONACYT).

This book has been made possible by the support provided by Vitro S.A. – a Mexican industrial group, whom I wish to thank for being willing to open their doors. I am deeply grateful to many executives, technical staff and other personnel in the company that spent much of their time hunting through their records for relevant data. It is not possible to mention them all here, but special thanks go to Luis Rendón, Antonio Pita, Jaime Parada, Serse Gilberti, Luis Cárdenas, Faustino Villarreal, José Garibay, Gerardo Valero, Enrique Canales, Bill White and Mike Sopp. They are however not responsible for the content of the present book.

Finally I wish to thank my father, my sisters Silvia and Mónica and my brother-in-law- Martín for their unconditional support and love. I wish to especially thank my husband Alexandre Vera-Cruz , with whom I shared the experience of doing a Ph.D. at the same time. This generated a common understanding and insights about the behaviour of Mexican firms, and contributed greatly to the final result. My love goes to my children Matías and Paula Vera-Cruz who were very flexible to my time and encouraged me to get to the end of the road.

1 Introduction

Technological capability building is an issue that has been widely discussed in the last 20 years by two different theoretical traditions based on firm-level empirical research. The first is the tradition of research on technological capability accumulation in industrial firms in developing countries (see for instance Dahlman and Westphal, 1982; Bell, 1984; Westphal, Kim and Dahlman, 1985, Katz, 1986 and 1987; Lall, 1987 and 1992; Bell and Pavitt, 1995). This tradition has concentrated on the learning processes involved in building up a minimum base of essential knowledge to engage in innovative activity. It is centered on the technical dimensions of that stage of accumulation and particularly on the learning processes at the individual level. However it has paid inadequate attention to two issues: i) the organizational and managerial aspects of that stage of accumulation; and ii) the later stage of accumulation as firms approach the international technological frontier and seek to build the more complex and integrated knowledge bases needed to make strategic use of that knowledge.

The second tradition is the strategic management literature about building core/strategic capabilities or competencies in firms at the international frontier in advanced industrial countries (see for instance Prahalad and Hamel, 1990; Teece, Pisano and Shuen, 1990; Pavitt, 1991; Leonard-Barton, 1995a). This literature has given considerable attention to organizational issues, but with reference to knowledge management in maintaining and renewing strategic innovative capabilities that already exist. The authors are particularly interested in how to manage strategic knowledge assets to move from simple to complex knowledge bases to renew the strategic capabilities, considering that all the organizational units already have the minimum base of essential knowledge for innovation. Processes of organizational learning, coordination of learning and knowledge integration have become important issues. However this body of literature has given little attention to how those strategic capabilities were initially accumulated.

Neither body of literature provides a very useful explanation on what has been going on over the last 10–20 years in the case of Vitro-Glass Containers.

1

Vitro-Glass Containers is a division of Vitro,[1] one of the few Mexican 'star Groups' that was able to achieve international success in a context of protected markets. Vitro is one of the main players at world level in several activities, such as glass containers, and became a multinational corporation in the 1960s.

Vitro-Glass Containers has built innovative technological capabilities in several technical-functions and has created different simple knowledge bases. It has been able to undertake activities in each technical-function that match with different stages of technological capability accumulation according to the taxonomies of Lall (1992) and Bell and Pavitt (1995). Many activities required to integrate different knowledge bases located in different organizational units as analyzed by Prahalad and Hammel (1990), Leonard-Barton (1995a) and Iansiti and Clark (1994). Vitro-Glass Containers has also implemented several organizational arrangements to promote learning processes at individual and organizational levels. However nearly 100 years after start-up Vitro-Glass Containers is still missing strategic capabilities. There was a long period from 1910 until 1970 spent building the minimum essential knowledge base. In the 1970s the firm started shifting beyond that and began a Transition Process towards building strategic capabilities. However even 25 years after starting that Transition Process, it has not been completed. Vitro-Glass Containers has built embryonic strategic capabilities but has failed to build the strategic capabilities to distinguish the firm competitively. The firm experienced difficulties in socializing the learning process at organizational level, coordinating different learning strategies pursued by different organizational units and in integrating knowledge across organizational boundaries.

The problems experienced by Vitro-Glass Containers generated needs for more explicit knowledge management oriented to supporting the identification and creation of the primary strategic capabilities rather than towards nurturing and renewing already built strategic/core capabilities. The differences in the learning processes across organizational boundaries highlighted the problem of integrating different stocks of knowledge and the importance of the organizational dimension in the technological accumulation process.

The central argument of this book is that there is no simple linear progress from the early stage of accumulation of the minimum levels of innovative capability to the management of knowledge as a strategic asset. Instead there is a complex Transition Process as firms build embryonic strategic capabilities on top of those minimum levels, and then stretch beyond these to develop strategic capabilities. As firms make this transition they have to build up deeper and broader stocks of knowledge and develop new types of knowledge

---

[1]   The group 'Vitro SA' is called here either Vitro or Vitro-Group, and 'Vitro Envases de Norteamérica' is called here Vitro-Glass Containers.

management. This Transition Process is a barely explored issue between the two theoretical traditions mentioned above.

This book addresses the following questions:

1. What are the characteristics of the long term process of technological capability building in late industrializing firms and what are the key issues of knowledge management in each stage of that process?
2. More specifically: What are the problems of the Transition Process? Why was the firm able to build innovative capabilities but not a set of strategic capabilities?
    2.1. To what extent was individual learning converted into organizational learning?
    2.2. To what extent was knowledge integrated across organizational boundaries?
3. What are the factors that influenced these and other features of knowledge management during the Transition Process?

The analysis of Vitro-Glass Containers shows that several features of the firm's approach to knowledge management affected that truncated transition.

1. *Limited efforts to convert individual learning into organizational learning.* The firm established many organizational arrangements to strengthen learning activities, however the accent was put on supporting individual learning rather than on the conversion from individual learning into learning at the organizational level. In addition the organizational arrangements established to facilitate that conversion have not worked, revealing that Vitro-Glass Containers had difficulties in changing its ways of doing things. Therefore there were failures in the sharing of tacit knowledge and the knowledge basically remained at the level at which it was acquired: individual, group or plant level. Knowledge also remained essentially as tacit, indeed little effort was put on codifying potentially codifiable tacit knowledge.
2. *Different learning strategies pursued by the firm and a limited coordination of learning.* Different organizational units pursued different learning strategies and learned at different speeds. Hence they created and accumulated knowledge of a different nature and depth. The coordination between those strategies was limited.
3. *Limited knowledge integration.* Vitro-Glass Containers experienced difficulties in integrating the knowledge internally across business function, plant and department; it also found it difficult to integrate knowledge with other divisions of the Vitro-Group to look for potential

synergy. The bridges between units to facilitate knowledge integration were indeed very weak.

4. *Instability of the knowledge creation process.* Vitro-Glass Containers accumulated knowledge in certain areas and it also built a number of embryonic strategic capabilities. However the directions of the knowledge accumulation and the intensity of the efforts to create knowledge in each area changed several times, which affected the gradual accumulation in any of them.

Two broader issues underlying those features of knowledge management were identified.

1. *The failure to consider the firm's knowledge as a system.* Vitro-Glass Containers lacked a systemic view to articulate mechanisms, organizational arrangements and on-going learning processes within the firm. The lack of interrelatedness occurred at the level of the organizational units, which worked quite independently of each other. The firm also did not take into account either the differences in the knowledge depths and learning strategies by different organizational units or the differences between the individual and organizational dimensions of the learning processes. The firm carried out a management of knowledge, but this was incipient and disconnected.

2. *The instability of the firm's dual technology strategy.* Vitro-Glass Containers pursued two technology strategies in parallel. It sought to rely on its innovative technological capabilities to be at the international technological frontier in some areas. At the same time it pursued a fast follower strategy. Both strategies were supported by decisions taken by the top management and received organizational support. However the organizational support for each strategy was unstable over the whole period, which affected the aims and efforts to manage the company's knowledge.

The problems described here are certainly not exclusive to Vitro-Glass Containers. They can be found in several Latin American firms that are world-level players. Certain problems are specific to the developing country context, others are most certainly related to the culture of the firm. However others are referred to in the literature on knowledge management about the largest and most innovative companies in the world. Firms like Vitro-Glass Containers are in transition from the type of problems of the learning processes analyzed in the literature on developing countries to the type of problems analyzed in the strategic management literature about the most innovative firms. Neither of those bodies of literature individually provides very useful explanations or insights to help analyze and overcome that Transition Process. The aspects of the Transition Process analyzed in this book should be much better understood if the insights of research on strategic management in advanced industrial countries, or technological learning in developing countries, are to be useful for firms at late stages of 'catching up'.

The research is based on a firm-level case study of a Mexican firm: Vitro-Glass Containers, in a mature industrial sector: glass containers. Data were gathered at plant, division and corporate level through direct observation, interviews and records. Several plants and organizational units of the firm located both in Mexico and the US were included in the case study.

This book uses a particular focus to analyze the process of technological capability building. The research has looked at the problems that limited the building of strategic capabilities rather than stressing the positive things that the firm did as is the focus of the strategic management literature. Therefore the research looked at the negative aspects of the firm's behavior to identify the difficulties encountered in converting individual into organizational learning, coordinating learning, integrating knowledge and creating knowledge, and thus identify the reasons why strategic capabilities were not built. This allows identification of the problems which the firm must overcome in order to be able to compete on the bases of knowledge. The firm also had positive aspects which were considered but were emphasized less in this book.

This book is based on a detailed case-study of the internal organizational characteristics and behaviors of the firm. Little attention was paid to the effect of the environment on firm's behavior. The relationship between micro, meso and macro levels is not systematically explored. However it is evident that they had considerable importance. For instance, the instability of the firm's dual technology strategy which influenced several aspects of knowledge management in the firm was itself influenced by patterns of competition in the glass container industry and by changes in the firm's macroeconomic policy context in Mexico.

This book is organized in three parts. Following this introduction, Part I contains a review of the literature, and the analytical framework of this book on which the discussion of the case study draws. Chapter 2 reviews literature related to the technological capability building, and concentrates on the broader aspects of that process. As mentioned above, this process has been examined from two points of view that are reviewed here. First, the literature on developing countries examines the long term process of building the minimum essential technological capabilities to survive in the market. Second, the strategic management literature examines the process of maintaining and renewing core capabilities to be able to maintain technological advantages. The analytical framework for the analysis of technological capabilities is presented at the end of the chapter. Chapter 3 reviews the strategic management literature in more detail, focusing on a number of knowledge management issues, particularly the role of the conversion of individual into organizational learning, the coordination of learning and knowledge integration in building strategic capabilities. The analytical framework for the analysis of knowledge management and the conceptual design of this book is presented at the end of the chapter. This Part I also includes the methodology adopted to conduct the case study, which is described in Chapter 4. Finally Chapter 5 presents an overview of the technological trends in the glass container industry, summarizes the main characteristics of the Mexican and US markets and outlines the case study firm.

Part II contains an analytical narrative of the capability building process of Vitro-Glass Containers. Chapter 6 describes how the firm built the minimum essential knowledge base from 1909 to 1970; Chapter 7 presents how the firm evolved, but not very effectively, towards building strategic capabilities and describes the problems of making the Transition Process between 1970 and 1990; and Chapter 8 describes some problems encountered in a changing economic and technological environment which further hampered the Transition Process.

Part III draws upon the analytical narrative and the analytical framework of this book to discuss the problems in knowledge management underlying the truncated Transition Process. Chapter 9 examines the main characteristics of the conversion of individual into organizational learning, the coordination of the learning strategies, the integration of knowledge and the knowledge creation process in Vitro-Glass Containers and discusses to what extent they explain the failure to build strategic capabilities to distinguish the firm competitively and complete the Transition Process. Chapter 10 discusses two factors that influenced the key features of knowledge management in the firm, the failure to consider the firm's knowledge as a system and the instability of the firm's dual technology strategy, and analyses to what extent they contribute to explain the difficulties in building strategic capabilities.

Finally, Chapter 11 summarizes the main features of the knowledge management that contribute to explain the truncated Transition Process of Vitro-Glass Containers. It also presents a number of more general issues related to the case study and suggestions for future research.

PART ONE

Theoretical and Contextual Background

2 Building Technological Capabilities in Different Theoretical Traditions

2.1 INTRODUCTION

This book addresses two issues: (i) the long term process of building up technological capabilities; (ii) knowledge management in a large firm which is undergoing a Transition Process towards competing at the technological frontier, but is still behind that frontier.

The first issue has been the focus of attention of the literature about learning and technological accumulation in developing countries's firms (DCL), and has also been addressed by the Strategic Management Literature (SML) about building core capabilities in firms at the international frontier in advanced industrial countries. The second issue, knowledge management, as part of that process of building technological capabilities, recently became a very relevant issue and has been examined in detail by the SML, based on the experience of the most innovative firms in the most technologically dynamic industries. Therefore this book is drawing on two different theoretical traditions based on firm-level empirical research: (i) the field of learning and technological accumulation in DCL, and (ii) the SML, and particularly that literature more related to knowledge management in maintaining and renewing core capabilities.

This chapter reviews the DCL and SML in relation to the long term process of building up technological capabilities, and concentrates on the broader aspects of that process. Chapter 3 reviews SML related to a number of knowledge management issues as a specific part of that process.

Section 2.2 reviews the DCL regarding building technological capabilities and indicates the limited empirical treatment of the links between technological knowledge and organizational factors, and of the specific problems confronting firms that are undertaking a Transition Process towards being able to compete at the technological frontier. Section 2.3 reviews the SML concerned with maintaining and renewing core capabilities/competencies in the most innovative firms. It indicates the limited insights into how to build the first core capabilities/competencies. Section 2.4 presents the analytical framework that is used in this book for the analysis of technological capabilities.

2.2 TECHNOLOGICAL CAPABILITY BUILDING IN DEVELOPING COUNTRIES LITERATURE

This section reviews the DCL about technological capabilities, describes the emergence of this concept, the focus on technological knowledge and the taxonomy developed. The aim is to reveal that this DCL contains a limited empirical treatment of the links between technological knowledge and organizational factors, and a limited treatment of the specific problems confronting firms that are undertaking a Transition Process towards competing at the technological frontier.

2.2.1 The Emergence of the Concept of Technological Capabilities

Building up technological capabilities has been the focus of attention in the DCL in the last 20 years. Technological capability was defined in the early 1980s as 'the ability to make effective use of technological knowledge ... It inheres not in the knowledge that is possessed but in the use of that knowledge and in the proficiency of its use in production, investment and innovation' (Westphal, Kim and Dahlman, 1985:171). This concept was interchangeable with other concepts that referred to the same idea, such as technological effort (Dahlman and Westphal, 1982; Lall, 1987) or technological capacity (Bell, 1984; Scott-Kemmis and Bell, 1985; Katz, 1986 and 1987). Later on the concept of technological capabilities became more widely used.

From very early times the concept of technological capabilities has referred to a stock of technological knowledge as well as the use of that knowledge, which is an organizational dimension. The organizational/institutional dimension is more clearly stated by Bell and Pavitt (1995:71) when they referred to technological capabilities as the 'domestic capabilities to generate and manage change in technologies used in production, and these capabilities are based largely on specialized resources ... [which] need to be accumulated through deliberate investment – a management problem'. The focus on technological capabilities to generate and manage changes emerged in the context of maintaining competitiveness in a changing environment (Bell and Pavitt, 1995:76).

Firms build technological capabilities through learning processes, so technological learning refers to the dynamic process of acquiring technological capabilities. Firms learn over time, accumulate technological knowledge, and can progressively undertake new activities and acquire new capabilities.

One of the main concerns of the DCL was to illustrate at the firm level that there had been an 'indigenous technological effort' which had resulted in the accumulation of technological capabilities.

2.2.2 Focus on Technological Knowledge

In general the focus of the DCL has been on the learning processes to establish a base of technological knowledge that did not previously exist, as opposed to renewing a base of knowledge already accumulated or to using that knowledge base in a different way. The various authors analyze how firms move from having the abilities to operate plants to being able to undertake innovation activities. The ultimate achievement is to be a 'technologically mature firm' with the ability to 'identify a firm's scope for efficient specialization in technological activities, to extend and deepen these with experience and effort, and to draw selectively on others to complement its own capabilities' (Lall, 1993:268–9). Bell, Ross-Larson and Westphal (1984:107) observed that the majority of 'infant industries' from developing countries never achieve maturity because of their failure to build up adequate technological capabilities.

In addition, the idea that firms lack the basic technological knowledge explains the focus on the analysis of the acquisition of technological capabilities, defined as the ability to develop different types of technological activities, and not on the building of technological competencies in specific knowledge fields or disciplines, as highlighted in the case of the SML in Section 2.3.

2.2.3 Taxonomy of Technological Capabilities

However 'before full "maturity" is achieved, firms vary in their mastery of the various functions involved' (Lall, 1993:269), so it is possible to identify stages. Lall (1992), based on the idea that technological capabilities are the mastery of technological activities, and drawing on Dahlman and Westphal (1982), Katz (1984), Dahlman, Ross-Larson and Westphal (1987) and Lall (1987), presents a taxonomy of technological capabilities based on the major firm-level technological capabilities by technical-function. The technical-functions cover the main technological activities. Different degrees of maturity of those capabilities are also presented, which are measured by the type of activity undertaken in each technical-function.

Bell and Pavitt (1995:83–8) developed Lall's framework of technological capabilities. The columns set out the main technological capabilities by technical-function. Investment activities refer to generating technical change and managing its implementation during large investment projects; they include activities related to both decision-making and control, and preparation and implementation of projects. Production activities refer to generating and managing technical change in processes and production organization, and in products. In addition there are two supportive technical-functions: developing linkages and interaction with firms and institutions, and producing capital goods.

The rows set out the main technological capabilities by degree of difficulty as measured by the type of activity from which the technological capability arises. The distinction between routine production capabilities and innovative technological capabilities is a key issue, based on the distinction between 'the kind of knowledge and skills required to operate given production systems, and the kind of knowledge required to change them' (Bell and Pavitt, 1993:165). The routine production capabilities are an 'inner core' already accumulated (Lall, 1987:231) and required to be in the market, but firms can also build different 'depths' of innovative technological capabilities. The taxonomy includes four stages of accumulation of technological capabilities: routine production capabilities, and three 'depths' or levels of innovative technological capabilities. 'A basic level of capabilities may permit only relatively minor and incremental contributions to change, but at the intermediate and advanced levels, technological capabilities may result in more substantial, novel, and ambitious contributions to change' (Bell and Pavitt, 1995:83).

It is recognized that it is neither possible to judge whether a particular technical-function is simple or complex nor whether the stages show a necessary sequence of learning. Lall (1993:267) pointed out that 'though the very nature of technological learning ... would seem to dictate that mastery would proceed from simpler to more difficult activities, different firms and different technologies adopt different sequences', therefore the table does not show a necessary sequence of learning. In the same sense, Bell and Pavitt (1995:88–9) referred to the limitations of conceiving technological accumulation in terms of broad stages and the need to open the research about strategies for accumulating technologies at the firm level. They pointed out that firm-level, industry-level and country-level differences can determine a wide variation in the rate of accumulation and the level of sophistication of the activities developed by functional areas. Despite these assertions, the table reveals an idea of sequence, and the limitations of such an approach are not further developed.

In addition Lall (1987:17) recognized that the 'classification has dealt with strictly technical aspects of an enterprise. However organizational capabilities have to accompany technological ones'. Even though both the technological and organizational/institutional factors are recognized as part of the technological capabilities, the interaction between both dimensions is a key issue hardly treated in that literature. Most of the work is focused on the accumulation of technological knowledge, which is only the technical knowledge dimension of the accumulation of technological capabilities.

2.2.4 Empirical Work

There is a growing empirical literature on technological capabilities. Some representative studies of the issues highlighted in this section are briefly reviewed below.

Two large projects were the basis of the evolution of the framework about technological capabilities in the DCL. One was the Research Program in Science and Technology of IDB/ECLA[1] directed by Jorge Katz. This included comparative research at the firm-level of metalworking industries from six Latin American countries. The results are partly summarized in Katz (1986 and 1987). The other was the research project on 'The acquisition of technological capability', financed by the World Bank and directed by Carl Dahlman and Larry Westphal. This project, drawing on the former, covered a number of firm-level studies from four developing countries: India, South Korea, Brazil and Mexico. The results are partly summarized in Dahlman and Westphal (1982), Westphal, Kim and Dahlman (1985) and Lall (1987), and more conceptually in Dahlman, Ross-Larsen and Westphal (1987). Both projects shared common grounds and countries.

In the case of the firm-level studies of Latin American firms, although differences by type of firm, nature of the production process and market structure were found (Katz, 1986:244–75), the focus was on demonstrating that firms learned and built technological capabilities. They were able to assimilate the technology transferred from advanced industrial countries and generate improvements to that technology. Some cases even exported technology, as in the case of Usiminas described by Dahlman and Fonseca (1987) and the exports of industrial plants from Argentina analyzed by Katz and Ablin (1978).

These studies generated a tradition of looking at firm-level and a huge body of research based on case-study methodology has sought to identify the key characteristics of the learning processes, technology transfer processes, and factors that stimulate and hamper innovations. (See for instance Villavicencio, 1990; Villavicencio and Arvanitis, 1994; Pirela et al. 1991; Pirela, 1996; Unger, 1985).

The studies of India by Lall (1987) and Korea by Westphal, Kim and Dahlman (1985), originally related to the project directed by Dahlman

---

[1] IDB is the Inter-American Development Bank and ECLA is the UN Economic Commission for Latin America.

and Westphal and using the same framework, contributed to enrichment of the conceptualization of technological capabilities in the DCL. The research of Scott-Kemmis and Bell (1985) in Thailand has also contributed to identify key characteristics of the learning processes and key issues of the process of building technological capabilities in developing countries.

After the two large projects, the research in Latin America was mainly pointed in two directions: (i) identifying the sources of competitiveness of Latin American industries confronting the new economic environment (see for instance Unger, 1994; Casar, 1989; Clavijo and Casar, 1994; Katz, 1996; Capdevielle, Cimoli and Dutrénit, 1997); and (ii) analyzing the characteristics of the National System of Innovation (see for instance Katz and Bercovich, 1993; Dahlman and Frischtak, 1993; and also Kim, 1993 about the Korean case) and the role of some features of the Import Substitution Industrialization that hamper or stimulate competitiveness (see for instance Pérez, 1992 and 1996; Fajnzylber, 1990 and 1991; Corona, Dutrénit and Hernández, 1994; Casalet, 1994; Lara, 1994; Aboites and Soria, 1999; Tirado, 1994; Vera-Cruz, Villa Soto and Villegas de Gante, 1994; and also Kim, 1997b about the Korean case). Several of these studies were conducted in order to identify differences between industries and between types of firms in terms of level of accumulation of technological capabilities, business and technology strategies, structure of linkages and industrial policies required to support their competitiveness (see for instance Katz, 1996; Dutrénit and Capdevielle, 1993; Unger, 1994; Pirela et al. 1991 and 1993). However, there is no empirical treatment of firm-level studies of the problems that confront firms, that are in a Transition Process towards competing at the technological frontier, in going beyond the level already achieved. Neither have those studies analyzed the links between the technological and organizational dimensions of technological capability building

The research into the process of catching up by the newly industrializing countries in East Asia describes the stages from acquiring foreign technology to building increasingly more innovative technological capabilities and catching up (see for instance Hobday, 1995; Kim, 1997b; Kim, Lee and Lee, 1987; Amsden, 1989; Enos and Park, 1988; Nakaoka, 1993). For example, Hobday (1995) describes how firms from Taiwan learned and moved along three stages, from being original equipment manufacturers, to producing their own designs, and finally to creating their own brands. He focuses on the specific strategies used by firms to progressively assimilate foreign technology in order to develop design capabilities, to catch up and also leapfrog competitors at international level, as in the case of Singapore. Nakaoka (1993) describes successful cases of capital good firms that acquired technological capabilities by stages in Korea, Taiwan and Japan. He emphasizes the role of the domestic market and the strategy related to the world market in the learning process. Enos and Park (1988) and Amsden (1989) focused on the accumulation of engineering capabilities based on skilled human resources. In general most of these authors analyze the deliberate technology strategy followed by these firms to sequence the learning activities, and the role of the government in supporting that process. The successful cases clearly considered learning to be a costly and time consuming process that requires a deliberate strategy to acquire technological capabilities, as defined by Bell (1984:190). The description has followed basically the tradition of the DCL. In general the authors focused on the accumulation of stocks of technological knowledge, and much less on the process of specialization of knowledge bases, the integration of knowledge across organizational boundaries and other organizational issues that certainly contributed to that success.

In contrast Kim (1995, 1997a) introduced a new framework to analyze the process of building capabilities by Korean firms. In the description of how Hyundai and Samsung sequenced their learning processes in stages until they caught up, he gives greater attention to the role of organizational factors in the process of knowledge creation. Firms not only followed a deliberate and persistent technology strategy, which gradually changed as the firm acquired technological capabilities from a creative imitation to innovation, they implemented an active 'management of dynamic learning' or knowledge management. This included specific mechanisms to manage tacit and codified knowledge and convert individual into organizational learning, which were different at each stage of the acquisition of technological capabilities. The learning process was managed in such a way that different internal components of the knowledge system were articulated to strengthen the knowledge building process.

However in his book, Kim (1997b) tried to stress that 'successful technological learning ... requires an effective national innovation system' (1997:219). The driving forces of this process were basically external, only crisis construction was defined as an internal driving force. The description presented in the case studies (Kim, 1997b:105–89) and the implications for corporate management (1997b:229) showed that firms not only implemented a 'crisis construction' to expedite technological learning, they also carried out an active management of knowledge that changed according to the stage of accumulation. However the focus on the national innovation system conducted him to stress that the building of technological capabilities at the firm-level depended basically on external conditions. 'Crisis construction' without the type of knowledge management conducted by those firms probably did not yield the same result; neither would the external conditions have contributed to catch up without the specific mechanisms used by those firms and the features of dynamic firms that he describes (Kim, 1997b:233). But those issues were not brought into the conclusions about the characteristics of the process of acquiring technological capabilities.

The focus of attention on firms from catching up countries explains Kim's concern for analyzing the process of creation of new knowledge at international level, instead of the concern for using the existing knowledge that distinguishes most of the DCL. This concern is revealed in his definition of technological capabilities as 'the ability to make effective use of technological knowledge to assimilate, use, adapt, and change existing technologies. It also enables one to create new technologies and to develop new products and processes in response to the changing economic environment' (Kim, 1997a:86). The definition of technological capabilities to include the capacity to assimilate existing knowledge and the capacity to create new knowledge is much closer to the focus of the strategic management literature about technological capabilities than the definitions used by other DCL.

Apart from the works already mentioned, there are several others studies that cover different issues of the process of acquiring technological capabilities (see for instance Enos and Park, 1988; Enos, 1991; Pack 1992; Fransman and King, 1984; Fransman, 1986; Herbert-Copley, 1990), but few studies underline the importance of managerial and organizational issues in that process. Between these studies, Tremblay (1994) analyzes the wider aspects of organization and management in the study of the relationship between technological capability and productivity performance of Indian firms.

Even though the firm-level works cover a broad range of industries, there are no studies concerning the building of technological capabilities in the glass container industry in developing countries. This book presents evidence of the process of building technological capabilities by a firm in this industry.

This review of the DCL suggests the following conclusions:

1. It contains basically an empirical/descriptive story of the capability building process and a taxonomic treatment of the material.
2. It is difficult to classify firms by stages because firms undertake activities of different innovative nature by technical-function. Even within the same technical-function, there are different levels between different organizational units of a firm, as analyzed in Chapter 9. Therefore, How can it be said that a firm has advanced innovative technological capabilities if it presents different stages in a number of different technical-functions? What activities are critical to building the knowledge base and to classifying firms by stages? Which technological capabilities are critical in those taxonomies?
3. The DCL is mainly concerned with the building of the minimum essential knowledge base to survive in the market, which requires the building of innovative technological capabilities. Less attention has been put on the specific problems confronting firms that are undertaking a Transition Process towards competing at the technological

frontier. Those firms have accumulated the minimum essential knowledge base, have acquired advanced innovative technological capabilities in certain technical-functions and specific fields, and probably have different types of problems from firms that are only building basic and intermediate innovative technological capabilities. This is an issue not addressed by the DCL but which is examined in this book.

4. The focus of the DCL has been on technological learning and on the accumulation of technological knowledge rather than on the interaction between technological and organizational factors. However certain organizational/institutional factors affect the creation of technological knowledge. Therefore the focus on the accumulation of technological knowledge is narrow in order to analyze the process of building technological capabilities. The practices, behavior and some features of the knowledge management are also a stock that should be renewed to contribute to that process. Some points remain unclear in that literature, What are the necessary internal conditions for learning? What, how, and how much to learn? How the capabilities that matter might be built? Even though organizational/institutional factors are said to be important in building technological capabilities, few studies have actually examined their interaction with the accumulation of technological knowledge. Kim (1995, 1997a, 1997b) is the unique clear work in this area. It is the aim of the present book to analyze this issue.

2.3 RE-BUILDING CORE CAPABILITIES IN THE STRATEGIC MANAGEMENT LITERATURE

This section reviews the Strategic Management Literature concerned with maintaining, nurturing and renewing core capabilities/competencies by the most innovative firms. Special attention is put on three issues: (i) the different concepts that the SML uses to approach the re-building or renewing of a distinctive capability to compete; (ii) the fact that this literature analyzes firms that have already accumulated a significant base of knowledge; and (iii) the fact that its focus is on both technological knowledge and organizational issues. The aim is to indicate the limited insights into how to build the primary core/strategic/distinctive capabilities or competencies.

2.3.1 Core, Strategic or Distinctive Competencies/capabilities

In recent decades dramatic changes have occurred in technology, economy, and the organization of production and management that have challenged the basis of competitive advantage of the most innovative firms. Academic researchers and management consultants have produced a significant amount of literature examining how firms can align themselves to those changes and maintain a competitive advantage. They share the idea that firms compete on the basis of distinctive competencies, capabilities or routines that are accumulated over time (see for instance Nelson and Winter, 1982, Prahalad and Hamel, 1990; Teece, Pisano and Shuen, 1990; Pavitt, 1991; Leonard-Barton, 1992a and 1995a). This literature is based on firm-level research and is built up on the idea of Penrose (1959) that firms are a bundle of resources, and Polanyi's work about tacit knowledge (1962). This has opened up a new way of thinking about strategic management linked to the resource-based approach.

There is a common idea in this SML that knowledge allows the creation of capabilities and those capabilities determine the ability to do things. Knowledge and knowledge-creating activities are the basis on which to create, sustain and re-build technological capabilities (see for instance Leonard-Barton, 1992a; Dosi and Marengo, 1993; Prahalad and Hamel, 1990; Teece, Pisano and Shuen, 1990).

Some of that knowledge is essential simply to survive or to achieve parity with the competition, as asserted by Leonard-Barton (1995a:xi). Other assets of knowledge are strategic in the sense that no ready market exists for them (Teece and Pisano, 1994:541) and they differentiate a company strategically (Leonard-Barton, 1992a:111). These assets of knowledge determine the core capabilities or competencies which, in turn, determine the ability to survive, adapt and compete in a changing environment.

The center of attention of this SML is the world's largest firms that compete at the technological frontier – organizations that have already accumulated a significant base of knowledge and have built distinctive or core competencies/ capabilities and compete on the basis of technological advantage. In this context the authors are interested in how firms can maintain, nurture and renew distinctive or core capabilities to respond to shifts in the business and technological environment. In this sense when this SML refers to building core capabilities it has in mind the re-building of core capabilities as opposed to building the 'first' or primary core capabilities, or in other words the firm's initial stocks of core capabilities.

Nelson and Winter (1982) developed a more theoretical treatment of the firm-specific or distinctive competencies. Based on the work of Simon (1959) on bounded rationality, and the idea of March and Simon (1958) about the routinized behavior of organizations, they defined a firm as a repository of knowledge, dependent on the firm's past history. The firm stores the knowledge generated by learning in organizational routines (Nelson and Winter, 1982:99). Routines refer to the regular and predictable aspects of a firm's behavior (Nelson and Winter, 1982:14), they are relatively simple decision rules and procedures used to guide actions in a context of bounded rationality. The knowledge embedded in routines cannot be fully captured in codified form, it has a tacit dimension. As Nelson and Winter (1982:134) pointed out, 'much of the knowledge that underlies the effective performance is tacit knowledge of the organization, not consciously known or articulable by anyone in particular'. Several routines are seen as the source of distinctiveness and therefore of competitiveness of firms.[2]

Prahalad and Hamel (1990) introduced the notion of core competencies as the source of a firm's advantage in a changing environment and so as a key issue of the corporate strategy. They asserted that 'the real sources of advantage are to be found in management's ability to consolidate corporate-wide technologies and production skills into competencies that empower individual businesses to adapt quickly to changing opportunities' (Prahalad and Hamel, 1990:81). Core competencies are not only a bundle of skills and technologies, they include the integration of technologies and coordination of production skills in a distinctive way. They pointed out that 'core competencies are the collective learning in the organization, especially how to coordinate diverse production skills and integrate multiple streams of technologies' (Prahalad and Hamel, 1990:82). They require organizational arrangements to integrate the knowledge, to organize the work and to share understandings and work across organizational boundaries. Corporate managers play an important role in building core competencies. Therefore core competencies are based on technological and organizational dimensions. The pattern of internal coordination and learning is difficult for competitors to imitate, so it has a tacit component. They define competencies at two levels, as a set of technological fields (e.g. optic/media in Phillips and optic/imaging and microprocessors controls in Canon) or as a functional capacity, a capacity to do something (e.g. the capacity to miniaturize in Sony and Casio). Even though the organizational dimension is considered in the analysis, the empirical definitions of core competencies are essentially based on the technological dimension.

Patel and Pavitt (1994) discussed the concept of core competencies proposed by Prahalad and Hamel from the point of view that large firms are typically active in many technical fields and 'firms have substantial technological competencies outside what would appear to be their core areas' (Patel and Pavitt, 1994:7). This introduced difficulties in defining the firm's technology strategy to build core competencies. They found that large firms require to maintain some in-house competencies in background technologies to interact with suppliers and customers, and also to develop complex products in the

---

[2]   According to other authors, routines also generate rigidities and could contribute to hamper the re-building of core capabilities. This issue is referred to in Section 3.2.

future which require the integration of different knowledge bases (Patel and Pavitt, 1994:18-24). Therefore a broad range of technological competencies should be built to maintain and renew competitive advantages. Along the same lines, Leonard-Barton (1995a:4) defined three types of technological capabilities that contribute to creating a sustainable advantage: core, enabling and supplemental technological capabilities. Core technological capabilities are those capabilities that distinguish the firm competitively; enabling capabilities are those capabilities which do not give a particular competitive advantage but are necessary to a company as a minimum basis for meeting the competition, such as world-class quality in manufacturing; and supplemental capabilities only add value to core capabilities but could be imitated. The enabling capabilities can be compared with the innovative technological capabilities analyzed by the DCL, as described in Section 2.2.

Teece, Pisano and Shuen (1990) elaborated the basis of the dynamic capabilities perspective, later developed by several authors (see for instance Teece and Pisano, 1994, Teece et al., 1994; Iansiti and Clark, 1994; Leonard-Barton, 1992a, 1992b and 1995a; Dosi and Marengo, 1993). Building upon the resource-based approach, this perspective has stressed both the dynamic dimension of the capability building process and the role of organizational capabilities in that process. These authors stress the mechanisms by which firms accumulate and dissipate new skills and capabilities and the forces that limit the rate and direction of that process, more than the bundle of re-sources *per se* and the strategies for exploiting existing firm-specific resources emphasized by the resource-based approach.

A competence or a capability is seen by this perspective as a firm's ability to solve both technical and organizational problems. A firm's core/distinctive competence is defined by Teece et al. (1994:18) as 'a set of differentiated technological skills, complementary assets, and organizational routines and capacities that provide the basis for a firm's competitive capacities in one or more businesses'. 'These people are good at X activity' summarizes the idea.

A distinctive competence has to be a difficult-to-replicate or difficult-to-imitate competence or capability (Teece and Pisano, 1994:541). Such a capability is based on routines which, as in Nelson and Winter (1982), involve a strong tacit dimension that often cannot be readily articulated. Therefore routines are the basis of the firm's distinctiveness. As Teece, Pisano and Shuen (1990:20) have asserted, 'it is the routines themselves, and the ability of management to call upon the organization to perform them, that represents firms' business capability'. There is not a market for those distinctive competencies, they cannot be bought, therefore they must be built (Teece and Pisano, 1994:541).

The dynamic focus of this perspective is based on stressing the importance of continually developing new capabilities as well as exploiting old ones in the context of a shifting environment. Dynamic capabilities are defined by Teece and Pisano (1994:541) as 'the subset of the competencies/capabilities which allow the firm to create new products and processes, and respond to changing market circumstances'.

Based on the idea that knowledge is the foundation of capability and problem solving is the basic unit of knowledge creation (Dosi and Marengo, 1993), problem solving is considered the primary driver of the generation of new capability (Iansiti and Clark, 1994:559). For this reason the more empirical works are based on the analysis of problem solving during new products development (see for instance Clark and Fujimoto, 1991; Iansiti and Clark, 1994; Iansiti, 1998; Nonaka and Takeuchi, 1995). Pisano (1997) uses a similar approach to analyze the new process development.

Coming from an organizational learning perspective, Cohen and Levinthal (1990) elaborated a different perspective on firm-specific competencies. They pointed out that firms develop an 'absorptive capacity', an ability to absorb existent external knowledge and in turn generate new knowledge. The absorptive capacity depends on two elements: i) prior knowledge, which confers the ability to recognize the value of new information, assimilate it and apply it to commercial ends; and ii) intensity of effort, which is related to internal organizational mechanisms to develop an effective absorptive capacity (Cohen and Levinthal, 1990:128-31). Therefore the organization needs a significant base of knowledge to be able to use, assimilate and create new knowledge. Moreover the absorptive capacity is an organizational capability related to a specific knowledge base, as Cohen and Levinthal (1990:148) pointed out, the 'absorptive capacity tends to be specific to a field or knowledge domain'. The critical component of the absorptive capacity is firm-specific and therefore cannot be bought and quickly integrated into the firm (Cohen and Levinthal, 1990:135). As Nelson and Winter (1982) asserted, much of the detailed knowledge of organizational routines is tacit, so it is acquired only through experience. In this sense the absorptive capacity needs to be internally developed.

Even though the SML uses a number of concepts, many of them are alike. For instance, as Teece, Pisano and Shuen (1990:29) pointed out, 'core competencies, as raised by Prahalad and Hamel, are identical to our concept of capabilities/resources'. Moreover as Dodgson (1993:383) pointed out, routines (Nelson and Winter 1982), core competencies (Prahalad and Hamel, 1990), firm-specific capabilities (Teece, Pisano and Shuen, 1990), firm-specific competencies (Pavitt 1991), core technological capabilities (Leonard-Barton, 1992b and 1995a), and the absorptive capacity (Cohen and Levinthal, 1989 and 1990) are alike approaches. They use different concepts to express a common idea: the 'uniqueness of firms's knowledge and learning', which has a strong tacit component. While codified knowledge, which includes words, books, technical specifications, designs, equipment, software, log-books, patents, etc. is easy to acquire by competitors; tacit knowledge is acquired by individuals through experience and cannot be codified. Hence tacit knowledge is unique, is difficult to imitate or to copy and so is the source of distinctiveness. Therefore tacit knowledge is the base of the core capabilities/competencies of firms.

In this literature there is a theoretical discussion behind the stress on tacit knowledge as the source of competitiveness. These authors are discussing firms as repositories of knowledge instead of information processors. At the base of the approach of the firm as an information processor (see for instance Coase, 1937; Alchian and Demsetz, 1972; Williamson, 1985) is the perception that all knowledge is codifiable, there is no tacit knowledge, so knowledge can be reduced to information (a discussion of this issue is presented in Fransman, 1994; and Nonaka and Takeuchi, 1995:8). On the contrary, tacit knowledge is a central element in explaining a firm's distinctiveness if firms are seen as repositories of knowledge. The distinctiveness cannot be easily codified, otherwise it could be copied and the competitive advantage would be lost. The distinctiveness has to be based on firm-specific knowledge that is tacit, is embedded in firms's routines and is difficult to copy.

Leonard-Barton (1992a:114) introduced another source of firm distinctiveness when she asserts that 'a core capability is an interrelated, interdependent knowledge system'. This knowledge system comprises four interdependent dimensions: (i) employee knowledge and skills, (ii) physical technical systems (e.g. equipment, software), (iii) managerial systems (systems of education, rewards and incentives), and (iv) values and norms. The first two dimensions are a dynamic knowledge reservoir, or competence, and the latter two are mechanisms for controlling or channeling knowledge. Because of the interrelationship between the four dimensions, such systems are difficult to imitate. It is not possible to copy a system, and copying isolated mechanisms and fitting them into another knowledge system does not necessarily generate the same results. Therefore it seems that the firm-distinctiveness is based on the system itself rather than on tacit knowledge. This systemic view has implications for management. Based on the idea of Senge (1990:15) that successful leaders are systems thinkers, able to see 'interrelationships, not things, and processes, not snapshots', she stressed that it is necessary to adopt a system thinking or to have an organic learning system (Leonard-Barton, 1992b:24). Porter (1996:70) also stressed that advantages come from the system of activities or functions. Referring to the Southwest Company, he pointed out that its 'strategy involves a whole system of activities, not a collection of parts. Its competitive advantage comes from the way its activities fit and reinforce one another'.

2.3.2 Technological or Organizational Capabilities/competencies

Within this literature some authors have stressed organizational capabilities or competencies, while others have emphasized technological capabilities. The dynamic capabilities perspective has mostly focused on organizational capabilities in a broad sense (see for instance Teece, Pisano and Shuen, 1990; Teece and Pisano, 1994; Teece et al., 1994; Chandler, 1990). However even focusing on organizational capabilities/competencies, the definition of core/distinctive competence includes both an organizational/economic dimension and a technical dimension. Organizational/economic competence involves allocative, transactional and administrative competencies. Technical competence includes the ability to develop and design new products and processes, and to operate facilities effectively; and the ability to learn (Teece et al., 1994:19).

Other authors within this perspective have focused on more specific organizational capabilities. For instance, Clark and Fujimoto (1991), Iansiti and Clark (1994) and Henderson (1994) analyzed the capability for integration as a dynamic organizational capability. Moreover they considered that the capability for integration is the basis for the process of building and renewal capabilities. As Clark and Fujimoto (1991:340) pointed out, 'in a competitive environment, integration is the underlying source of superior performance'. Integration is seen as the capacity to merge new knowledge with deep accumulated knowledge (Iansiti and Clark, 1994:602). It is basically a specific organizational capability. They analyzed the internal integration of that knowledge across internal boundaries, and the external integration across firm's boundaries. Henderson (1994) used a similar approach, but she analyzed integration in terms of both organizational boundaries (internal and external) and technological boundaries. She described how the recent drug discovery process required the integration of different therapeutic areas and scientific disciplines that are located across the firm (1994:610). She analyzed the organizational arrangements that allow the integration of that fragmented knowledge and the creation of a new technological competence. Iansiti (1998) analyzed one, even more specific, organizational capability, the capability for technology integration, which is part of the capability for integration defined in Clark and Fujimoto (1991) and developed in Iansiti and Clark (1994). Iansiti (1998:5) defined technology integration as the 'capability of conceptualizing how a multitude of emerging possibilities might be used coherently to define a product that makes business sense'. It is reflected in integrated products, which should have a good match between technology and context (Iansiti: 1998:75). Von Hippel (1994) focused on the integration of knowledge about customer needs and preferences into the product development process as another specific capability for integration.

Other works have focused attention on the importance of different organizational capabilities, such as the ability to coordinate specialized units (Lawrence and Lorsch, 1967), and the ability to absorb existent knowledge and generate new knowledge (Cohen and Levinthal, 1989 and 1990) described before.

A series of work has focused on the pivotal role of technological competencies, closely related to R&D activities, in the core competencies of the firm. Miyazaki (1993 and 1994) empirically analyzed how firms change the nature of their knowledge by combining different fields of knowledge (e.g. optics and electronics) and creating a new competence in another technological field (e.g. optoelectronics). Firms have certain technological competencies which they can combine to create a new one. She focused on the technological boundaries of the firm more than on organizational boundaries. She recognized that there are several types of competencies, such as those related to production, marketing, finance as well as organizational and technological competencies, the interaction among which determines the competitive advantage of the firm. She admitted that the organizational competence plays a role in coupling the set of competencies. However she asserted that the technological competence forms the foundation of the firm's core competence (Miyazaki, 1993:33).

Along the same lines, Nelson (1991:349) pointed out the importance of technological competence when he said that 'R&D capabilities may be the lead ones in defining the dynamic capabilities of a firm'. Mitchell and Hamilton (1988:16) asserted that the importance of R&D in knowledge building is related to its potential to open new opportunities when R&D is conducted for strategic positioning. Patel and Pavitt (1994:5) argued that the accumulated technological competencies constrain the directions of the firm's search, so the differentiated nature of technological competencies is one of the most important factors in explaining the coherence and the boundaries of the firm.

Leonard-Barton used the concept of core technological capabilities; however she pointed out that the 'technological capabilities rest less upon technical information *per se* and more upon all the activities and systems that create that technical knowledge' (Leonard-Barton, 1995a:260). Therefore in her approach technological capabilities include a technological dimension and an organizational dimension, and the behavior of firms related to that organizational dimension is very important in the process of building up technological capabilities.

Focusing either on the technological or on the organizational dimension, all the authors recognize that both dimensions are required to build core capabilities. The description by Iansiti and Clark (1994:560) of the organizational capability for designing and developing dies used in the production of body panels for automobiles clearly illustrates the interrelation between each dimension. The four dimensions of the knowledge system described by Leonard-Barton are used to classify the knowledge in that description. The knowledge that underlies that capability includes:

1. Employees's knowledge and skills, such as knowledge related to the fundamental properties of the die and its production system, e.g. an understanding of metallurgy, the flow of metal under pressure, etc. (fundamental knowledge); how the fundamental concepts can be operationalized into effective actions, e.g. knowledge of techniques of die design, die modeling, etc. (industry-specific and firm-specific knowledge); the skills of die designers in anticipating processing problems, e.g. know how.
2. Technical systems, such as customized software that allows for rapid and effective testing.
3. Managerial systems, such as patterns of communication and informal interaction between die designers and manufacturing engineers that allow for early identification of potential problems.
4. Values and norms, such as an attitude of cooperation that facilitates coordinated action between the die designers and the tool makers who will build the dies.

To sum up, technological competencies is a concept most frequently used in two types of analysis: (i) theoretical discussion of tacit knowledge as a firm specific competence (see for instance Dosi and Marengo, 1993; Teece et al., 1994; Winter, 1987); and (ii) empirical work about the combination of different knowledge specialization (see for instance Prahalad and Hamel, 1990; Miyazaki, 1994; Patel and Pavitt, 1994). In contrast the concept of capabilities is most frequently used when focusing on: (i) the ability to do things, which is called technological capabilities but which includes both a technological knowledge dimension and an organizational dimension (see for instance Leonard-Barton, 1992a and 1995a); and (ii) organizational capabilities instead of technological capabilities (see for instance Teece, Pisano and Shuen, 1990; Teece and Pisano, 1994; Henderson, 1994; Iansiti, 1998).

Despite the differences between the concepts of capabilities and competencies, these concepts are usually used in the same way and at many times are indistinguishable. There is some consensus that the process of maintaining, nurturing and renewing core capabilities or competencies requires continual reconfiguration of a bundle of resources through learning processes. Sharing knowledge within the organization and integration of knowledge across organizational boundaries is seen as one feature. Specific purpose and long term support by managers to create knowledge and build core capabilities are considered crucial. As Leonard-Barton (1995a:xi) pointed out 'through systematic decision making and actions, both routine and strategic, core technological capabilities can be built and changed', as firms compete on the basis of their ability to create and utilize knowledge, the management of knowledge becomes a central issue.

This review of the SML suggests the following conclusions:

1. All these authors assume the firm has identified its firm specific competencies, core competencies or core capabilities and they analyze how the firm can nurture, increase, integrate, combine or fuse the knowledge it has to create a more complex knowledge base. There is neither clear explanation of the technological and organizational problems to be overcome in order to build the primary core capabilities to compete on the base of knowledge nor a description of the specific activities that contribute to creating that core capability. How can firms identify their core competencies, firm specific competencies, knowledge base or the routines that matter? What activities are crucial to build the prior knowledge base and the primary core capabilities? What are the capabilities that are important and how might the firm build them?

2. The SML focuses on organizational aspects of maintaining, nurturing and renewing a significant base of technological knowledge that already exists. Therefore they analyze how to move from simple to more complex knowledge bases. It is basically an issue of knowledge management. Firms do not lack knowledge and through changes in the organization they can accelerate and improve the knowledge creation process and nurture and renew the knowledge base.

3. Apart from the technological and organizational competencies, other competencies can be important, particularly in the case of developing countries firms, such as marketing or coordination, or even such technical aspects as investment project management, however these are not analyzed.

4. The SML has developed different types of works. Some authors have developed a theoretical treatment of the material at a very abstract level (see for instance Nelson and Winter, 1982; Winter, 1987). Other authors have treated capabilities in a broad sense and tended to give general definitions that include the distinction between technological and organizational issues (see for instance Teece, Pisano and Shuen, 1990; Teece and Pisano, 1994). Yet others have treated capabilities/ competencies in a very specific way and have analyzed a specific technological competence, such as optoelectronics (Miyazaki, 1994) or a functional competence, such as miniaturization (Prahalad and Hamel, 1990). As Teece and Pisano (1994:538) pointed out, 'only

recently have researchers begun to focus on the specifics of how some organizations first develop firm-specific capabilities'. As Henderson (1994:609) and Iansiti and Clark (1994:559) pointed out, the SML have not identified the detailed capabilities that it is necessary to have. These authors are amongst those who are trying to fill this hole by focusing on the capability for integration as the base of the dynamic organizational capabilities.

2.4   TOWARDS A FRAMEWORK FOR THE ANALYSIS OF TECHNOLOGICAL CAPABILITIES

The description of the main issues of both bodies of literature has revealed several differences in the approach to technological capabilities by the DCL and the SML.

1. The concept of building technological capabilities has been used in two different ways, as illustrated in Figure 2.1. On the one hand, the DCL has focused on vertical movements up the y-axis towards building the minimum essential knowledge base. On the other, the SML has focused on horizontal movements from the top of the y-axis along the x-axis, nurturing and renewing strategic capabilities already built and combining knowledge bases.

Figure 2.1 Different meaning of 'building technological capabilities'

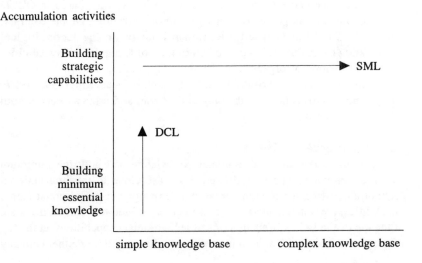

Accumulation activities

2. The type of treatment is different. The DCL contains a more empirical/ descriptive story of the building of technological capabilities and a taxonomic treatment; whereas the SML has developed a more theoretical treatment of the material, but at a very abstract level. For instance, the SML has been concerned with confronting knowledge with information, and has focused the discussion on this theoretical issue. Authors are discussing the firm as a repository of knowledge and not as an information processing unit. They assert that by creating and managing knowledge, basically tacit knowledge and not information and codified knowledge, the firm can build and renew its capabilities. In contrast the DCL, even sharing that argument, has been basically discussing a more empirical problem: the accumulation of abilities to do things, which requires the accumulation of stocks of knowledge and the development of organizational/institutional factors. Because the learning processes play a key role in the accumulation of those technological capabilities, these processes have been a focus of attention.

3. The knowledge depth of the firms analyzed is different. The SML studies firms that have already accumulated a deep base of knowledge, in contrast the DCL is concerned with firms that have a shallow knowledge base.

4. The role of the organizational and technological knowledge dimensions of the technological capability building is different. The SML considers both dimensions. It is perhaps more concerned with the role of the organizational dimension to strengthen the creation of technological knowledge to maintain and renew the core technological capabilities. As Pavitt (1997:2) pointed out, 'lack of technological knowledge is rarely the cause of innovation failure in large firms based in OECD countries. The main problems arise in organization'. On the contrary, the DLC has focused attention primarily on the technological knowledge dimension of the building up of technological capabilities in isolation of organizational issues. The shallow knowledge base of the firms analyzed contributes to explain this focus. Kim (1995, 1997a and 1997b) is perhaps the only author who addresses aspects of both dimensions.

Firms in a transition process
However firms that have accumulated knowledge and built the minimum essential knowledge base, and even more are close to the international technological frontier in some areas but have not yet built core/strategic capabilities, are not considered by these bodies of literature. These firms are at the top of the DCL's firms in terms of technological capabilities, at the top of the y-axis of the DCL at least in some areas. But they have neither built any

strategic capability nor are they making substantial progress along the x-axis in Figure 2.1. They have not arrived at the situation that the SML uses as a point of departure. Therefore firms like those do not fit with the problems raised by either body of literature.

As illustrated in Figure 2.2 below, such firms are in the Transition Process area. They have already built the minimum essential knowledge base in several areas (vertical movements up the y-axis). They are making efforts to learn to move further to build embryonic strategic capabilities as a first stage towards building strategic capabilities (further vertical movements up the y-axis until the top), and making efforts to learn to move from simple to complex knowledge bases in certain areas (as illustrated by the curve key moving horizontally along the x-axis).

In the DCL area firms compete on the basis of production capabilities, largely acquired from elsewhere and reinforced by basic to intermediate innovative technological capabilities related to a simple knowledge base. This area has been the main concern of the DCL. In the SML area firms compete on the basis of innovative technological capabilities, and core/strategic capabilities based on diverse and complex knowledge bases and knowledge integration. This area is the focus of attention of the SML. The Transition Process area represents a stage of transition from building the minimum essential knowledge base to building strategic capabilities and beginning to compete on the bases of knowledge. This Transition Process and the specific organizational and technological problems confronting firms during the process of building the primary strategic capabilities have been barely analyzed in either the DCL or the SML. This is the focus of this book.

Therefore, neither DCL nor SML provides an adequate framework to analyze two particular issues. First, the long term accumulation process to arrive at a level to be able to build strategic capabilities, a stage that is the point of departure of the SML but which is not considered at all in most of the DCL. Second, the specific organizational problems related to the management of knowledge that firms present in each stage of accumulation, particularly the differences between the stage of building the minimum essential knowledge base and the Transition Process from that stage to building strategic capabilities. However these bodies of literature provide some ideas that are drawn on to develop the analytical framework that is used in this book.

Technological capabilities
As in Kim (1997a:86), technological capabilities are defined in this book as 'the ability to make effective use of technological knowledge to assimilate, use, adapt, and change existing technologies. It also enables one to create new technologies and to develop new products and processes in response to the changing economic environment'. This concept is congruent with the

Figure 2.2 Transition Process: an unexplored area by DCL and SML

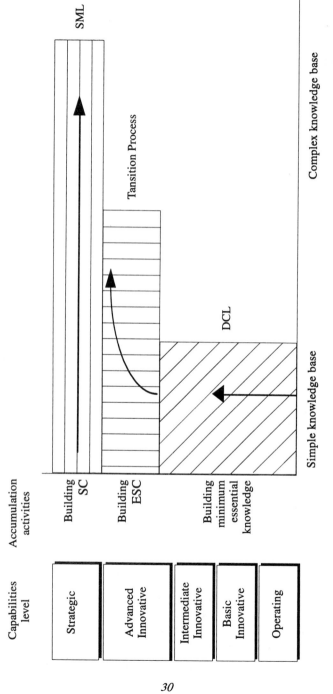

Notes:
SC = Strategic Capabilities, ESC = Embryonic Strategic Capabilities.
DCL = Developing Countries Literature, SML = Strategic Management Literature.

definition of technological capabilities used by Bell and Pavitt (1995), which includes the accumulation of technological knowledge and the development of organizational/institutional factors. Learning will be understood as a process, the process that allows the firm to build technological capabilities. Therefore firms create their knowledge base through learning processes, which take time, are costly and require a deliberate learning strategy (Bell, 1984). This book uses the taxonomy of technological capabilities presented in Bell and Pavitt (1995), which distinguishes routine production capabilities and three levels of innovative technological capabilities (basic, intermediate and advanced).

The concept of a knowledge base will be used in two senses. First, to refer to the whole knowledge accumulated in the firm. Second, in a narrower sense, to refer to the knowledge accumulated in specific fields, such as electronics, mechanical engineering or glass composition.

Strategic capabilities and embryonic strategic capabilities
Based on the concept of core capabilities/competencies used by the SML, this book will define the concept of strategic capabilities. Strategic capabilities are those innovative technological capabilities that are used to distinguish the firm competitively, to compete on the base of knowledge. They give a competitive advantage. They are built and rebuilt in the SML area of Figure 2.2. However a distinction between strategic capabilities and embryonic strategic capabilities will be made. Embryonic strategic capabilities are those advanced innovative technological capabilities that are still incipient, they are not used to distinguish the firm competitively. They include a deeper stock of knowledge accumulated more in some technical-functions, technical areas or knowledge fields than in others, and which can be the base on which to build strategic capabilities. Embryonic strategic capabilities are built in the Transition Process area.

Stages of building technological capabilities and the transition process
Within these concepts, three stages of building technological capabilities are defined, according to the level of accumulation of innovative technological capabilities (basic to advanced) and the use of the innovative technological capabilities (for distinguishing the firm competitively or not). One first stage consists of 'building the minimum essential knowledge base to survive in the market', which corresponds to the DCL area in Figure 2.2. It is referred to in this book as 'building the minimum essential knowledge'. Another superior stage consists of 'building, nurturing and renewing strategic capabilities', which corresponds to the SML area in Figure 2.2. It is referred to here as 'building strategic capabilities'. Finally there is another stage in between: the 'Transition Process from building the minimum essential knowledge to building strategic capabilities', which corresponds to the Transition Process area. This

stage is referred to in this book as the 'Transition Process'. The main characteristics of these stages of building technological capabilities are presented in Table 2.1.

This book analyzes particularly the characteristics of the Transition Process, a stage unexplored by the DCL and SML. Both the technological knowledge and the organizational dimension are crucial to complete the Transition Process and build strategic capabilities.

Table 2.1 Stages of building technological capabilities

Stages	Building the minimum essential knowledge base	Transition Process	Building strategic capabilities
Definition	Stage of accumulation where the firm has built technological capabilities to reduce costs, improve the quality, and upgrade the equipment to achieve parity with competitors	Stage of accumulation from building the minimum essential knowledge base to build strategic capabilities to distinguish the firm competitively	Stage of accumulation where the firm has already built strategic capabilities which distinguish the firm competitively, and continually looks to maintaining, nurturing and renewing them
Characteristics	i) accumulation of: • routine production capabilities • basic to intermediate innovative technological capabilities • simple knowledge base	i) accumulation of: • routine production capabilities • intermediate innovative technological capabilities in certain technical-functions and advanced in others • simple knowledge bases ii) emergence of embryonic strategic capabilities in some technical-functions, technical areas or knowledge fields	i) accumulation of: • routine production capabilities • advanced innovative technological capabilities in all the technical-functions • complex knowledge bases ii) emergence of strategic capabilities in some technical-functions, technical areas or knowledge fields
Literature	DCL mostly refers to this stage	—	SML refers to this stage

33

3 The Role of Knowledge Management in Re-building Strategic Capabilities

3.1 INTRODUCTION

As referred in Section 2.3, there has recently been heightened interest in the SML in understanding how firms can sustain, nurture and re-build strategic technological capabilities.

These strategic capabilities are based on the ability to create new knowledge and integrate it with the existing knowledge base. The process of knowledge creation is the center of attention and issues about the management of knowledge are playing an increasingly important role in the explanation of the effectiveness of this process. The management of knowledge facilitates the process of creation and renewal of knowledge and thus of the strategic technological capabilities. Therefore the management of knowledge has become a key organizational issue in the nurturing and renewing of strategic technological capabilities. The discussion in the SML has moved from technology strategy and technology management issues to knowledge management issues.

This chapter reviews some of the SML examining the role of knowledge management in the process of knowledge creation and in building strategic capabilities. Different aspects of the knowledge management are considered relevant to support the competitive advantages of firms in a changing environment. Section 3.2 reviews the literature that examines the conversion of individual into organizational learning. Section 3.3 reviews the literature dealing with coordination of learning and knowledge integration. This review aims to identify a set of variables permitting the assessment of key features of the knowledge management process. Section 3.4 presents the framework for analyzing the knowledge management process that is used in this book. Finally, Section 3.5 presents the conceptual design of this book.

3.2 LEARNING AT THE INDIVIDUAL AND ORGANIZATIONAL LEVELS

Learning is defined as the process through which firms create knowledge and acquire technological capabilities. As Teece et al. (1994:11) pointed out, 'learning is a process involving repetition and experimentation which enables tasks to be performed better and quicker, and new production opportunities to be identified'.

Technological learning takes place at two levels: individual and organizational. As Simon (1996:176) pointed out, 'all learning first takes place at individual level, inside individual heads; an organization learns only in two ways: (a) by the learning of its members, or (b) by ingesting new members who have knowledge the organization did not previously have'. Thus the definition of learning, and therefore knowledge, is after all an individual issue. However individual learning is a social phenomenon, what an individual learns is very much dependent on what is already known by other members of the organization.

Organizational learning is not considered the sum of the individual learning of the organizations's members. As Hedberg (1981:6) pointed out, 'although organizational learning occurs through individuals, it would be a mistake to conclude that organizational learning is nothing but the cumulative result of their members' learning. Organizations do not have brains, but they have cognitive systems and memories ... organizations' memories preserve certain behaviors, mental maps, norms, and values over time'.

There are several issues related to organizational learning and connected with the conversion of individual into organizational learning, and there is an increasing interest in this process from different disciplines and theoretical perspectives (see for instance Hedberg, 1981; Fiol and Lyles, 1985; Levitt and March, 1988; Huber, 1996; Dodgson, 1993; Cohen and Levinthal, 1990; Cohen and Sproull, 1996; Garvin, 1993; Senge, 1990; Argyris and Schön, 1978; Nonaka and Takeuchi, 1995). The SML reviewed in Section 2.3 also refers to learning, knowledge and strategic capabilities. However most of the works do not address the issue of conversion of individual into organizational learning. Either they assume that individual learning becomes organizational learning and they discuss learning in general, or that it is one of a number of key factors which combine to maintain, nurture and renew core capabilities. The overall literature that approaches the conversion of individual into organizational learning is unrelated and there is little agreement on what organizational learning actually is (Huber, 1996:125).

Two main bodies of literature covering different issues are reviewed here. First, SML related to organizational learning and the features of a 'learning organization'. Second, SML related to the role of tacit and codified knowledge in a 'knowledge building company'.

3.2.1 The Emphasis on Organizational Learning and the 'Learning Organization'

There are several works about organizational learning, mostly theoretical, and they give several definitions of organizational learning. Some of them focus on behavioral changes while others look at new ways of thinking; some stress the sharing of information while others focus on building shared visions. Coming from a behavioral perspective, Levitt and March (1988:320) pointed out that 'organizations are seen as learning by encoding inferences from history into routines that guide behavior'. From the management studies and organizational science literature, Argyris and Schön (1978:3) stated that 'organizational learning involves the detection and correction of error'. They define three levels of learning: single-loop, double-loop, and deutero-learning (learning to learn), according with the way to detect and correct errors. Dodgson (1993:375) describes learning at organizational level 'as the ways firms build, supplement and organize knowledge and routines around their activities and within their cultures, and adapt and develop organizational efficiency by improving the use of the broad skills of their workforces'. He stressed that the importance lies in not only what a firm knows or what skills it possesses, but how it uses them (Dodgson, 1993:383). In the same way Marengo (1991:130) asserted that organizational learning is the process of generation of new competencies and improvement of the old ones. Cohen and Levinthal's (1990) absorptive capacity can also be seen as a measure of organizational learning, considering it is a set of collective abilities developed through learning activities. As they pointed out 'these abilities collectively constitute what we call a firm's "absorptive capacity"' (Cohen and Levinthal, 1990:128).

Huber (1996:126) challenged the treatment of organizational learning by most of the literature and, also from a behavioral perspective, asserted that 'an entity learns if, through its processing of information, the range of its potential behaviors is changed'. He argued that there are four basic learning-related processes that determine four attributes of organizational learning. These attributes are the following: (i) existence: 'an organization learns if any of its units acquires knowledge that it recognizes as potentially useful to the organization'; (ii) breadth: 'more organizational learning occurs when more of the organization's components obtain this knowledge and recognize it as potentially useful'; (iii) elaborateness: 'more organizational learning occurs when more and more varied interpretations are developed, because such development changes the range of potential behaviors'; and (iv) thoroughness: 'more organizational learning occurs when more organizational learning units develop uniform comprehension of the various interpretations of organizational learning' (Huber, 1996:126-7). Knowledge acquisition is the learning-related process by which knowledge is obtained and determines the existence of organizational learning. Information distribution is the process by which information from different sources is shared and determines the existence and breadth of the organizational learning. Information interpretation is the process by which distributed information is given one or more commonly understood interpretations, and it determines the elaborateness and thoroughness of the organizational learning. Finally the organizational memory is the means by which knowledge is stored (Huber, 1996:127). Due to the processes of specialization and departmentalization, organizations frequently do not know what they know, therefore the construction of an organizational memory is a key element for organizational learning (Huber, 1996:150). This framework contributes to clarifying the links between individual and organizational learning, setting more specific issues related to organizational learning and bringing elements to evaluate its scope.

Another line of work focuses on the characteristics of a 'learning organization'. It is based on the ideas about the nature of the organizational learning developed by Senge (1990). Senge defined and popularized the notion of 'learning organizations' as places 'where people continually expand their capacity to create the results they truly desire, where new and expansive patterns of thinking are nurtured, where collective aspiration is set free, and where people are continually learning how to learn' (Senge, 1990:1). He suggested five sets of characteristics called 'component technologies' to achieve this result: systems thinking, personal mastery, mental models, shared vision and team learning.

Based on those ideas Garvin (1993:80) proposed a new definition of a 'learning organization', 'a learning organization is an organization skilled at creating, acquiring, and transferring knowledge, and at modifying its behavior to reflect new knowledge and insights'. These 'learning organizations' have to carry out five activities: systematic problem solving, experimentation with new approaches, learning from their own experience and past history, learning from the experiences and best practices of others, and transferring knowledge quickly and efficiently throughout the organization (Garvin, 1993:81). Garvin stressed the idea that each activity has to be managed as a system, which includes a mind-set, a set of mechanisms and a pattern of behavior. This idea is very similar to the 'organic system view' of the core capabilities and the four subsystems described by Leonard-Barton (1992a:114 and 1992b:24). Only if learning is managed deliberately across the different activities, can the organization be a 'learning organization' and continually keep competitive advantage. As Garvin (1993:81) asserted, companies have to 'actively manage the learning process to ensure that it occurs by design rather than by chance'. Several specific mechanisms are mentioned for transferring knowledge, or in other words for converting individual into organizational learning, such as visits to other facilities, rotation of personnel, training, and some specific forms of codification of tacit knowledge (Garvin, 1993:87).

With a different focus of attention, the literature on innovation has identified a set of learning mechanisms, for instance, learning by using (Rosenberg, 1976), learning by R&D (Cohen and Levinthal, 1989), learning from customers (von Hippel, 1988), learning by interacting (Lundvall, 1988 and 1992), learning from own experiences, learning from competitors, learning from searching information, and also learning by licensing, by training, by hiring key individuals, by carrying out reverse engineering, etc. Each of these mechanisms reflects a different nature of learning and they cover a broader range of areas of learning than the classic learning by doing (Arrow, 1962). Another line of works has been concerned with identifying the sources of knowledge for innovation. Two representative works were the Yale survey and the Pace questionnaire, summarized in Levin et al. (1987) and Arundel, van de Paal and Soete (1995), respectively. Learning mechanisms and sources of knowledge have been used indistinguishably, although their nature is different.

Cohen and Levinthal (1989) distinguished the different nature of the concepts when analyzing the dual role of R&D – as a source of innovation and as a process of learning. They asserted that 'while R&D obviously generates innovations, it also develops the firm's ability to identify, assimilate and exploit knowledge from the environment ... [which is] a firm's "learning" or "absorptive capacity" ' (Cohen and Levinthal, 1989:569). These two roles of R&D, which have generally not been differentiated by the literature, contribute to firm's competitiveness. Tidd, Bessant and Pavitt (1997:108) presented another aspect that is hidden by the indiscriminate use of both concepts, they asserted that 'it is important to distinguish knowledge of what technological development are being undertaken by competitors, from knowledge of how the innovations can be made to work in practice ... the former can be obtained quickly through information-gathering activities, whilst the latter requires extensive investments of resources and time in benchmarking and learning activities'.

The literature on innovation has approached learning mechanisms at the firm level without taking into account the extent to which and by what means individual learning is converted into organizational learning. The literature related to organizational learning has been concerned with those issues and an important topic when analyzing, for instance, learning by hiring key individuals, is where, when and how the knowledge possessed by these hired individuals is socialized at the organizational level.

What is clear is that just as learning in broad terms requires an investment and a deliberate strategy (Bell, 1984:190), the conversion of individual into organizational learning also requires a deliberate strategy and specific efforts.

3.2.2 The Role of Tacit and Codified Knowledge and the 'Knowledge Building Company'

Building upon the Strategic Management Literature described in Section 2.3, on the organizational learning literature and on the distinction between tacit and explicit knowledge proposed by Polanyi (1966), Nonaka and Takeuchi analyzed the characteristics of what they call a 'knowledge building company'. Based on the idea that knowledge is a product of learning, they focus on knowledge instead of learning. They criticized the organizational learning approach for avoiding the issue of how knowledge is created, and for not taking into account that the process of knowledge creation is also a learning process. They also criticized the resource-based approach for missing a 'comprehensive framework that shows how various parts within the organization interact with each other over time to create something new and unique' (Nonaka and Takeuchi, 1995:49). Unlike those bodies of literature, Nonaka and Takeuchi focused attention on the process of knowledge creation, on the specifics of how organizations create new knowledge. They developed a model of organizational knowledge creation that relates tacit and explicit knowledge with individual and organizational knowledge, which is broadly presented in Nonaka and Takeuchi (1995) and summarized in Nonaka (1994) and Nonaka and Konno (1998). The organizational knowledge creation is seen as a capability of the firm. Even though they raised some differences with respect to the organizational learning theorists, they recognized that their 'knowledge building company' is very similar to the 'learning organization' described before (Nonaka and Takeuchi, 1995:45). Both approaches share several common issues, particularly the focus on the conversion from individual learning into organizational learning.

Nonaka and Takeuchi postulate that the organization creates new knowledge through building tacit and explicit (codified)[1] knowledge and through the dynamic process of conversion between these two dimensions of knowledge. Codified knowledge is the knowledge that 'can be articulated in formal language including grammatical statements, mathematical expressions, specifications, manuals, and so forth'. On the contrary, tacit knowledge 'is hard to articulate with formal language. It is a personal knowledge embedded in individual experience' (Nonaka and Takeuchi, 1995:viii). To be communicated and shared within the organization, tacit knowledge has to be codified in some way, has to be converted into words or numbers that anyone can understand (Nonaka and Takeuchi, 1995:9). Therefore codification is the basis for sharing tacit knowledge.

---

[1] The concepts of explicit and codified knowledge are both used but are indistinguishable. Nonaka and Takeuchi use explicit knowledge but, to keep consistency with the concepts used in this book, the term 'codified' knowledge will be used from here on.

Nonaka and Takeuchi use a narrow definition of tacit knowledge and several degrees of codification, as described in Table 3.1. They aimed to stress the different ways of codifying the knowledge adopted by Japanese firms. The Japanese firms use symbols, analogies, etc. to codify tacit knowledge. These types of codes represent a semi-codification of the tacit knowledge, only understood by them. Therefore in their approach the distinctiveness of the firm is based on both tacit knowledge and semi-codified knowledge.

The SML referred to in Section 2.3 also uses a narrow definition of tacit knowledge to stress the distinctiveness of the firms, which is based only on tacit knowledge (see for instance Nelson and Winter, 1982, Teece, et al. 1994; Winter, 1987; Dosi and Marengo, 1993).[2] Following Nelson and Winter (1982), Nonaka and Takeuchi assert that the capability for organizational knowledge creation at a firm is a collection of tacit knowledge which enables firm's members to use the codified knowledge.

Table 3.1   The distinction between tacit and codified knowledge in the SML

Tacit knowledge	• Non codifiable
Codified knowledge	• Verbally codified Words, symbols, analogies, etc. • Documented Written documents, grammatical statements, mathematical expressions, specifications, designs, manuals, equipment, software, etc.

The creation of knowledge and the growth of the knowledge base depend on the interaction between tacit and codified knowledge, and not only on the accumulation of isolated tacit or codified knowledge (Nonaka and Takeuchi, 1995:70). According to Nonaka and Takeuchi (1995:62–9), organizational knowledge creation takes place primarily through the dynamic process of the following four modes of knowledge conversion:

---

[2]   There is another body of literature discussing how information technology increases the knowledge codification and to what extent this changes the ratio of codified to tacit knowledge (see for instance Senker, 1995; Dosi, 1996; Foray and Lundvall, 1996; Cowan and Foray, 1997). In this line, Nightingale (1997) analyzes empirically the extent to which computerization has not led to the universal codification of tacit knowledge. Some authors (see for instance David and Foray, 1994) actually consider that practically all tacit knowledge is codifiable, in which case the dichotomy presented in the table does not represent their view.

1. From tacit to tacit, which is called socialization and is the process of sharing experiences and creating tacit knowledge.
2. From tacit to codified, which is called externalization and is the process of articulating tacit knowledge into codified forms.
3. From codified to codified, which is called combination and is a process of systematizing concepts into a knowledge system and involves the combination of different bodies of codified knowledge.
4. From codified to tacit, which is called internalization and is the process of embodying codified knowledge into tacit knowledge.

Organizational knowledge creation takes place between three levels: individual, group or team, and the organization. New knowledge starts with an individual, who is the creator of knowledge, and then that individual's personal knowledge is transformed into organizational knowledge which is valuable to the firm as a whole (Nonaka and Takeuchi, 1995:13). Individuals learn through the four modes of knowledge conversion and, as more individuals are involved, the conversion from individual into organizational knowledge becomes faster and more effective. The organizational knowledge creation is then a spiral process starting at the individual level.

The model was constructed from empirical evidence gathered in case studies of Japanese firms and aimed to elaborate a new theory of knowledge building. In addition they pointed out several specific organizational arrangements, such as teamwork and strategic rotation of personnel, used by the case-study firms, which facilitate both the transformation of individual knowledge into group and organizational knowledge, and the integration of knowledge through different internal boundaries of the firm.

Building on that approach, Nonaka and Konno (1998) emphasized the key role of shared spaces (physical, virtual or mental), which they called 'Ba' (a Japanese concept), as a foundation for knowledge creation. They added that knowledge actually resides in these shared spaces (Nonaka and Konno, 1998:41).

The work of Nonaka and Takeuchi is very helpful in understanding a wide spectrum of issues related to the process of knowledge creation and a number of specific mechanisms used to manage the knowledge to facilitate that process. They described in detail a number of mechanisms to facilitate the sharing of knowledge and the process of learning at organizational level. They have clearly shown the relationship between the modes of knowledge conversion and their contribution to the conversion of individual into organizational learning. However some issues remain unclear. In their examples it does not matter where codified knowledge come from, it seems that it does not matter if the effort to acquire tacit knowledge from external or internal sources is different. Firms do not seem to need external sources of knowledge. They basically have the tacit knowledge and the codified knowledge, as firms have knowledge in other SML reviewed in Section 2.3. They mentioned that external knowledge has to be transformed, enriched and translated to fit the company's self-image and identity in order to create new knowledge (Nonaka and Takeuchi, 1995:11), however it is not made clear how firms do this.

The review of the literature about learning at individual and organizational levels offer some suggestions:

1. The 'learning organization' and the 'knowledge building company' perspectives share common grounds, for instance, they intend to explain how firms can maintain, nurture and renew competitive advantages. They use the same mechanisms and similar behaviors to get their result. There is also common ground with the SML referred to in Section 2.3 on core capabilities.

2. The works extract normative recommendations based on successful cases. However the extent to which individual mechanisms introduced in other contexts work is unclear. As Leonard-Barton pointed out (1992b:26), a learning laboratory is a system; the activities, values and managerial practices 'operate as a system ... emulating just parts may never produce true learning laboratories'. The 'organic system view' has to be developed at the level of all the subsystems that form the core capabilities, and each of those subsystems has to be internally consistent (Leonard-Barton, 1992b:25). This systemic view was also clear in Garvin's approach to the 'learning organization'. Teece and Pisano (1994:550) also mention the interrelatedness between routines when analyzing the scope of imitation. They asserted that 'imitation can be hindered by the fact that few routines are "stand-alone"; coherence may require that a change in one set of routines ... requires changes in some other'.

3. Both bodies of literature describe mechanisms to facilitate the conversion of individual into organizational learning, but they do not consider that the firm could have an uneven distribution of stocks of knowledge in different areas (e.g. deeper in production than in marketing, deeper in glass composition than in glass formation), which would make the interaction between these areas and so the knowledge conversion process difficult. They do not consider that the learning strategies followed by different areas within the firm can be significantly distinct, which also affects the knowledge creation activities.

4. The more empirical literature stresses the description of successful cases. For instance, Nonaka and Takeuchi analyzed the four modes of

knowledge conversion when they actually happened. They did not consider the situation of firms where those knowledge conversion processes were incomplete, particularly firms where codifiable knowledge remained tacit, or where the tacit knowledge has simply not yet been codified. In relation to the reasons for the lack of codification, Teece and Pisano (1994:550) pointed out that 'deep process understanding is often required to accomplish codification. Indeed if knowledge is highly tacit it indicates that underlying structures are not well understood, which limits learning because scientific and engineering principles cannot be as systematically applied'. The lack of codification is an issue which is not developed further by these authors nor is it considered by Nonaka and Takeuchi.

5. Some issues related to the problems that firms confront when they are actually undertaking the conversion between tacit and codified knowledge and between individual and organizational learning remain unexplored. The authors neither raise the problems of the internal coherence between the set of mechanisms established to facilitate that conversion, which are related to analyzing the whole system of knowledge including the different subsystems, nor the practical difficulties in establishing new way of doing things. These issues are discussed in this book. In relation to the latter issue, several authors have pointed out the different rhythm of change in organizations and technology (see for instance Nelson, 1994; von Tunzelmann, 1995: 407–9). Several organizational theorists have stressed the rigidity of the behaviors, the difficulties involved in trying to change them and the organizational inertia. Along these lines, Leonard-Barton (1995a:34–5) refers to the core rigidities as the difficulty involved in changing the core capabilities based on the ingrained organizational routines. There are some very practical problems inherent in the conversion of individual learning into organizational learning, such as the difficulties in changing the existing way of doing things or routines and fitting in new routines with old ones. As Tidd, Bessant and Pavitt (1997:41) pointed out, 'routines are firm-specific and must be learned. Simple copying what someone else does is unlikely to help ... there is no substitute for the long and experience-based process of learning'. In this sense, what is learned from external sources has to be internalized, but this is not an automatic process, it takes time. External knowledge has to be integrated with the firm's own routines. However there is a problem of change, integration and coherence in the whole set of routines. As mentioned before, this topic has been highlighted in Teece and Pisano's (1994:550) paper in relation to the difficulties of imitating, but at a very abstract level. Nonaka and

Takeuchi's work pointed out that in order to be internalized external knowledge has to be translated to fit the firm's identity. However it seems that there is no problem in integrating old tacit knowledge with the new. Individuals acquire tacit knowledge through experience, then they can share it with others and transform it from individual to group and organizational knowledge. What is not clear is what are the conditions, mechanisms and specific problems related to the integration of new tacit knowledge with old knowledge, and new routines with those already established.

DCL has given very little attention to organizational learning. The focus of attention has been on the vertical movements referred to in Section 2.4 from operating to building the minimum essential knowledge base, and not on changing and integrating a shallow knowledge base. There has been a broad emphasis on individual learning to accumulate, but without taking into account the individual and organizational levels. Even though at an early stage in the development of this literature, Bell (1984:188) pointed out that learning 'refers to the acquisition of additional technical skills and knowledge by individuals and, through them, by organizations', the extent to which individual learning was converted into organizational level has not been an issue, or was assumed to be something that happened automatically.

Kim (1995, 1997a and 1997b) is the unique author, undertaking empirical work, identified in the DCL who deals directly with problems related to organizational learning. He used Cohen and Levinthal's (1990) and Nonaka and Takeuchi's (1995) frameworks to analyze the process of learning, the creation of knowledge and the accumulation of technological capabilities by Korean firms. Unlike Nonaka and Takeuchi, he used the concept of organizational learning and described some specific mechanisms used by those firms to carry out the conversion between tacit and codified knowledge and to transform individual into organizational learning. He presented some ideas about organizational learning in a catching-up country.

Like Nonaka and Takeuchi (1995), Kim followed a quite linear description of the successful process of new product development by these Korean firms. The successful cases established several mechanisms to facilitate knowledge conversion and transform individual into organizational learning, which in turn contributed to the spiral of knowledge conversion. Because of the necessity to move through stages, Kim described the use of different mechanisms at each stage by those firms. However it seems that the firms in question did not have problems associated with different level of technological capabilities by technical-function or an uneven knowledge by field or by organizational unit. There were apparently no restrictions or difficulties in integrating knowledge between different organizational units within the firm or between internal and external sources. Neither was there a problem in changing the way of doing things and linking the new practices learned from foreign firms to their own established practices. Everything appears to have worked harmoniously to contribute to the gradual process of catching up. In this sense, even though Kim added the specificity of firms from a catching up country, his work carries the same type of limitations referred to in the works of Nonaka and Takeuchi and the organizational learning theorists.

3.3   COORDINATION OF LEARNING AND INTEGRATION OF KNOWLEDGE

Since the beginning of this century large firms, and later most firms, have followed a process of knowledge specialization by product-division, business function and department (see for instance, Chandler, 1990; von Tunzelmann, 1995). This specialization has set the problem of deciding which activities to maintain internally, how to coordinate the activities undertaken by different units, and how to integrate specialized knowledge located in different organizational units.

There are different lines of approach to the coordination of activities. In a broad sense, when discussing the market as coordinator of economic activities, Coase (1937:38) defined a firm as a form of coordination of economic activity. He asserted that a firm exists where the cost of coordinating economic activities is lower than would be achieved by the market. In relation to the coordination of activities and the boundaries of the firm, particularly the definition of which activities have to be internalized and the scope of the vertical integration, Williamson (1975 and 1985) developed the approach of transaction costs. He pointed out that 'a transaction occurs when a good or service is transferred across a technologically separable interface' (Williamson, 1985:1). The costs of the transaction arise from bounded rationality and the possibility of opportunistic behavior. He asserted that in attempting to economize on transaction costs people select structures to govern the cost of transactions, which are called governance structures (Williamson, 1985:13). Coordination of activities is seen within the context of contracts and is a problem of organizational structure and governance. Teece (1976:13) also pointed out that vertical integration facilitates the coordination of activities to reduce costs. Considering innovation activity in the explanation of vertical integration, Teece (1986) asserted that the costs of coordinating among independent stages would be greatest when innovation is systemic and there is a high degree of interdependence among stages. The coordination of change across more than one internalized stage facilitates systemic innovation and then vertical integration is more conducive to innovation activity. The coordination of the flows of information was the focus of attention by Aoki. Based on Arrow's (1974) work, Aoki (1986) focused on problems of coordinating production, and developed a model of coordinating information flows.

Other lines of studies are concerned with the coordination of learning. They share the insight that increasingly complex organizations and innovation activities need to integrate knowledge across organizational and technological boundaries, such as between business-functions, between organizational units within the same business function, between technical functions and between knowledge fields. Managers have different perceptions about the world and understanding about innovation activity, organizational units have to play different roles in the overall innovation activity of the organization, and units have followed different paths of learning. For these and other reasons the organizational units follow different learning strategies and build different knowledge bases. Hence coordination of learning within different units is required to be able to integrate knowledge and build strategic capabilities. In dealing with this issue, Chandler (1990) established a relationship between the organizational structure and the characteristics of individual and organizational learning. He pointed out that the structure of the organization defines the way in which individuals and groups interact. Marengo (1991 and 1992) focused on one aspect of the coordination of learning activities across organizational boundaries and developed a model of coordination of the perceptions of the outside world. Lundvall (1988 and 1992) analyzed the coordination and interaction between user and producer of innovations, based on the work of Arrow (1974) about the information flow, and the work of Rosenberg (1976) about the interaction between user and producer. Von Hippel (1988) also analyzed different coordinating mechanisms between customers and suppliers in relation to innovation activity.

These studies have covered different issues of the coordination of learning. However as Dodgson (1993:388) and Pavitt (1997:12) recognized, the coordination of learning in a wider sense is unexplored. In general the SML, even the literature that focuses on the integration of knowledge, has not emphasized this point. Authors have assumed implicitly that there is some consistency between the learning processes on-going in different organizational units, and between the type and depth of knowledge located in those units. In distinct ways the authors have recognized the existence of differences within the firm, as revealed by the fact that organizations build strategic capabilities, which are different from other capabilities. Moreover these differences are purposely promoted and strategic capabilities have to be strengthened in relation to other non-strategic capabilities. However the problem of how to maintain an equilibrium between these areas of knowledge in order to be able to integrate knowledge and build strategic capabilities is not clear. In other words the problem of how and how much to coordinate the learning processes is not discussed.

The SML has focused on the fact that, today, nurturing and renewing strategic capabilities requires firms to solve complex problems, which demands the combination of deep knowledge bases. These deep knowledge bases should be accumulated by specialized units, therefore knowledge has to be integrated across different organizational units. This literature has analyzed to what extent knowledge is integrated, what are the types of knowledge integration, to what degree knowledge integration affects the performance of the firm and to what extent knowledge integration contributes to building core capabilities.

The process of knowledge specialization and the need to integrate knowledge across organizational boundaries refer to different aspects of the firm's activities. At the level of the whole set of business-functions, Porter (1996:70) asserted that 'while operational effectiveness is about achieving excellence in individual activities, or functions, strategy is about combining activities'. Competitive advantage comes from the 'fit among activities (functions)' rather than from the simple collection of activities. Integration between the R&D and the production functions has been a concern of the literature on innovation. Even though strong feedback between R&D and production is required to undertake successful innovations, there is consistent evidence about the difficulty of linking these activities by the large innovative firms (see for instance Rothwell, 1977; Cooper, 1988). At the level of corporate divisions, integration is associated with the fact that companies can find and exploit synergy across specialized knowledge bases located in different divisions (Leonard-Barton, 1995a:68). Within the technology function, Lawrence and Lorsh (1967) analyzed the process of knowledge specialization between the research and development activities, and stressed the need for coordination of these specialized units. As Iansiti (1998:11) asserted, this specialization is related to the fact that new products and processes are based on two different types of knowledge: domain-specific, which refers to disciplines and is associated with research activities; and context-specific, which refers to interactions between the domains and their application context and is associated with development activities. They are different knowledge bases and are usually located in different units, but they have to be integrated. At the level of the knowledge creation process, integration is the merging of new knowledge about the impact of possibilities with deep accumulated knowledge in the existing knowledge base of the organization (Iansiti and Clark, 1994:602).

Firms integrate knowledge all the time at different levels. They do it even without calling this activity integration, without any clear objective for doing it and without setting specific mechanisms to facilitate the process. However as Tidd, Bessant and Pavitt (1997:65) observed, 'internal structures and processes must continuously balance potentially conflicting requirements: (i) to identify and develop specialized knowledge within technological fields, business-functions and product divisions, (ii) to exploit this knowledge through integration across technological fields, business-functions and product divisions'. Due to this conflict, it is necessary to strategically manage knowledge, looking for the integration of knowledge across the organizational boundaries of the firm. In particular, it is necessary to change the way of organizing the process of knowledge creation across the organization to allow that integration. The opening of the disciplinary and organizational boundaries of that process is a relevant issue.

The concept of knowledge integration has a varying scope in the literature. For some authors it is only one amongst several issues involved in building strategic capabilities (see for instance Leonard-Barton, 1995a; Prahalad and Hamel, 1990; Miyazaki, 1993), in building a 'learning organization' (Garvin, 1993), in creating a 'knowledge building company' (Nonaka and Takeuchi, 1995) or in developing an 'absorptive capacity' (Cohen and Levinthal, 1990).

In contrast, for other authors the integration of knowledge plays a much more central role. It is the base on which to build dynamic capabilities (see for instance Clark and Fujimoto, 1991; Iansiti and Clark, 1994; Henderson, 1994). These authors concentrate more on elaborating the concept of knowledge integration and its different dimensions. Integration is analyzed in the context of problem solving activities, which are considered to be the basic units of knowledge creation. These authors differentiate between internal and external integration of knowledge. Internal integration refers to problem solving activities that focus and manage internal assets (Iansiti and Clark, 1994:565-6). It is basically analyzed in the context of project implementation and relates to the linking of existent specialized skills, knowledge bases, and technical and managerial systems. Clark and Fujimoto (1991:251-2) developed an index of internal integration which estimates the extent to which the different subgroups involved in development activities are managed and coordinated to achieve a well-integrated, coherent product. This index was critical in explaining performance differentials in the automobile industry. External integration refers to problem solving activities that span the boundary between the firm and its external environment. It is basically analyzed in the process of concept development of projects, and it is related to the generation of options using external sources of information and to the ability to evaluate those options according to the existing knowledge base (Iansiti and Clark, 1994:565). External integration includes two dimensions: (i) integration of knowledge of the market and the customer base, termed customer integration, and (ii) integration of knowledge of emerging technologies, termed technology integration. Iansiti (1998:119) defined technology integration as the integration of domain-specific and context-specific knowledge. Following Clark and Fujimoto (1991), he measured the technology integration capability by a similar index. The technology integration index refers to activities performed during the technology integration stage, before the technical concept is established, whereas the internal integration index (and overlapping problem solving) refers to activities after the establishment of the technical concept (Iansiti, 1998:47).

Knowledge integration also has different meanings. It is seen as the action of linking:

1. Different 'knowledge specialisms', technological fields or disciplines (see for instance Miyazaki, 1993; Prahalad and Hamel, 1990; Patel and Pavitt, 1994; Henderson, 1994). Knowledge fusion refers to the creation of a new technological field that emerges through the combination of two already existing technological fields, as in the case of optoelectronics analyzed by Miyazaki (1993 and 1994).
2. Specialized skills, knowledge bases and technical and managerial systems (knowledge in a broad sense) located in different units, business-functions or divisions of the company. This is what is meant by internal integration which is much more focused on organizational issues. It is used by Clark and Fujimoto (1991), Iansiti and Clark (1994) and Henderson (1994).
3. Internal capabilities with external sources of knowledge. This is the meaning of external integration used by Iansiti and Clark (1994), Henderson (1994) and Iansiti (1998).

A set of integrative mechanisms is described by several of the authors reviewed here to facilitate the integration of knowledge. They are extracted from empirical studies and are the base for normative recommendations. The most recurrent in the SML are listed in Table 3.2.

This review of the literature surrounding the coordination of learning and knowledge integration suggests the following considerations:

1. Even though this literature mentions the existence of differences in the learning strategies between organizational units, authors assume that those differences do not limit the coordination of learning and the integration of knowledge.
2. The literature focuses on firms that have a substantial base of knowledge. There is no problem associated with lack of knowledge in some organizational units or knowledge fields. The emphasis has been put on issues related to the management of knowledge and the implementation of mechanisms and promotion of behaviors conducive

to integrating knowledge. For instance the literature about knowledge integration concentrates on the organizational arrangements to integrate pre-existing knowledge in order to generate new knowledge, as highlighted in Section 2.3 in relation to the SML's focus on renewing the firm's knowledge base instead of building the first strategic capabilities. This is clear in the scope of external integration which does not include knowledge from competitors because firms are looking for new technical concepts; it is also revealed in the approach to customer integration which refers to future customers and new needs.

3. There is little empirical treatment of the problems of coordinating learning to support the integration of knowledge and the building of strategic capabilities. Many authors mention this issue but they do not elaborate the problem in detail. This focus results from analyzing successful cases and not those where there are problems.

4. The DCL has analyzed neither the coordination of learning nor processes of knowledge integration.

Table 3.2   Integrative mechanisms mentioned in the SML

- Teamwork based on cross-functional and cross-discipline teams
- Overlapping problem solving among different stages of the projects and among the engineering and manufacturing functions
- Overlapping of knowledge, redundancy of knowledge, or shared knowledge and expertise
- Boundary spanning or integrators: individuals who stand at the interface between different specialized units, knowledge bases or internal and external knowledge
- Project-focused organizational structures and processes
- Small teams with broad task assignments and a 'heavyweight' product manager
- Strategic rotation of personnel
- Informal communication networks

3.4   TOWARDS A FRAMEWORK FOR THE ANALYSIS OF KNOWLEDGE MANAGEMENT ISSUES

This chapter has reviewed literature about the role of different aspects of knowledge management that are considered relevant to support the competitive advantages of firms in a changing environment. Several authors have pointed out a number of similar mechanisms to support different organizational processes. For instance, the organizational arrangements to facilitate knowledge integration outlined by Iansiti and Clark (1994), Clark and Fujimoto (1991) and Henderson (1994) are similar to those described by Garvin (1993) and Senge (1990) to build a 'learning organization'; by Nonaka and Takeuchi (1995) to analyze the knowledge creation process; by Prahalad and Hamel (1990) to develop a strategic architecture that guides the process of building up core competencies; and by Leonard-Barton (1995a) to analyze the management of knowledge to nurture and re-build core technological capabilities. The descriptions of the same mechanisms to share, convert, integrate and create knowledge reveal the interrelation between several factors that contribute to maintain, nurture and re-build strategic capabilities, and the systemic nature of the strategic capabilities. This also reveals the still incipient understanding of this complex system.

The empirical evidence used by these studies illustrates the process of creation of new knowledge by the most innovative firms. This SML has focused on the characteristics and mechanisms for managing the creation of new knowledge and its integration with the already existing knowledge base. This literature brings a broad picture of the organizational factors that facilitate the process of utilization, creation and renewal of knowledge. In contrast it has not been concerned with issues related to the process of making effective use of existing knowledge to operate, assimilate, adapt and improve existing technologies. This issue is central to analyzing the characteristics of knowledge management in firms that do not play at the technological frontier.

In fact knowledge management can be centered around three issues: (i) creating new knowledge; (ii) utilizing, adapting and changing existing knowledge; or (iii) with a short term focus, only utilizing existing knowledge. This research refers to these three dimensions of knowledge management.

This book draws on the understanding of problems and overcoming them, rather than only on describing successful projects to identify the best mechanisms and practices that contribute to the success. The processes and mechanisms associated with the management of knowledge described by the SML are used here as a sort of benchmark.

The analytical framework used for the conversion of individual into organizational learning, and for the analysis of the coordination of learning and knowledge integration deserves more consideration. That framework is elaborated below.

3.4.1 About the Conversion of Individual into Organizational Learning

The literature about tacit and codified knowledge which is reviewed above does not provide an adequate framework for analyzing empirically problems related to the lack of knowledge codification. This book builds upon several ideas from that literature to develop the following analytical framework.

An important feature of the case study discussed in this book is that the firm neglected to codify substantial bodies of codifiable knowledge. For this reason this book uses a more flexible definition of tacit knowledge than that used by the SML reviewed here, which includes two broad categories: non codifiable tacit knowledge and codifiable tacit knowledge. Codifiable tacit knowledge refers to both verbally codified and non-codified knowledge. Unlike the SML this book uses a more rigid definition of codified knowledge, which only corresponds to written documents, software, equipment, specifications, etc. Verbal codification is considered as an incomplete codification of knowledge as it is difficult to explain details in words and some details are forgotten, and also because it is difficult to repeat the same ideas with the same level of accuracy. Additionally this book uses a framework which highlights the fact that there is some non-codified knowledge, which is in principle codifiable. This framework is described in Table 3.3.

Table 3.3 Distinction between tacit and codified knowledge used in this book

Tacit knowledge	<ul><li>Non codifiable</li><li>Codifiable tacit knowledge Verbally codified and non-codified</li></ul>
Codified knowledge	<ul><li>Documented Written documents, grammatical statements, mathematical expressions, specifications, designs, manuals, equipment, software, etc.</li></ul>

The level of tacitness of knowledge and the possibility that it may become codifiable changes over time: what is non codifiable this year may become more codifiable next year. Over time the amount of knowledge increases, new tacit knowledge is acquired, some of today's non codifiable tacit knowledge becomes codifiable in the future and the amount of codified knowledge increases. However as Cowan and Foray (1997:600) pointed out, 'codification is never complete, and some forms of tacit knowledge will always continue to play an important role'. In firms that neglect codification, new codifiable tacit knowledge will surely remain non-codified. The extent to which and the rate at which codifiable tacit knowledge is codified depend on several factors, such as the economic costs and benefits of the codification (Cowan and Foray, 1997:600–1), the extent to which valorization of the knowledge is considered likely to become relevant in the future (Levitt and March, 1988:327), or people's unawareness of the tacit dimensions of their knowledge (Leonard and Sensiper, 1998:113).

Over time it is difficult to say which tacit knowledge will strictly always be non codifiable. There is some knowledge that is non codifiable in each period of time, the most recurrent example being how to ride a bicycle, which has a strong non codifiable component. This book neither looks for discrimination between different types of tacit knowledge nor does it try to analyze the relationship between tacit and codified knowledge. The focus is that both tacit and codified knowledge are complementary and are required for building technological capabilities, and that there is always codifiable tacit knowledge that remains uncodified.

This book uses the modes of knowledge conversion between tacit and codified knowledge described by Nonaka and Takeuchi (1995) and examines in more detail two modes: (i) the conversion from tacit to tacit knowledge (sharing); and (ii) the conversion from tacit to codified knowledge (codification).

This book uses the general ideas described in Section 3.2 to analyze the processes of learning at individual and organizational level. However it looks at the details of the coherence between the learning mechanisms and the organizational arrangements explicitly designed to learn from others which have been designed for other purposes but affect the learning process at organizational level.

Therefore this book looks at the overall knowledge system from a broader perspective than the literature referred to before, and examines a wider range of factors that affect the knowledge system.

3.4.2 About the Coordination of Learning and Knowledge Integration

This book builds upon the literature reviewed in Section 3.3, however it changes the lens to analyze the organizational processes. The focus is on the problems of coordinating the learning when there are differences in learning strategies between organizational units.

This book analyzes the integration of knowledge as one issue of knowledge management and not as the base on which to build strategic capabilities. This book uses basically the second meaning of knowledge integration referred to above, as the action of linking specialized skills, knowledge bases and technical and managerial systems located in different units, business-functions or divisions of the company. The third meaning of external integration will refer here to knowledge from competitors, a source of knowledge not considered in the SML.

To sum up, the conversion of individual into organizational learning, the coordination of learning and the integration of knowledge are crucial processes in building strategic capabilities. This book analyzes to what extent they occur and what are the factors that influence the scope of these features of knowledge management. This is done on the basis of a case study of a single firm that is undergoing a Transition Process.

3.5   CONCEPTUAL DESIGN OF THIS BOOK

Chapters 2 and 3 constitute the theoretical foundations of this book. The DCL and SML reviewed have made major contributions to the analysis of the process of building technological capabilities, but leave several issues unclear, particularly those related to firms in a Transition Process. This book intends to begin to address those issues. Based on the DCL and SML already reviewed and on the framework built upon them, this book analyzes the long term historical process of the building up of technological capabilities of a firm with a depth of understanding about the internal knowledge management process. This is achieved by drawing on the knowledge management literature to analyze the long term process of capability building. This book analyzes the specific problems of the Transition Process, which are different from those arising from building the minimum essential knowledge base and from building strategic capabilities.

Based on the analytical framework described in Sections 2.4 and 3.4, Part II presents a detailed description of the long term process of building up technological capabilities in the case study firm. Under the heading of technological capabilities a description of the creation of technological knowledge and of the organizational/institutional factors which affect that process are presented. Chapters 6 to 8 are organized according to the stages in the building up of technological capabilities in the following way: Chapter 6 contains an analytical description of how the firm built the minimum essential knowledge base to survive in the market; Chapter 7 presents how the firm evolved, but not very effectively, towards building strategic capabilities, and describes the problems of making the Transition Process; Chapter 8 describes some problems encountered in a changing economic and technological environment which further hampered the Transition Process.

Part III contains an analysis of the problems in the knowledge management to complete the Transition Process. It focuses on the features of the knowledge management that explain the truncated Transition Process and some factors influencing those features. The features, factors influencing and their links with the Transition Process are presented in Figure 3.1 below.

Figure 3.1 Links between knowledge management and the Transition Process

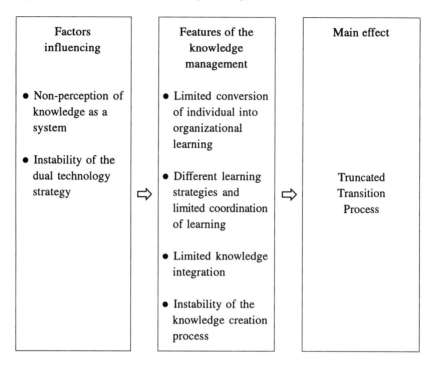

Factors influencing	Features of the knowledge management	Main effect
• Non-perception of knowledge as a system • Instability of the dual technology strategy	• Limited conversion of individual into organizational learning • Different learning strategies and limited coordination of learning • Limited knowledge integration • Instability of the knowledge creation process	Truncated Transition Process

Chapter 9 analyzes the four key features of the knowledge management and Chapter 10 analyzes two factors that influenced these key features of the knowledge management.

4 Methodology

4.1 INTRODUCTION

This book is based on firm-level research developing a detailed case study of the long term process of building up technological capabilities with a depth of understanding about the internal knowledge management. The case study is the Glass Container Division of the Mexican Vitro Group. This is one of the larger and most successful Mexican industrial groups which is internationally competitive but yet is behind the technological frontier.

The analysis of the case aims at clarifying questions about the characteristics of the long term process of building technological capabilities, the specific problems of the Transition Process, the key features of the knowledge management that limit the building of strategic capabilities and some factors influencing them.

The SML reviewed in Chapters 2 and 3 is also based on firm-level research, using case studies and questionnaire methodologies. That literature stressed the positive things that firms did to maintain and renew strategic capabilities. The authors mostly analyzed successful cases and projects to identify the behaviors and mechanisms underlying them. By this means they extracted the characteristics of the process of building strategic capabilities, of a 'learning organization', or of a 'knowledge building company' to generate normative recommendations.

This book has used a different perspective to analyze the process of building strategic capabilities. This research has looked at the problems that mitigated against the building of strategic capabilities. The firm's behavior is a key element in the process of building technological capabilities because this process involves both the accumulation of technological knowledge and a set of activities and systems that create that technological knowledge. Hence particular attention was put on identifying firm's behavior associated with successful and failed development projects. The identification of behavior associated with projects was based on carrying out several and highly diversified interviews about each project. The interviews included personnel involved from different business-functions and from different departments within each function; personnel in different hierarchical positions, from machine operator to the Divisional President; and personnel from different plants, including Mexican and American subsidiaries. These diverse sources of information about the same projects allows officially established mechanisms, organizational arrangements and procedures to be distinguished from actual behavior.

This research looked at the negative characteristics of the firm's behavior to identify the problems in converting individual into organizational learning, coordinating the learning, integrating the knowledge and creating knowledge in order to identify the reasons for not building strategic capabilities. This allowed identification of the problems the firm has to overcome in order to be able to compete on the basis of knowledge.

The information utilized in the case study was collected in 1995 and 1996 during the pilot study and the field work in Mexico and the US. The main sources of information are interviews carried out within the firm, which were complemented with unpublished documents provided by the firm, and firms's Annual Reports. Further details of the methodology are described below.

4.2   BROAD RESEARCH STRATEGY

This book is based on firm-level research and aims at clarifying questions about the long term process of building technological capabilities. Why was it that the firm could accumulate knowledge but could not build strategic capabilities? What were the key features of knowledge management and how did they limit the building of strategic capabilities?

The research strategies selected to conduct the study were a case study combined with a retrospective study. The selection of the research strategies was based on the fact that this book is addressing what Yin (1994:4–9) describes as 'how' and 'why' questions, and also on the fact that the study addresses issues not yet thoroughly researched (Leonard-Barton, 1995b:40). The case study allowed several sources of evidence to be included, and the retrospective study contributes to a better understanding of the bases of the problems that the firm faces today. Therefore even though this book refers to a case study methodology, it is understood that this includes both research strategies. The particular research questions and the selection of a single case study were oriented to carrying out an exploratory type of study in order to gain insights into new problems (Yin, 1994:41).

The case was selected from a set of Mexican firms with similar characteristics, such as participation in the international market, being a first player at international level, using patents to protect their intellectual property, etc.

A pilot study was conducted to support the selection of the case to be studied. Accessibility and availability of documentation were the key issues in making the choice between the possible options. This pilot study provided empirical observations and insights into the basic issues being studied. This information was also used in parallel with a review of relevant literature and industrial publications to improve the final research design.

4.3   SOURCES OF DATA

The information utilized in the case study was collected in 1995 during the pilot study and in the summer of 1996 during the field work carried out in Mexico and the US. The main sources are described below.

1.   *Interviews*. They were the main source of information. Two types of interviews were conducted: (i) open-ended, in which the key respondents were asked for facts, their opinions about them and insights (Yin, 1994:84), these interviews also contributed to identification of key issues; and (ii) focused, in which a set of questions were followed to cover specific topics of the case study, these questions were basically approached as open-ended questions, but some structured questions were also included.

2.   *Casual meetings, informal conversations and attendance at meetings.* These contributed to generate insights and to make more precise information obtained during the interviews.

3.   *Direct observation.* The observation during the field work of problems that arose in the production line and the way plant and technical personnel interacted to solve them gave insights into difficulties, behaviors, links, etc.

4.   *Archival records.* Organizational charts, list of products and clients, job descriptions, industrial census, etc. helped to corroborate and rectify points in the information collected via the interviews.

5.   *Documentation.* Several types of documentary information were collected and used in the research, for instance, Annual Reports, memoranda, minutes of meetings, progress reports, conference proceedings, newspaper and other articles appearing in the mass media, some specific publications of the firm and a few studies that referred to other aspects of the firm. These documents served to corroborate and enrich the evidence obtained from other sources (Yin, 1994:81) and to rectify the timing of the events.

4.4   COLLECTING INFORMATION THROUGH INTERVIEWS

The focus of the collection of information was individual's and firm's behavior over time. Due to the difficulties inherent in asking for behavior *per se*, interviewees were asked for anecdotes about specific development projects.

The types of behavior were basically identified through these stories. The following steps were followed during the field work to collect information.

1. Identifying and selecting development projects
    1.1 Key informants and managers of the technical-functions were asked for relevant projects through open-ended interviews.
    1.2 Projects were selected in order to build a sample that included:
        • development and continuous improvement projects
        • both recent projects and others from the 1970s and 1980s
        • successful and less successful projects.

The selection of the projects took into account that the projects had been completed. This was to avoid failure to complete a project or its interruption being confused with the firm's actual behavior associated with the implementation of the projects (Leonard-Barton, 1995b:46). Some projects are intricately described in this book, others not but all the projects were drawn on to identify the firm's behavior. The development projects listed in Table 4.1 were included in the case study, the boxes refer to the specific place in the book where some of these projects are described:

Table 4.1   List of development projects included in the case study

The project with Heye Glas about the positioning in bottle thickness	(Boxes 7.1 and 10.2)
The development of an electronic control system for the IS machine	(Boxes 9.2, 9.5 and Section 7.4.1.2)
The change in the glass formula	(Box 7.2)
The pasted machine for glassware products and the 'VII system'	(Box 6.2)
The case of coupling new plunger mechanisms with the molding equipment	(Boxes 9.4 and 10.1)
Coupling equipment from different technology sources	(Box 9.1)
The design of an IS machine by Fama	——
The team for continuous improvement to develop a fine adjustment of the take-out mechanism	——
The design of a kit to increase the speed of the ceramics cycle	——
The acquisition of a feeder mechanism with Emhart Glass	(Section 8.4.1)
The coupling of two IS machines in line: the tandem IS machine at Anchor Glass Containers Corporation	——

2. Identifying the learning mechanisms and organizational arrangements to learn currently established in the firm
    2.1 In-depth interviews with current managers of the technical areas were conducted. The managers were asked about the learning mechanisms and organizational arrangements promoted and established to learn. A structured questionnaire was completed.
    2.2 With this information a list of learning mechanisms and organizational arrangements was added to the interview guide for the development projects.
3. Accessing information about firm's activities in the past
    3.1 In-depth interviews were conducted with retired personnel who had played key roles in the technical areas, in operations or at the managerial level.
4. Identifying individual's and firm's behaviors over time, and the key features of knowledge management
    Due to the complexity of this issue and the interaction between several factors, it was necessary to obtain information from multiple levels and perspectives in the firm. The following methodology based on interviews about the projects was implemented:
    4.1 Interviews with the leader of each project. Projects leaders were asked about the history of the projects. The interviews were focused with some structured questions, and in particular they were asked about the extent to which the learning mechanisms and organizational arrangements listed previously by managers were used.
    4.2 Interviews with other key participants in the project team. These were oriented to obtaining different views about several aspects of the projects. This group of interviews covered personnel from different business-functions, departments, hierarchical positions, and plants – including Mexican and American plants. The use of multiple informants provided more details, suggested issues that had been inadequately covered in other interviews, allowed the validation of information by checking information given by one informant against that from another, and also allowed discrepancies in some of the information to be resolved (Glick et al., 1995:142). In some cases a second round of interviews with key participants was carried out to correct certain issues. Most of the discrepancies in information from different participants were solved by the second round of interviews.
    In addition open-ended and focused interviews with personnel not participating in the project teams were conducted to explore different issues. These interviews covered a broad range of personnel from

different hierarchical positions in the firm, ranging from the machine operator to the Divisional President; from different business-functions and also from different departments within each function; and from different plants.

By carrying out interviews at different levels, and by corroborating the learning mechanisms and organizational arrangements listed by managers during the interviews with the views of several participants in the projects, it was possible to obtain a much more clear idea about the actual behavior of the firm.

5. Corroborating information

Key informants were used to corroborate the information obtained from other personnel during the field work. This was the basis used to identify misunderstandings or issues not deeply or correctly described. With this continuous feedback several interviewees were asked for more precision about certain behaviors. Some key informants were selected due to their lead position in the firm or in the processes analyzed. Other key informants emerged spontaneously due to their own interest in the issues being analyzed in the research. The firm's Annual Reports and some published documents were also used to corroborate and enrich the evidence obtained.

6. Sites and interviewees

The case study covered a number of different sites, including different business activities, towns and countries. The sites listed in Table 4.2 were visited and included in the study.

Table 4.2 Sites included in the study

- Monterrey plant, in Monterrey, Mexico
- Querétaro plant, in Querétaro, Mexico
- Mexico II Plant, in Mexico City, Mexico
- Fama, in Monterrey, Mexico
- Corporate Headquarters, in Monterrey, Mexico
- Technical Center and Corporate Headquarters of Anchor Glass Containers Corporation, in Tampa, Florida, US
- Excellence Center of AGCC, in Cincinnati, US
- Elmira Plant, in Elmira, New York, US

The case study covered sixty-nine interviewees, fifty-four in Mexico and fifteen in the US. A summary of the job position of the interviewees is given in Table 4.3.

Table 4.3 Main job positions of the interviewees

	Mexico	US
Glass Container Plants Plant managers; engineering and job change department managers; maintenance and molding leaders; Upkeeps[1]; machine operators; mechanics	13	6
Direction of Technology of Vitro-Glass Containers Director; managers of several departments; project leaders; designers and project engineers	17	9
At divisional level Divisional President; manager of the strategic planning department of the Marketing Direction; staff	4	
At the corporate level Corporate Director of Technology; Director of Technology of other division and ex-Corporate Director of Technology (1987–90); managers and staff of different departments of the Corporate Technology Direction	5	
Fama (internal machine manufacturer) Director, managers of the production engineering and marketing departments	3	
Retired and ex-personnel Upkeep from 1930 to 1980; technical plant leader and later Director of Technology of Vitro-Glass Containers from 1954 to 1985; managers of different departments of Fama from 1945 to 1990; ex-Corporate Director of Technology (1978–87); ex-Director of Fama (1980s)	7	
Civil servants; personnel form industrial associations and researchers	5	
Total interviewees	54	15

---

[1] This is the name used in the industry for the technician in charge of fixing the machine's problems.

4.5   ANALYZING CASE STUDY EVIDENCE

The interviews and some published documents were the basis on which the story of the process of building technological capabilities was developed, and by which the firm's behaviors were identified along with the problems over building strategic capabilities. The description of the projects was used to identify similarities and changes over time in the firm's behavior.

The analytic strategy was to develop a historical narrative for organizing the case study. This helped to identify the causal links to be analyzed and to explain the reasons why the Transition Process was not completed. As Van de Ven and Huber (1995:xii) pointed out, 'change processes are themselves composed of events with antecedents and consequences, and when these are understood and connected in the form of a story or historical narrative, an understanding of the process is often the result'.

On the basis of the historical narrative, the case study data were analyzed by building an explanation of the case. The explanation-building was based on stipulating a set of casual links about the case. Several iterations contributed to the final explanations. Because the links are complex and difficult to measure in any precise manner, explanation-building was also developed basically in narrative form (Yin, 1994:110).

The methodological details of how qualitative data gathered during the field work were processed to build interpretative tables are described by table in Chapters 9 and 10.

4.6   WRITING THE CASE STUDY

The case study is written following a linear-analytic structure. The evidence is presented in two ways:

1. 'An analytic chronology', which is basically the historical narrative of the process of building technological capabilities but including the key analytical issues of this book, is presented in Chapters 6, 7 and 8.
2. 'A theory-building structure', which aims to interpret the story, to link some issues with the theoretical debate in the literature, and to present several factors that explain why the firm did not complete the Transition Process, is presented in Chapters 9 and 10.

A number of drafts of the case study report were sent to a key informant for review. Initially the 'analytic chronology' of the long term process of building technological capabilities, as it was reconstructed in this book, was sent for reviewing. This key informant provided additional details and corrected inaccuracies. Later on the interpretation of the facts included in the analytical chapters (theory-building) was sent to the same key informant to gain his reactions and to try to evaluate the extent to which the interpretation was sensitive to the firm's problems.

5 Overview of the Technology, the Industry and the Firm

5.1 INTRODUCTION

Why study firm's behavior in the glass container industry in Mexico? The Mexican glass container industry is small in relative terms. It is an industry worth around 800 million dollars per year. It represented only 0.8 per cent of manufacturing GDP in Mexico in 1995 and 0.4 per cent of the manufacturing exports. However it has a number of features that make it of interest to study.

First, it is a traditional industry rooted in 1909 that has grown quickly over the century. The yearly average growth rate of the industry from 1970 to 1993 was 5 per cent, higher than the 3.8 per cent of the manufacturing sector in that period. Second, the industry has increased its orientation towards the international market. Glass container exports increased from 9.4 million dollars in 1975 to 127 in 1992 and to 157 in 1995. Its export coefficient has grown from 4.4 per cent in 1975 to 14.6 per cent in 1992. The Mexican glass container industry is characterized as a 'rising star' according to the CAN 20 database.[1] Moreover it is one of the nine sectors that reported increased productivity, a high growth of production rate and an improvement in trade balance in the period 1980–91.[2] Third, Vitro-Glass Containers (VGC), the main producer, is a world player. It was the third producer at international level in the mid-1990s. It has been a multinational firm since the late 1960s, with subsidiaries in Latin America and the US. It has always had a particular technological culture related to its own history. Its founders were strongly influenced by American entrepreneurs at the beginning of the 1900s. Since the earliest days, they pushed the organization to introduce state-of-the-art technology, which behavior has continued until today. It never was a typical Import Substitution Industrialization (ISI) firm. During the ISI period it took advantage of the protected market, but at the same time it competed in the

---

[1] CEPAL (1995).
[2] Capdevielle, Cimoli and Dutrénit (1997:11).

international market. This duality has influenced its technological and business strategies.

The main purpose of this chapter is to present a background about the technology, the industry and the firm for this book. Section 5.2. describes the technology for making glass containers. Section 5.3 summarizes the main characteristics of the industry. Section 5.4 describes the Mexican and US glass container markets, where the case study firm has subsidiaries. Finally Section 5.5 presents a profile of the case study firm.

5.2   THE TECHNOLOGY

This section summarizes the main features of the technology for glass container making. Section 5.2.1 outlines the process of glass container making. Section 5.2.2 describes the main characteristics of the glass container forming stage and the IS machine, where this book is essentially concentrated. Section 5.2.3 describes the technological trajectory, leaders and trends of the industry.

5.2.1 The Process of Glass Container Making

Glass container making can be summarized in the following way: primary and selected secondary raw materials are melted in furnaces and fed to continuous, automatic processing machines that press and blow, or blow and blow, the molten glass into glass container molds. The containers can then be annealed and later decorated, sandblasted, and/or polished in post-forming secondary treatments. Figure 5.1 below shows the main stages of the glass container making process.

The primary raw materials are silica sand, soda ash and limestone. Soda ash accounts for approximately 70 per cent of the total raw material volume. Secondary raw materials include potash, lead oxide, boric oxide, oxidizing or reducing agents, and agents that provide specific properties and colors. Cullet (excess or waste glass from an earlier melt or recycled glass articles that can be charged to the glass furnace) has become an increasingly large proportion of the glass batch, up to 25 per cent.[3] It allows energy saving and reduces the emission.

The manufacture of glass containers is a continuous operation with most furnaces fueled by natural gas. The new energy source is based on the oxygen process, the diffusion of which is still limited due to the price of the equipment. Half of total plant energy consumption is due to the melting stage.

---

[3]   USITC (1993:1).

Some of the main technologies in the industry are: (i) melting, particularly the design of furnaces; (ii) chemical formulation of glass to determine the glass batch; (iii) glass formation, particularly equipment and process technologies; and (iv) control of the processes.

Figure 5.1 The glass container making process

Raw materials
⇩

Batch preparation	The raw materials are chosen according to the glass formula and mixed.

⇩

Melting	The glass batch is transformed from solid to molten glass in the furnace.

⇩

Glass conditioning	The molten glass is thermally conditioned in the forehearth to control its temperature. The shape and weight of the gob is determined according to the container type to be made by the gob feeder. Through the feeder mechanism the IS machine is feed with glass gobs.

⇩

Glass container forming	The gob falls into the blank mold of each section of the IS machine, where the parison[4] is obtained by blow or by plunger press. The blank-mold is inverted and the parison is transferred to the blow-mold where by means of air blowing acquire the final form. The container is transferred by the take-out mechanism to a dead-plate to be cooled. Finally the 90 degree push-out mechanism moves the container to the conveyor belt.

⇩

Annealing	The container receives a thermal treatment to achieve room temperature.

⇩

Surface treatment	The container receives a chemical treatment to form a permanent coating to increase its strength.

⇩

Inspection	The containers are inspected to detect faults, such as break, blur, choked neck, etc.

⇩

Post-forming	Several processes can be undertaking, such as decorating, labeling, polishing or sandblasting of the containers.

⇩

Packaging	Product handling.

⇩
Glass containers

Source:
Compiled from Catve (1989 and 1995).

---

[4] The parison is glass given an approximate shape in this preliminary forming process.

5.2.2 The Glass Container Forming Stage and the IS Machine

The IS machine is the most diffused machine used to form the glass container. It was launched on the market in 1925. The name refers to the operation of Individual Sections, each of which constitutes a complete machine unit and can be operated independently.

The success of the IS machine in persisting in the market is associated with its versatility in terms of: (i) number of sections, from two to eighteen; (ii) number of mold cavities per section: from simple to quadruple; and (iii) range of products, from containers of 2ml to 5l. It is also a universal machine that can be operated using different processes. Three basic processes of fabrication are used for glass container formation with the IS machine.[5]

1. *Press-Blow process for wide mouth containers.* This is a process in which the parison is hollowed out with a plunger. Then it is blown to the final shape of the ware by mechanical means. This was the first process used in the IS machine and is called the '62 process'. It is basically used to produce wide mouth containers for the food industry.
2. *Blow-Blow process for narrow neck containers.* This is a process in which the blank-mold is blown to form the parison, and then blown again to produce the final shape of the ware by mechanical means. It is used to produce narrow neck containers for drinks and liquids.
3. *Narrow-Neck-Press-Blow (NNPB) process for narrow neck containers.* This is quite a new process introduced in the late 1980s, as described in Section 8.2.2 and Box 7.1. The parison is hollowed out with a plunger as in the Press-Blow process. The use of the Press-Blow process allows the amount of glass used in narrow neck containers to be reduced resulting in production of lightweight containers, permitting increased machine speed. It also improves the glass distribution in the container, increasing the product quality. However the narrow neck of the container causes the process of penetrating and pressing by the plunger to be a more complex and precise machine task than is the case of the wide mouth containers.

In general the IS machine has thousands of pieces and eleven mechanisms of pneumatic operation which are controlled by a time drum. The time drum is used to start up and stop each section and control the functioning of the machine mechanisms. There are two types of time drum: the original mechanical control and the electronic control introduced in the 1970s, as highlighted in Section 7.4.1.2. The electronic control allows a larger number

---

[5] Based on Catve (1989 and 1995).

of functions to be controlled by section than the mechanical time drum, and gives more precision in the mechanisms movements.[6]

5.2.3 Technological Trajectory, Leaders and Trends

The industry has mainly progressed on technological trajectories of process innovation. Equipment technology has been crucial. The forming of the glass is the most important part of the production process. There were three important innovations in the early decades of the century: the Owens automatic machine in 1903, the automatic gob feeder in 1915 and the IS machine in 1925.

In 1903 Michael Owens, from the Toledo Glass Co., patented the first automatic bottle machine. The machine could both gather molten glass by suction and blow glass automatically. It was a breakthrough in the concept of making bottles. It allowed an increase in productivity and reduced the cost of the bottles. This innovation made it possible to mass produce bottles and jars of uniform height, weight and capacity which improved product quality and allowed the introduction of high speed filling in the food, dairy and beverage industries, increasing productivity in these industries also.[7]

The Owens Bottle Machine Co. (later Owens-Illinois) was created by the Toledo Glass Co. to produce bottles and to license others to use Owens machines.[8] The Owens Bottle Machine Co., being a glass container maker, did not allow a quick diffusion of the innovation in the US. There were also other hindrances to the diffusion, such as the high capital cost associated with the machine and the high royalty payments imposed by the firm. The Beech-Nut Packing Co., an American food producing firm, did not have access to containers produced by Owens machines. It was interested in improving the glass container production method to obtain containers of a similar quality and productivity to those produced with the novel Owens machine. Semi-automatic machines were on the market, using either a hand-gathering system or a stream flowing feeder. An automatic feeder could convert them into fully automatic units to compete with Owens machines. The Beech-Nut Packing Co. funded R&D activities to look at the problem of automatic feeding of glass to forming machines. In 1912 it formed a new company to design and build new and improved glass-working machinery, named Hartford Fairmont Co.[9] In 1915 Karl Peiler, an employee of that firm, was granted a patent for an automatic gob feeder. The Hartford Fairmont Co. started

---

6   Catve (1995:35).
7   Meigh (1972:48).
8   Meigh (1960:32).
9   Meigh (1960:37).

manufacturing the gob feeder. In 1922 Hartford Fairmont joined the Corning Glass Works to form Hartford Empire Co. (later the Hartford section of the Emhart Corp., and later Emhart Glass). The Hartford Empire Co. was granted the first patent for the IS machine in 1925, which was invented by Henry Ingle. This was the origin of the Emhart Glass IS machine technology which today is widespread.

The Owens Machine Bottle Co. continued improving its Owens machines, for instance, in 1920 it introduced the Owens rotated AW machines. These machines were equipped with the Graham system based on a gravity flow stream feeder.[10] However by 1920 the Owens Machine Bottle Co. recognized the supremacy of the Hartford Fairmont feeder and began to use it. After the successful market introduction of the IS machines, Owens-Illinois – a merger of the Owens Machine Bottle Co. and the Illinois Glass Co. – acquired the Hartford Empire IS machines and later developed its own technology. This was the origin of the now common Owens-Illinois IS machine technology.

Since the 1940s the IS machine has dominated the equipment technology. The innovation activity in equipment has been oriented to developing ways to increase the speed, efficiency, machine throughput and machine coordination, and to reduce downtime and defects. The production capacity of the machine has increased from 40 to 500 bottles per minute. The increase in the number of sections and cavities, and the introduction of the electronic control have also contributed to the improved performance. The changes in the production methods and glass forming equipment have been accompanied by changes in the chemical composition of the glass.[11] For instance the Owens machines required a less viscous glass than that used by hand-workers or by the semi-automatic machines.[12] The automatic gob feeder changed again the viscosity of the molten glass required.

Todat there are two main technologies of IS machines: Owens-Illinois and Emhart Glass. Owens-Illinois, with its more robust machines that allow high productivity, dominates the US market and several developing countries, such as Mexico. Owens-Illinois sells technology and so supplies machines only to its licensees. Emhart Glass, with its more flexible equipment, dominates the European market. It sells machines, complementary equipment and technology. Most of the firms world-wide pertain to one club or the other. Heye Glas uses a different equipment technology and is particularly strong in the NNPB technology of double cavity.

The IS machine technology determines all the complementary equipment to be used. Several changes in complementary equipment and other stages of

---

[10] Meigh (1972:61).
[11] Meigh (1972:11).
[12] Meigh (1972:46).

the glass container production process have followed the innovations in the IS machine. From the 1980s small organized suppliers of machine mechanisms have been an important source of improvements to the IS machine. This has put pressures on glass container makers to develop the abilities to couple these mechanisms to their IS machines.

The description of the evolution of the glass forming machine revealed the key role of machine users at the beginning of the century. Firms changed their main activity from users to producers, and vice versa, revealing that knowledge about the container production process was an essential base for production of machines. For instance, the Beech-Nut Packing Co. was a food producing firm that became a machine producer. The Toledo Glass Co. changed from being a glass products maker to being a machine producer and then to being a producer of containers using its own machines. The emergence of specialized suppliers of machine mechanisms in the 1980s, many of whom were former users, such as Quantum and Imtec, reveals again the central role of the users in the innovation process in the industry. Actually the vertical disintegration process has not been completed in the glass container industry world-wide. Several companies are vertically integrated to produce the specialized machines used to make glass containers, as described in more detail in Sections 5.3 and 10.3.3.

In terms of product innovations, lightening by the NNPB process, increasing strength by improving the surface condition, labeling and decoration have been areas of improvements.

The industry has followed basically a technological trajectory of a scale intensive sector according to the taxonomy of Pavitt (1984). Specialized suppliers of equipment and components (independent or vertically integrated), and in-house technological activities carried out by design departments, production engineering departments and operating experience have been sources of innovation. However many firms, apart from the largest players, can be considered to be supplier dominated, following a strategy more dependent on innovations introduced by those specialized suppliers of equipment.

In the most recent decades there has been little research into glass container production.[13] Today the glass container industry uses a mature technology. Competitiveness is based on the control of the whole process of container production and the combination of improved mechanisms developed by small suppliers using standard IS machines. A new trend in the industry is to combine different technologies to obtain better performance from the equipment, which includes acquiring the mechanisms for one technology and coupling them to another technology. This makes knowledge in mechanical engineering essential.

---

[13] Interviews with managers of AGCC's Technical Center and of Dirtec.

R&D activities are concentrated on ultralightweight, increased container strength (e.g. coatings), processing and batch melting technology improvements.[14] At present, lightweighting and recycling have reduced materials and energy consumption and solid waste disposal. The lightweighting, as a result of the introduction of the NNPB process, has reduced the glass container's weight by around 20 per cent in relation to the early 1980s.[15] The recycling has allowed increased use of cullet in the glass batch. Alternative raw materials are being tested to reduce the glass formula costs. A common view in the industry is that more strategic research should be oriented to changing the glass forming process rooted in 1925.[16]

5.3   THE INDUSTRY

The glass container industry is conformed by the establishments primarily engaged in manufacturing glass containers for commercial packing and bottling, and for home preserving. The codes of the industry are the following:

Table 5.1   Definition of the industry

SIC Code	3221 Glass Containers
Parent Division	D. Manufacturing
Parent Major Group	32 Stone, clay, glass, and concrete products
Parent Industry Group	322 glass and glassware, pressed or blown
SITC Code	665 Glassware

The main characteristics of the glass containers industry are outlined in Table 5.2 below.

The barriers to entry in the industry are high, the following barriers are particularly important:

1. *High capital investment.* It is an industry associated with high fixed costs and it is an increasingly capital-intensive business (the cost of a new furnace exceeds 50 million dollars, the cost of an IS machine is around two million dollars). A typical glass container plant costs about 70 million dollars to build.[17] Such conditions are beneficial for the largest players and magnify the importance of proprietary technology.

[14] USITC (1993:5).
[15] 'The Future Lies in Quality Management Systems' (1991:16).
[16] Interview with the Director of Dirtec and managers of AGCC's Technical Center.
[17] 'Glass: a Clear Vision for a Bright Future' (1996:10).

2. *High costs of transportation.* Glass containers are a local business. In particular bottles and jars have traditionally been manufactured locally because of the low value/weight ratio and high costs of shipping empty containers. Transportation costs are estimated as representing 10 per cent of the import value.[18] In contrast perfume and pharmaceutical flasks have high or medium value/weight ratio and are economically suitable for exporting.

Because of the high costs of transportation, the local specifications of the product and the importance of prompt delivery, glass container production facilities must be located close to customers. Raw materials, labor and capital are equally important in the cost structure of the containers, they represent one-fourth each. Energy and other costs represent the other one-fourth.[19]

Table 5.2 Characteristics of the glass container industry

- The product is an input
- The technology is idiosyncratic, highly specialized
- The life cycle of the industry has reached a mature stage
- Low or negative growth, except in emerging economies
- General abundance of raw materials
- The production process is capital intensive, however labor and materials represent a high percentage of the production cost
- Economies of scale
- High barriers to entry in the industry
- Energy intensive production
- The glass container industry throughout the world is highly concentrated (except in Germany, where there is more competition), however large oligopolies coexisted with medium-size firms
- A local or regional business

The structure of the industry world-wide is different. The European industry is conformed by few large groups and small and medium-size businesses (Papadopoulos, 1990), while in the US there are only large firms. Markets are also different. The European market has traditionally required flexible production to supply a highly specialized demand. The US market is very large and less diversified and thus has required long production runs. Several Latin American markets have a diversified demand that requires small production runs as in Europe.

---

[18] USITC (1993:9).
[19] Morgan Stanley & Co. (1995:Table 11) for the costs structure of a 16 oz. glass bottle in 1994.

Oligopolies play at the international level. The main glass container producers of the industry at international level in 1995–6 were: 1st, Owens-Illinois (US); 2nd, Saint Gobain (France); and 3rd, Vitro-Glass Container (Mexico). These firms have subsidiaries in several other developed and developing countries. Owens-Illinois and Saint Gobain have occupied these positions for a long time. Vitro-Glass Container used to be ranked sixth at the international level and rose to third by its acquisition of the Anchor Glass Container Corporation in 1989. In 1997 it fell back to sixth place after divesting itself of the American company in December 1996.

The product mix of the large producers world-wide is different because firms have pursued different strategies of diversification. The main strategies are outlined below.

1. *Vertical integration.* Some firms are vertically integrated to produce the machines, such as Owen-Illinois (US), Vitro-Group (Mexico), Toyo Glass (Japan) and Heye Glas (Germany).
2. *Diversification in glass.* Some firms have diversified into other glass related businesses, sharing some core technologies, such as Saint Gobain (France), Owens-Illinois (US) and Vitro-Group (Mexico).
3. *Diversification in packaging.* Some firms have followed a strategy of diversifying into other packaging materials (e.g. plastic and cans), such as Owens-Illinois (US), Rockware (UK), Consumer Packaging (Canada) and Vitro-Group[20] (Mexico).

Mergers between players in the world (joint ventures or acquisitions) are the means to enter the industry. This way of entry is related to the mature life cycle of the industry, a decreasing demand, the oligopolistic character of the market, and a new type of relationship established with clients based on long term contracts. In 'emergent economies' the rate of substitution of other materials for glass is lower than in industrial advanced countries. Hence, large international players have tended to carry out mergers with local firms to supply those markets.

5.4   THE MEXICAN AND THE US GLASS CONTAINER INDUSTRY

Vitro-Glass Containers, the case study firm, is the main producer in the Mexican market. In 1989, with the acquisition of AGCC, it became the second largest producer in the US market. It has regularly exported to the US since

---

[20] This is a still incipient business.

the 1930s. Therefore in the period analyzed in this book, from 1909 to 1996, VGC has been an important player in both markets. Hence this section will describe both markets. Section 5.4.1 traces the historical evolution of the Mexican glass container industry and draws attention to the salient characteristics of the economic and policy context, which need to be taken into account in interpreting the process of building technological capabilities by VGC. It also describes the main trends of the Mexican glass container industry in recent years. Section 5.4.2 presents a brief description of the main trends of the US glass container industry.

5.4.1 The Mexican Glass Container Industry

This Section contains a brief description of the history and trends of the glass container industry. Particular attention is given to the description of the evolution of the industry in the economic and policy context, main players, market structure, main markets and recent changes in the sources of competitiveness.

5.4.1.1 Brief history of the glass container industry

The origin of the industry

The history of the industry has its roots in 1909 with the creation of the first company of the Vitro-Group: 'Vidriera Monterrey' at Monterrey, and it was associated with the evolution of the Mexican beer industry.

'Vidriera Monterrey' was created as a result of the vertical integration of the Cuauhtémoc brewery. It was set up as an independent company and it was the origin of the Vitro-Group, parent of Vitro-Glass Containers. However beer and glass containers were related businesses created at Monterrey by a group of families. In these and other related businesses a powerful industrial group, later called the 'Monterrey Group',[21] had its origins.

The glass container industry began in the context of an incipient industrial development at Mexico. The government established a number of stimuli to promote the creation of industrial firms, however there were shortages in

---

[21] The 'Monterrey Group' is an informal network of independent groups located in Monterrey and engaged in different business, such as glass, beer, steel and petrochemical. It has its roots in the foundation of the Cuauhtémoc brewery by Francisco Sada. Francisco Sada invited Isaac Garza, his brother in-law, to join the brewery. These two with other families founded 'Vidriera Monterrey' to make the glass bottles and a steel company to make the bottle caps. Monterrey companies continue to share many common business and some board members. Some of the directors of these companies have owned approximately 20 per cent of the common shares outstanding, many of them are Francisco Sada's descendants. (Nichols, 1993:168).

infrastructure, inputs and qualified human resources. The local government offered several other stimuli to reorient capital from trade to the industry. Therefore Monterrey was a locus for industrial development.

All the firms of the 'Monterrey Group' had strong connections with the US. Monterrey town was first connected by train to the US in 1882, and it was not until the end of the 1880s that it was connected to Mexico City. In the case of the glass container industry, the Vitro-Group's founders were entrepreneurs related to the US glass industry in two main ways: (i) several of the founders or their sons studied in the US, and (ii) two founders were American entrepreneurs related to glass companies. The Vitro-Group's founders were directly influenced by the fluorescence of the innovation activity in the US at the beginning of the 1900s. In particular they closely followed the transformation in the glass industry associated with the radical innovation of the Owens machine in glass bottle production, described in Section 5.2.3, and the innovative dynamic it stimulated in the glass industry world-wide. An example of the interrelations between business and with the US was the appointment of Roberto G. Sada – an MIT-trained engineer and the grandson of the Cuauhtémoc brewery founder – to run the glass container plant in 1909.

After several years of intense instability associated with the Mexican revolution, from 1915 to 1920 there was an increase in glass container demand and production. In 1921 the market dropped following an economic and social crisis in the country. At that time prices for domestic production were higher than for imports motivating an increase in imports. In 1922 the government protected the glass bottle industry with a duty. During the 1930s the demand for glass containers grew dramatically because of an increase in the domestic market. In addition in 1933 the industry started the exportation of bottles to the South of the US.[22]

The industry during the ISI

From the late 1940s until the early 1970s the general economic and policy context changed dramatically. After World War II the Import Substitution Industrialization was adopted as a development strategy to support industrial development. The ISI implemented a commercial protection based on tariff and non-tariff protection, fiscal and credit stimulus, frequent exchange rate controls, and devaluation mainly since the 1970s.

The promotion of industrial development was based on protection and subsidies. The idea was to progress from substituting consumer goods, to intermediaries to capital goods; and from importing goods to producing

---

[22] Fernández (1993).

and finally to exporting them. The industrial development was supported by development of infrastructure based on public investment. However the industrial policies were essentially horizontal, with few vertical policies by industrial sector until the end of the ISI. The last stages of the ISI – substituting capital goods and exporting goods – were not successfully accomplished.

The ISI was not only a development strategy to support industrial development, it was an ideology, culture or set of attitudes. In particular, the ISI promoted little attention to competitiveness, efficiency, technological upgrading, and export activity, and a great dependence on government support.[23]

During the ISI period a heterogeneous industrial structure was created: on the one side a traditional sector far from the international technological frontier, and on the other a modern sector closer to but still quite far behind the technological frontier. Due to problems in the industrial structure firms, even in the modern sector, became more vertically integrated and they horizontally diversified more than they would otherwise have done, and plants were small in size according to the international patterns.[24] Although there were differences between the traditional and modern sectors, both shared the ISI ideology and behaviors.[25]

The Mexican industry observed high rates of growth after the 1950s. Because of the dynamic domestic demand, the limited support to export activities and the institutions and behaviors associated with the ISI, industrial production was mostly oriented to satisfying the domestic market. In the early 1970s the ISI observed the first symptoms of crisis associated with the difficulties to accomplish the lasts stages of substituting capital goods and exporting. A set of stimuli for the capital goods industry and new policies to promote exports were introduced.

The glass container industry grew during these decades as a response to the increasing domestic demand. From 1970 to 1975 production saw high rates of growth, as illustrated in Figure 5.2. The industry recuperated after the crisis of 1975–6 and recovered its growth until 1980.

In spite of the anti-export bias of the first stages of the ISI, the glass container industry had been exporting since the 1930s. The geographical and cultural closeness to the US of the main producer, described in Sections 6.1 and 6.2, contributes to explaining this behavior. The main producer was part of the modern sector referred to above. However exports were not significant in value until the 1970s.

---

[23] Pérez (1996).
[24] Katz (1995).
[25] See for instance Chudnovski (1996), Katz (1995) and Pérez (1996).

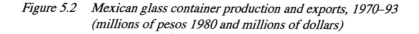

Figure 5.2   Mexican glass container production and exports, 1970–93
(millions of pesos 1980 and millions of dollars)

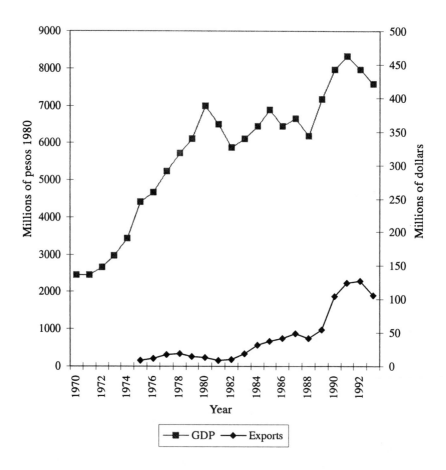

Source:
Based on ILET's database.

The crisis of the 1980s and the opening up of the economy

In the 1980s there was a radical change in the economic and policy context.
A severe crisis in 1982 was followed by a macroeconomics adjustment and a
change in the development strategy. The new strategy was based on the opening up of the economy to foreign competition, a reduction of the participation
of the State in the economic activity and an increase in internal competition.

The process of opening up the economy, which started in 1987, was furthered in the 1990s and a regional market was established through the signing of the NAFTA agreement. In December 1994 there was a new crisis in the Mexican economy, which again reduced the level of the domestic market, but recovery from which was faster than in 1982.

The contraction of the domestic market in the 1980s and the on-going change in the development strategy affected the whole industrial sector. Overall the manufacturing industry looked to foreign markets to compensate for the reduction in domestic demand, in particular exports observed an increased trend from 1985.

The trade liberalization policy from the late 1980s, the de-regulation of markets and the privatization of public assets changed the conditions of competition. Also when the frontiers were opened new rules of competition, prices and quality, as well as lower costs were needed for survival in the international market, and moreover to achieve parity with potential new foreign entrants in the domestic market.

In general there was a change in the industry towards modernization and internationalization over this period. However because of the heterogeneity of the industrial structure, firms reacted and adapted to the changes in different ways.[26] The international competing firms, which already had experience in such activity, led the export dynamics in the 1980s. They were also faster at establishing associations with international players to acquire technology, to gain access to commercialization channels, to agree the distribution of the regional market with US and Canadian firms, and even in penetrating the NAFTA market by acquiring US firms.[27]

The crisis at the beginning of the 1980s reduced the domestic demand for glass containers, as can be seen in Figure 5.2. Actually glass container demand fell in 1981, revealing early signs of the crisis. The industry, but mainly the largest producer, reoriented its production towards the international market following the pattern described above. Even though this firm had exported from the 1930s, from the early 1980s exports became increasingly important, as can be seen in Figure 5.2. This strategy was supported by the policy to stimulate export firms established by the Government after the crisis, and the export experience the largest producer already had in the US and Latin American markets. Glass container exports increased from 9.4 million dollars in 1975 to 127 in 1992 and 157 in 1995, and the export coefficient grew from 3 per cent in the 1970s to 7 per cent in 1985 and to 14.6 per cent in 1992. The increase in exports partially explains the recuperation of the GDP since 1983. In contrast imports have never been significant in this market.

---

[26] See for instance Casar (1994) and Katz (1995).

[27] Pozas (1993:29–62).

The dynamic of the glass container industry during the 1990s was also affected by changes in the structure of demand. The glass container industry was threatened by containers made from other materials, such as plastic, aluminum and tetrapack, which put increasing pressure on the search for cost reduction, quality increase and product innovation. These factors furthered the increase in the level of competition and the search for higher efficiency, and generated an absolute reduction in the demand of glass containers. This helps to explain the contraction of production in the early 1990s observed in Figure 5.2.

In the 1990s the export dynamics continue to be good but the dynamics of the production have been lower. Today the glass container industry represents approximately 50 per cent of the glass GDP and 0.8 per cent of manufacturing GDP in Mexico. In spite of the export performance, glass container exports only represented 0.4 per cent of the manufacturing exports in 1995 (without including the 'maquila' activities).

The change of the ISI as a strategy for development in Mexico, and the whole of Latin America, has been faster than the change in the institutions. Although several new mechanisms, regulations and institutions were established according to a market economy, the new coexist with the old inherited from the ISI. As asserted by Pérez (1996), there is a 'legacy of ISI policies' in terms of behaviors, beliefs and industrial heterogeneity.[28] Even the modern sector with its international competing firms preserve that legacy and have a mixture of old and new practices.[29] The rigidities against changing the way of doing things and the coexistence of new and old practices are issues addressed in this book at the firm-level, particularly in Section 9.3.2.

5.4.1.2 Trends of the market

Glass, plastic, coated paper-board and aluminum tinplate are the basic materials used to make containers for packaging food, beverages, medicines and perfumes. The size of the Mexican packaging market in 1994 was around 700 million dollars and 18.300 million containers. The Mexican market is smaller than the US market, it represents around 8 per cent of the US market by number of pieces and 14 per cent in value. The structure of materials used in containers is also different. Mexican consumers demand more containers made of glass than American consumers. In 1990 glass containers represented 30 per cent of the Mexican packaging market, as Table 5.3 illustrates. Glass participation fell to 24 per cent in 1994, however it was still higher than the 18.6 per cent observed in the US market.

---

[28]   See also Katz (1995), Fajnzylber (1990) and Chudnovski (1996).
[29]   Katz (1995).

Table 5.3 Trends in the Mexican packaging market, 1990 and 1994 (%)

Material	1990	1994
Cans	37.0	43.0
Glass	*30.0*	*24.0*
Plastic	22.0	22.0
Cartons	11.0	11.0
Total packaging market	*100.0*	*100.0*

Source:
Adapted from Grupo Financiero Bancomer (1995:42), which is based on INEGI.

The Mexican demand for glass containers has grown from 4.300 million containers in 1987 to 4.900 million containers in 1994.[30] This growth was a result of the increase from 1987 to 1990 which was higher than the reduction that occurred between 1990 and 1994. The value of the market between 1987 and 1994 did not change significantly due to the reduction in the price of the glass containers. Price reduction and negative growth in the 1990s reveal the maturity of the market.

The process of substituting cans and plastic bottles for glass, an international trend since the mid-1980s, has been slow in Mexico due to the consumption structure that is still focused on low-cost returnable glass bottles. For instance, glass represented 97.8 per cent of the total containers of the soft-drinks market in 1991, and fell to 78 per cent in 1994,[31] while in the US it represented less than 10 per cent in the last year. This market characteristic creates a demand for specialty label bottles that on average are re-used 40 times. Therefore Mexico has been slowly following the international trend to reduce the use of returnable glass bottles and increase the use of non-returnable plastic containers and cans.

The players and the market structure

There are six competitors in the Mexican market: one large firm (VGC), which is the most diversified firm and dominates all the product markets

---

[30] Grupo Financiero Bancomer (1995:45), based on INEGI.
[31] Grupo Financiero Bancomer (1995:43), based on Goldman Sachs, Packaging Market Research.

excepting beer; two medium-size (Nueva Fanal and Sivesa), owned by the two large Mexican brewers (Modelo and Cuauhtémoc-Moctezuma), which control the beer market; and three small firms, which are rather specialized. The production capacity is presented in Table 5.4.

The industry is highly concentrated. The three larger firms held 93.8 per cent and the small firms held 6.2 per cent in 1996.[32] Historically VGC, the largest producer, has had a market share of 80 per cent. In recent years there has been an increase in the competition from small firms and the brewery-owned firms. By 1996 VGC's market share was 67.8 per cent, lower than in the 1980s. The market share of the larger producers is shown in Table 5.5.

Table 5.4   Production capacity by producer, 1995

Producers	Plants	Furnaces	No. of lines	Tons/day
VGC[a]	*8*	*24*	*75*	*4788*
Nueva Fanal [b]	1	4	20	1100
Sivesa	1	2	6	440
Fev. Mexicali	1	1	1	90
Latino Americana	1	2	3	60
Vidrio Formas	1	2	NA	40
Total	*14*	*35*	*105*	*6518*

Notes:
a.   VGC was going to stop a furnace in Vimex (III/95) and to add a furnace in Vimosa (I/96), increasing 85 tons in 1996.
b.   The new plant in San Luis Potosí is not included.
Source:
Adapted from charts of the Strategic Planning Department of VGC's Marketing.

In general, competition has increased among domestic producers due to an increase in client power and the search for flexibility, price reduction and more client-producer interaction. In spite of the opening of the economy, imports have not been a threat in the case of the main markets. They represented only 2.3 per cent of the demand in 1993. VGC is the unique producer that competes in the international market. Its export sales to the US face considerably more competition.

---

[32]   Interview with a manager of the strategic planning department of VGC's Marketing Direction.

Main markets

The main markets for glass containers in 1987 and 1994 are presented in Table 5.6. Soft-drinks, beer, food, and wine and liquor are the main markets.

The most relevant change was the increased importance of the soft-drinks market in 1994 in relation to beer. This was associated with the substitution of cans for glass in the beer market and the dynamics of the soft-drinks market, which compensated the substitution of plastic and cans for glass in this market.

Table 5.5   Market share by main producer, 1996 (%)

Producers	Market share (%)
VGC	*67.8*
Nueva Fanal	16.0
Sivesa	10.0
3 small producers	6.2
Total Mexican market	*100.0*

Source:
Adapted from charts of the Strategic Planning Department of VGC's Marketing Direction.

Table 5.6   Mexican sales by end-use, 1987 and 1994 (%)

End-use	1987	1994
Soft-drinks	22.5	39.9
Beer containers	37.1	23.6
Food containers	17.8	17.4
Wine and liquor	14.9	12.5
Others (chemical, cosmetic, household, health, industrial, medicinal, and toiletry products)	7.7	6.6
Total	*100.0*	*100.0*

Source:
Adapted from Grupo Financiero Bancomer (1995:45), which is based on INEGI.

VGC, the largest and most diversified firm, participates in all the product markets. Food and soft-drinks are its main markets, and the generic non-returnable bottle is its main product, as Table 5.7 below illustrates. VGC produces only surpluses for the beer market. The other large producers have a different mix of products. Nueva Fanal and Sivesa specialize in the beer market because of their vertical integration condition. Sivesa also supplies the soft-drinks market via the Femsa Group, its parent company, which also produces coke.

Table 5.7   Mix of products of the Mexican large producers, 1996

Products	VGC	Nueva Fanal	Sivesa
Generic non-returnable*	41.9	—	9.7
Food	22.6	4.6	—
Soft-drink	16.9	—	22.4
Medicine	7.7	—	—
Beer	5.2	86.5	67.9
Perfumes	3.3	—	—
Wine	2.2	8.9	—
Others	0.2	—	—
Total sales	100.0	100.0	100.0

Note:
* The generic non-returnable bottle is produced through the NNPB process and is used mainly for soft-drink and food products. Products are differentiated by the label.
Source:
Adapted from charts of the Strategic Planning Department of VGC's Marketing Direction.

The market structure of the client industries is different to other countries. There is a duopoly in the brewing industry, and few oligopolies that compete or coexist with hundreds of small and medium-size firms in the soft-drinks and food industries. The market power of the demand side has been historically low because of the fragmented base of those industries and the ISI policies. Glass container has been a market dominated by producers, particularly the largest producer.

Changes in the source of competitiveness

The structure in the costs of glass container production is conformed by more or less equal parts of raw materials, capital and labor, and a smaller percentage of energy, as described in Section 5.3. VGC has a quite similar cost structure to the US firms. According to this firm, when there is a devaluation the cost structure changes; however this is temporary and the structure is soon readjusted. The labor cost in Mexico is cheaper than in the US and Europe, but it does not generate advantage because Mexican plants have a large inefficiency in the use of this factor. In some periods of time the energy prices in Mexico have been lower than abroad. However this advantage has been outweighed by the poor quality of the service associated with interruptions and variations in the voltage. The rate of recycling and then the use of cullet in the US and more especially in Europe is higher than in Mexico, which allows them to save on energy costs during the glass melting process. This is considered to be a disadvantage in the Mexican case.[33]

During the ISI period, domestic firms were protected against imports. The tariff for glass containers was 15 per cent and was negotiated under the C category of the NAFTA agreement. Tariffs for imports from the US and Canada have been reduced in annual stages of 1.5 per cent since 1994. On 1 January 2003 this product will be free. However competitiveness historically was not based on high tariff. Large Mexican glass container producers are part of the modern sector of the industry, they use state-of-the-art technology and operate the equipment with a reasonable level of efficiency. For instance VGC built expertise to produce short production runs for small niche markets, including niches in the US market, and decided to offer a reasonable quality and price to its clients to support its monopolistic position. All this reduced the incentive for foreign companies to enter the Mexican market. Actually the high tariffs of the past had overprotected the industry, producers were competitive without that protection. Once the economy was opened tariff reductions associated with NAFTA agreement allowed costs to be reduced through a reduction in the price of inputs.[34] Therefore domestic producers are still competitive even with a lower tariff. Finally geographical advantages and transport costs also restrain the competition from import or from the establishment of potential competitors in the country.

For the main markets the major potential competition comes from alternative packaging such as metal, plastic and coated paper-board containers. Conversely domestic producers feel their perfume and pharmaceutical business is being threatened. The tariffs are being reduced and they have competition from foreign firms, such as Saint Gobain, Bormioli and Wheaton.[35]

The largest producer has been the sole packaging alternative for most Mexican bottlers. The firm has enjoyed a strong advantage in negotiating with its fragmented customer base.[36] Recently the market has moved towards greater differentiation. Under these trends and in conditions of a more competitive market flexibility of production becomes more important than

---

[33] Interview with personnel from the technology planning area of Ditac.
[34] Interview with the Director of Dirtec.
[35] Interview with a manager of the strategic planning department of VGC's Marketing Direction.
[36] Morgan Stanley & Co. (1994).

scale. But VGC and the other large producers use technology for long production runs. For instance, the tons/day per furnace are 200 at VGC, 220 at Sivesa and 275 at Nueva Fanal.[37] Conversely the tons/day per furnace of the small producer are much lower, e.g. 30 at Latino Americana or 20 at Vidrio Formas. Even though large producers have built the capabilities to produce short runs, the scale constitutes a disadvantage in the new market conditions, particularly when the competition from other materials is increasing the pressure for cost reductions.

During the ISI and in conditions of a closed economy clients were not important, it was the domain of the producers. Flexibility was a requirement but the monopolistic position of VGC reduced that pressure. At present in an open economy client requirements are a key variable and flexibility has become a key attribute of the production process. This has changed the conditions of competition in favor of the small producers. Table 5.8 below lists the main attributes of large and small producers today.

Table 5.8   Attributes of the Mexican producers

Small producers	Large producers
• More production flexibility: they have small furnaces (20 to 30 tons/day) and they can run small batches	• Less production flexibility: the large furnaces (more than 200 tons/day) increase the costs of short production runs
•More proximity to their small clients: they establish almost personal relationships which allow more confidence and a better customer service	• They have close relationships with large clients, but their relationships with small clients are mediated through distributors
• Lower prices and quality: lower costs of transportation and logistic, and use of raw materials of lesser quality	• Higher price and quality: the large scale has determined an increase in the costs associated with the supply at national level, and use of better quality raw materials

Source:
Interview with a manager of the Strategic Planning Department of VGC's Marketing Direction.

---

[37]   The tons/day per furnace was calculated with the information contained in Table 5.4.

The different attributes reflect the changes in the conditions of the market competition and contribute to explaining the growth in market power of small producers in the last few years.

5.4.2 The US Glass Container Market

This section contains a brief description of trends of the US glass container market. Particular attention is given to the description of the main players, market structure and main markets.

Market trends

The size of the US packaging market in 1994 was around 80 billion[38] dollars and 220 000 million containers. Even though the US packaging market has increased from 150 000 million containers in 1980 to 220 000 in 1994, the demand for glass containers has declined from 46 000 to 41 000 million containers, reducing its contribution from 31.4 per cent in 1980 to 18.6 per cent in 1994. Since 1980 glass is being substituted for cans and plastic containers, as illustrated in Table 5.9. In 1995 the demand for glass containers was 41 000 million containers with sales of 5 billion dollars.

Table 5.9   Trends in the US packaging production, 1980–94 (%)

	1980	1985	1990	1994
Plastic	9.5	14.8	17	19.9
Glass	*31.4*	*23.7*	*20.3*	*18.6*
Cans	59.1	61.5	62.7	61.5
Total	*100.0*	*100.0*	*100.0*	*100.0*

Source:
Adapted from Grupo Financiero Bancomer (1995), which is based on Paine Webber (1995), Packaging Industry Annual Review.

The American glass container market is a mature market in a process of decline, as illustrated in Figure 5.3, as opposed to the still growing Mexican market.

---

[38] Billion is used here in the American meaning as one thousand million.

Figure 5.3   US glass container shipments, 1987–96 (millions of gross)

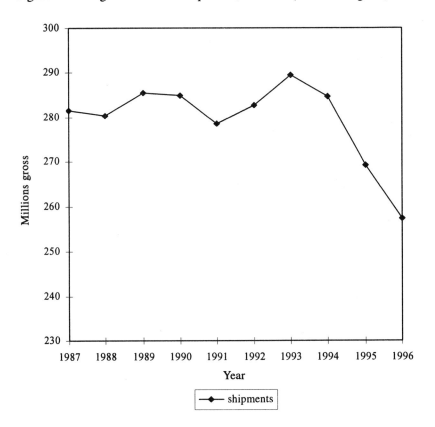

Source:
Based on the United States Department of Commerce, Economics and Statistics Administration,
Bureau of the Census, Current Industrial Reports: Glass Containers – 1996 Summary.

Over the past 16 years US glass container makers have undergone significant re-organization, consolidation and modernization of high cost capacity to achieve the required scale and efficiency to continue to compete. This process has been induced by the fall in demand for glass containers and intense competition from other rigid container products. As part of the consolidation process, the production capacity of the glass container industry has been sharply reduced by almost 50 per cent. Between 1979 and 1983 15 plants closed down and another 33 between 1983 and 1992.[39] At the same time

---

[39] 'Glass: a Clear Vision for a Bright Future' (1996:10).

productivity improvements have increased the pressure to make further capacity reductions to some extent. There were 68 plants operating in 1996 and the operating rates in the 1990s has been around 90 per cent.[40]

The way to enter the industry has been through acquisitions and joint ventures. The last new plant was constructed by Owens-Illinois in 1981.[41] The three new entrants were: (i) the Vitro-Group, who acquired Anchor Glass Containers Corporation in 1989; (ii) Saint Gobain, who established a joint venture with the Ball Corporation in 1995 and formed Ball-Foster; and (iii) the Consumers Glass Company (a division of Consumers Packaging, Canada), who in alliance with Owens-Brockway (a division of Owens-Illinois), bought Anchor Glass Containers Corporation in February 1997.

The new entrants have been firms with knowledge about how to produce bottles. They were keen to enter the US market, the biggest and most competitive market in the world. Two other important changes in the industry were the acquisition of Brockway by Owens-Illinois in 1988 and the acquisition of Kerr by Ball-Icon in 1991.

The players and the market structure

It is a highly concentrated market, as illustrated in Table 5.10. The combined market share of the top three manufacturers has increased from approximately 48 per cent in 1979 to 90 per cent in 1995.

Table 5.10   Market share by main producer, 1995

Producers	Number of plants	Market share (%)
Owens-Illinois	21	40
Ball-Foster	22	28
Anchor Glass Containers Corporation	14	22
Other	11	10
Total	*68*	*100*

Source:
Compiled from Donaldson, Lufkin & Jenrette Securities (1995).

Company market shares have remained essentially stable and share gains have largely been realized through acquisitions. Producers in the US glass container

---

[40]   Morgan Stanley & Co. (1995: Table 13).
[41]   'Glass: a Clear Vision for a Bright Future' (1996:15).

industry compete principally on the basis of price, service and quality. Almost all glass containers suffer intense competition from other rigid container products.

Imports increased in the 1980s. Imports as a percentage of the apparent consumption increased from nearly 3 per cent in 1987 to around 8 per cent in 1996. Mexico represented 40 per cent of the imports. In contrast size of exports to domestic shipments has remained very small.

Main markets

The main markets for glass containers in 1987, 1994 and 1996 are presented in Table 5.11. Beer and food are the main markets. The most relevant change in those years was the dramatic reduction in the soft-drinks market associated with the substitution of cans and plastic bottles for glass in this market. Such substitution has been much slower in the Mexican case as described in Section 5.4.1.2.

Table 5.11   US shipped units by end-use, 1987, 1994 and 1996 (%)

End-use	1987	1994	1996
Beer containers	30.3	36.7	45.0
Food containers	31.9	39.2	35.5
Wine and Liquor	10.1	8.5	9.2
Soft-drinks[a]	22.2	10.8	5.8
Others (chemical, cosmetic, household, health, industrial, medicinal, and toiletry products)	5.5	4.8	4.5
Total US market[b]	*100.0*	*100.0*	*100.0*

Notes:
a. The percentage of 1996 was estimated on data of 1995.
b. Includes exports.

Source:
Based on the United States Department of Commerce, Economics and Statistics Administration, Bureau of the Census, Current Industrial Reports: Glass Containers – 1997 Summary.

The substitution of cans and plastic for glass has been pronounced in the beer industry, however the erosion of the market share of glass has leveled off given that glass containers are the package of choice for premium beers. In 1996 of the total containers 69 per cent were of the narrow neck and 31 per cent were wide mouth. Most of the containers are non-returnable.

To sum up, the Mexican and US glass container markets are similar in the sense that both are dominated by large firms which produce mainly for the domestic market. Exports have represented an increased part of the Mexican production, while imports have been growing in the US case. However, in both cases production is oriented mainly to supplying the domestic market. These markets are different in other aspects. The Mexican market still observes a path of growth, high percentage of returnable bottles and a slow process of substitution of plastic and cans for glass. In contrast, the US market is mature and in decline, it is dominated by non-returnable bottles and a fast process of substitution.

5.5 THE CASE STUDY FIRM: VITRO-GLASS CONTAINERS

This section contains a brief description of the Mexican group Vitro and of its glass container division 'Vitro Envases de Norteamérica', named here VGC. This book is based on a case study of VGC. The description focuses on the main characteristics of the production structure, sales, exports, joint ventures and acquisitions.

5.5.1 The Vitro-Group: The Parent Company

Business profile

Vitro is the largest glass container manufacturer in Mexico. The group has its headquarters in Monterrey, Mexico, and came into being as a producer of bottles for the Cuauhtémoc brewery (now FEMSA). It was created in 1909 as a family owned firm with Mexican capital. It is now a publicly held company listed on the Mexican Stock Market (1976) and on the New York Stock Exchange (1991).

It was a 2.2 billion dollar Mexican group in glass-related activities in 1996. It was the 2nd Mexican group by sales in 1994,[42] and ranked 16th in Latin America by sales in 1996.[43] It is a multinational firm with subsidiaries in Latin America and the US, in fact it has facilities in seven countries. Vitro made half of its sales abroad in 1996.[44]

---

[42] Based on Garrido (1998:407–10, table 4). This position include the sales of associated firms, such as Grupo Financiero Serfin and CYDSA.

[43] Based on Garrido and Péres (1998:34–7, table 2). This position does not include the associated firms.

[44] Vitro SA (1996a). This percentage excludes Anchor Glass Containers Corporation's discontinued operations. AGCC was sold on 5 February 1997.

Production structure

The company operated through six divisions in 1995: (1) Glass Containers,
(2) Flat Glass, (3) Packaging (plastic, can and machinery), (4) Glassware,
(5) Home Appliances, (6) Chemicals, Fibers & Mining. Eighty-four per cent
of total sales were glass-related products. The glass container operations in
Mexico and the US generated 54 per cent of the Vitro-Group's sales, as shown
in Figure 5.4.

Figure 5.4   Sales by Vitro-Group's division, 1995 (%)

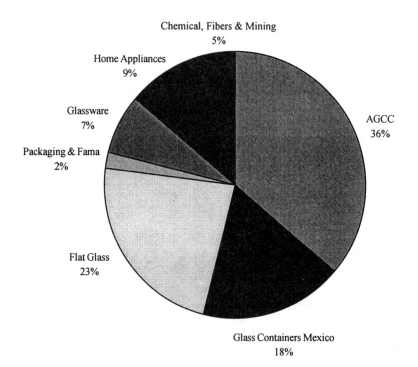

Chemical, Fibers & Mining
5%

Home Appliances
9%

Glassware
7%

AGCC
36%

Packaging & Fama
2%

Flat Glass
23%

Glass Containers Mexico
18%

Source:
Adapted from Vitro SA (1995).

The production structure of the Vitro-Group has changed recently. Figure 5.5
presents the contribution to the sales of four divisions of the Vitro-Group
over several years from 1936 to 1996. Glass Containers was the most important
division in sales from the earliest days until 1995. In 1996, with the divestment
of AGCC and after other investments in architectural and automotive glass,

Flat Glass became the largest division in sales. Home Appliances is also increasing its contribution to the sales. In spite of the changes, the Vitro-Group continues to be a glass group.

Figure 5.5 Sales by Vitro-Group's division, 1936–96 (%)

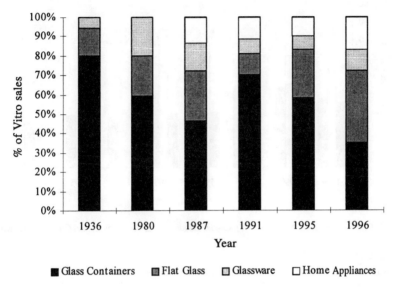

Source:
Own analysis of data in Vitro S.A. Annual Report (various years).

Vertical integration

The Vitro-Group is a vertically integrated company, except in the case of Home Appliances. Some business provides vertical integration, producing the raw materials, intermediate inputs and capital goods needed to manufacture the final products. In the case of the Glass Container and Glassware divisions the degree of vertical integration is higher, including the machinery. The internal production of raw materials has its roots in 1930 and the internal production of equipment was initiated in 1943.

Figure 5.6 shows the sales of the divisions that provide raw materials and equipment made inside the Vitro-Group. More than 70 per cent of the capital goods and around 30 per cent of chemical, fibers and mining were produced internally to supply Vitro-Group's requirements. Those divisions were integrated for 1996. The evolution of the aggregation of those divisions, under the heading of Chemical, Capital Goods and Packaging, reveals a reduction of the degree of integration from 1989 to 1996.[45]

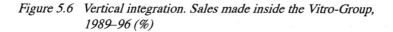
Figure 5.6   Vertical integration. Sales made inside the Vitro-Group, 1989–96 (%)

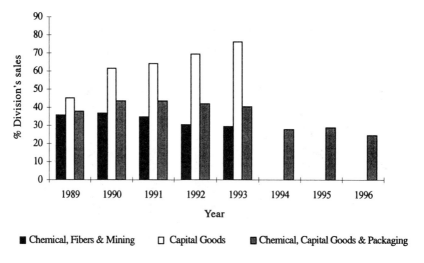

■ Chemical, Fibers & Mining   □ Capital Goods   ▨ Chemical, Capital Goods & Packaging

Source:
Own analysis of data in Vitro S.A. Annual Report (various years).

Sales, growth and exports

The Vitro-Group's sales have increased over time, as illustrated in Figure 5.7. The total sales of the Vitro-Group in 1995 were around three billion dollars. In 1996 the sales of the Vitro-Group were reduced to 2.2 billion dollars basically due to the divestment of AGCC.

The Vitro-Group has long experience in export activities. Exports steadily increased during the 1980s and 1990s. In 1995, exports as a percentage of the production of Mexican subsidiaries represented around 40 per cent. In 1995 the US was the main market for the Vitro-Group; around 60 per cent of the sales were made in the US. Anchor Glass Containers Corporation represented 59 per cent, and the exports of glass containers from Mexico represented 8 per cent of that total.

---

[45]   On 27 June 1997 Vitro sold 100 per cent of its interest in the subsidiaries engaged in the mining of sand and felspar (Vitro SA, 1998). This reduced the internal production of inputs and the degree of integration.

*Figure 5.7 Sales and exports of the Vitro-Group, 1977–96
          (millions of dollars)*

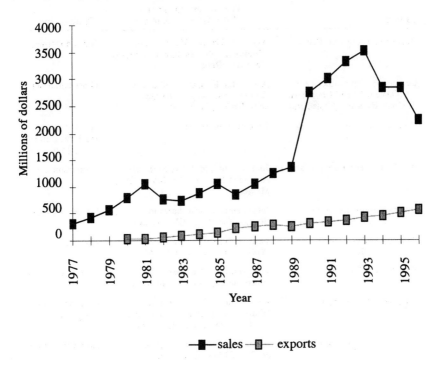

Source:
Own analysis of data in Vitro S.A. Annual Report (various years).

Joint ventures and agreements

Vitro has traditionally used joint ventures as a core component of its strategy to develop new, fast-growing product lines and to gain access to new markets. This strategy has also provided the company with access to leading-edge technology and allowed it to expand its distribution channels. Vitro's major alliance in the glass container business is with Owens-Illinois.

The motive for these joint ventures has changed over time. In the 1950s and 1960s, the objective was to have the best technology available for the domestic markets. But as Mexico began to change the need to export became more evident and the Vitro-Group began to look at how it could gain access to technology and to markets. The international associations and joint ventures in 1996 are listed in Table 5.12 below.

Table 5.12   Vitro-Group's international associations and joint ventures, 1996

Partner	Type of agreement and Vitro-Group's shares	Product line
Backus and Johnson (Peru)	Associated firm, 23% shares in 'Compañía Manufacturera de Vidrio del Perú', Peru	Glass container
Cervecería Centroamericana, SA (Guatemala) and Cervecería de Costa Rica, SA (Costa Rica)	Associated firm, 49.7% shares in 'Empresas Comegua, SA and subsidiaries', Guatemala	Glass container
Owens-Illinois (US)	Technical agreement	Glass container machinery and technology
Pechiney International (France)	Joint venture, 50% shares in 'Vitro-American National Can, SA de CV', Mexico	Aluminum can
Owens-Illinois Inc. (US)	Joint venture, 50% shares in 'Regioplast, SA de CV', Mexico	Plastic container
Pilkington, PLC (UK)	Joint venture, 65% shares in 'Vidrio Plano, SA de CV', Mexico	Flat glass
Ford Motor Company (US)	Joint venture, 62% shares in 'Vitro Flex, SA de CV', Mexico	Automotive glass
Vitchile, SA (Panama)	Joint venture, 51% shares in 'Vidrios Templados Colombianos, SA de CV'(Vitemco), Colombia	Automotive and flat glass
Whirlpool Corporation (US)	Joint venture in 'Vitromatic, SA de CV', 51% shares, Mexico	Home appliances
Delta Sourdillón (France)	Joint venture, majority holder in 'Acrotec, SA de CV', Mexico	Home appliances
Owens-Corning (US)	Joint venture, 60% shares in 'Vitro Owens Corning Fiberglass, SA de CV', Mexico	Fiberglass
The PQ Corporation (US)	Joint venture, 55% shares in 'Silicatos y Derivados, SA de CV', Mexico	Silica, metasilica, other chemical products
Kimble, Inc (US)	Joint venture, 51% shares in 'Envases de Borosilicato, SA', Mexico	Borosilicate containers
Solutia Inc. (US)	Joint Venture, 51% shares in 'Química M, SA de CV', Mexico	Polyvinyl Butyral
Celulosa y Derivados, SA (CYDSA) (Mexico)[46]	Associated firm, 49.9% shares	Chemicals, fibers and textiles
Grupo Financiero Serfin, SA (Mexico)[47]	Associated firm, 11.4% shares	Financial services

Source:
Adapted from Vitro SA (1996a).

Technology

On average the Vitro-Group spends 1.2 per cent of the sales in technology-related activities. Additionally it pays out around 0.6 per cent of sales to its technology licensor in the case of the glass container business.[48]

The Vitro-Group had 55 active patents and 19 applied for in the US in 1995. It also had 53 active and 25 applied for in Mexico.

A 'family group'

The Vitro-Group is a 'family group', there are many family members on the Board of Directors and they have control of the corporate executive positions. Generally the Chairman of the Board and the Chief Executive Officer (CEO) are from the family. Ernesto Martens became the Vitro-Group's first non-family President and CEO in 1985. This appointment was made as a way of reducing the family power. However from 1994 the family regained control. In 1994 Federico Sada was named CEO of the Vitro-Group and since 1995 has been President and CEO. His brother, Adrián Sada G., is the Chairman of the Board of Directors.

5.5.2 Vitro-Glass Containers

The Glass Container Division of the Vitro-Group is the largest glass container manufacturer in Mexico. It has had increasing experience of technology transfer to Latin American's subsidiaries and other companies since 1964. With the purchase of Anchor Glass Containers Corporation in 1989, VGC became the second largest player in the US glass container market[49] and the third largest in the world.[50] In 1996 the Mexican operations of VGC held a market share of 67.8 per cent. The US operations held a market share of 22 per cent in 1995.

---

[46] On 20 October 1997 Vitro-Group decided to divest itself of CYDSA, selling its shares to that company. The agreement included the sale of Vitro's shares possessed by CYDSA's owner. This operation was concluded on 15 December 1997 (Vitro SA, 1998).

[47] Vitro has not participated in the capitalization of Grupo Financiero Serffn since 1996. Hence its participation was reduced from 20 per cent to 11.4 per cent in June 1996, and to 6.8 per cent in 1997 (Vitro, SA, 1998). During 1998 the participation was further reduced to around 2 per cent.

[48] Interview with the Director of Ditac.

[49] In 1995 AGCC and VGC fell from second to third place in the US market after the joint venture of Ball Corporation and Saint Gobain, the acquisition of Foster Forbes and the constitution of Ball-Foster.

[50] This ranking changed in 1997 after the divestment of AGCC.

Production structure

In 1996 VGC consisted of 8 plants in Mexico (27 installed furnaces and 81 production lines); 14 plants in the US (30 furnaces and 80 production lines); 1 plant in Bolivia (1 furnace and 2 production lines), 2 associated firms with 3 plants in Guatemala, Costa Rica and Peru (5 furnaces and 16 lines), 1 distributor company in the US and 2 other minor companies. It had around 8,000 employees in Mexico and 5,000 in the US.

The Mexican plants are located strategically close to the largest towns, such as Mexico City, Monterrey, Guadalajara, Querétaro and Toluca. The Mexicali plant is located close to the US border.

Sales, growth and exports

The sales of VGC have increased over time, as illustrated in Figure 5.8. The glass container business was the seed of the company and until 1997 was Vitro-Group's largest business. In the 1970s the business grew significantly. In that decade growth was based on the expansion of the operations in Mexico to follow the dynamism of the domestic market. VGC created two new plants and increased the production capacity of the already operating plants. In the beginning of the 1980s VGC was affected by the Mexican crisis. 1982 to 1986 were years of instability and in 1987 it recovered the growth. New plants were created, reconverted or acquired. The increase of the sales in 1990 was related to the acquisition of Anchor Glass Containers Corporation in the US. From 1993 to 1995 VGC's sales were affected by both the Mexican crisis of 1994 and the contraction of the US glass container market in those years. The dramatic reduction of the sales in 1996 was associated with the divestment of AGCC in December, whose operations were excluded from the net sales that year.

The total sales in 1995 were 1.6 billion dollars, representing 54 per cent of total sales of the Vitro-Group. The glass container activities in Mexico generated 0.6 billion dollars and the activities in the US generated 1 billion dollars. Sales in Latin America represent 5 per cent of the sales in Mexico. In 1996 the total sales of VGC were reduced to 693 million dollars, which included only the Mexican and Latin American operations.

Exports have continually increased from 1981, following the reorientation of the industrial production towards the international market described in Section 5.4.1.1. By 1996, 70 per cent of the production of the Mexican subsidiaries was sold in the domestic market, 25 per cent in NAFTA markets and 5 per cent in Latin America.[51] Anchor Glass Containers Corporation produces and sells containers only for the domestic US market.

---

[51] Interview with a manager of the strategic planning department of VGC's Marketing Direction.

VGC has held a monopolistic position in the Mexican market. In spite of experiencing little competition in the domestic market, and the economic and policy context associated with the ISI, it has exported since very early on and has sought to be exposed to the conditions of the international market. It started its expansion in the Latin American market in 1964 by acquiring firms. In the 1980s it acquired firms in the US as well. At the beginning of the 1990s VGC became the third largest producer of glass containers in the world. These achievements are related to its particular culture and knowledge accumulation process which are analyzed in the following chapters.

Figure 5.8   Sales and exports of Vitro-Glass Containers, 1980–96 (millions of dollars)

Source:
Own analysis of data in Vitro SA. Annual Report (various years) and ILET's database.

PART TWO

The Process of Building up Technological
Capabilities from the Earliest Days on

Introductory Note

The building up of technological capabilities by Vitro-Glass Containers was a long process. From the outset to around 1970 VGC built up the minimum essential knowledge base to survive in the market. The main problems encountered by the firm were similar to those that can be found in the developing countries literature on learning processes and building technological capabilities. From the 1970s the firm started a Transition Process from building of the minimum essential knowledge base to building strategic capabilities.

The Transition Process was uneven. In some areas VGC had to build, nurture and combine different simple knowledge bases to undertake more complex innovation activities and as a result built more complex knowledge bases. Some of the main problems observed in this process were similar to those that can be found in the strategic management literature, particularly the literature about knowledge management in the largest companies in the world. However at the same time in other areas VGC had to continue its more gradual learning process to build up the minimum essential knowledge base. The Transition Process had two periods. First, from 1970 to 1990 there was a gradual process of knowledge accumulation that allowed the emergence of some embryonic strategic capabilities. In the second period during the 1990s the knowledge accumulation process was weakened, the embryonic strategic capabilities built previously did not progress to become strategic capabilities and new embryonic strategic capabilities emerged. The Transition Process regressed in some areas and went forward in others but it was not completed.

Part II contains a historical narrative of the long term process of building technological capabilities, focusing on the key analytical issues addressed in this book. Special attention is given to the process of building up internal capabilities, the use of external sources of knowledge, the characteristics of knowledge management, the interaction between the creation of technological knowledge and knowledge management, the directions of the knowledge accumulation and the results of this process. Part II is thus an analytical chronology.

The analytical chronology is organized according to the stages in building up technological capabilities to show the different types of problems that the firm had to deal with in each stage. Chapter 6 describes the process of build-ing the minimum essential knowledge base from 1909 to 1970; Chapter 7 describes the characteristics of the Transition Process towards building strategic capabilities from 1970 to 1990; and Chapter 8 describes some problems faced during the Transition Process in conditions of a changing economic and technological environment in the 1990s, specifically the difficulties to convert the embryonic strategic capabilities in strategic capabilities.

6   The Process of Building up the Minimum Essential Knowledge Base: 1909–70

6.1   INTRODUCTION

The main purpose of this chapter is to describe the process of building up the minimum essential knowledge base by Vitro-Glass Containers. This covers the stage of accumulation in which the firm built technological capabilities to reduce costs, improve quality, reduce consumption of raw materials and upgrade equipment to achieve parity with competitors. This stage is characterized by the accumulation of routine production capabilities and basic to intermediate innovative technological capabilities.

External sources of knowledge were very important from the outset. However VGC was gradually building routine production capabilities and innovative technological capabilities, and then combining external and internal sources of knowledge.

Even though the process of building up technological capabilities was a cumulative process, it took 60 years to build the minimum essential knowledge base. In this chapter it is argued that the depth of knowledge accumulated by technical-function was uneven, the speed of the learning processes across the organizational units was different, the effort to share the knowledge was small and there were difficulties in documenting the firm's knowledge. Those characteristics affected the process of building technological capabilities.

This introduction includes a brief description of the context, the technology strategy and the organizational structure of the Vitro-Group and VGC in the period analyzed. Section 6.2 describes the characteristics of the process of building in-house innovative technological capabilities. Section 6.3 describes the use of external sources of knowledge. Section 6.4 examines some of the efforts in knowledge management aimed at using the existing knowledge. Finally Section 6.5 presents the main conclusions.

The context and the technology strategy

VGC was created in 1909 which was a time of very weak industrial development in Mexico. The economic and political instability from 1909 until 1930 limited its capacity to settle in the business. From the 1930s to the 1970s the domestic market and the demand for glass containers grew steadily. In addition the implementation of the Import Substitution Industrialization in the 1940s brought some incentives to industrial development, as described in Section 5.4.1.1. Over this period VGC built its monopolistic position and enjoyed large profits in conditions of a closed economy.

The history of the creation of VGC reveals a concern for introducing state-of-the-art technology to solve technical problems. The technology strategy during the early decades was directed towards building the most elementary production knowledge, assimilating the foreign technology in operation and building the minimum essential knowledge base. It was basically a slow follower technology strategy.[1] However the firm was concerned with introducing the most relevant innovations introduced by the technology leaders at a quicker pace than would be expected from such a strategy. In the 1940s with the creation of Fama – the machine manufacturing plant – VGC redefined its targets and set up the goal of becoming 'technologically independent' of the technology suppliers.[2] From then on it followed basically a fast follower technology strategy and undertook some efforts to develop technology in certain areas.

The organizational structure

The organizational structure of the Vitro-Group has changed according to the growth strategies. Initially Vitro was created as a glass container company

---

[1]   There are many taxonomies of technology strategy (see, for example, Freeman, 1982: chapter 8; Porter, 1985). They share the idea that the accumulated knowledge of firms largely determines the technology strategies which are open to them. Following Freeman (1982) the firms's technology strategies can be defined as technological leadership, technological followership, imitation, or the firms can be just 'dependent' – or supplier dominated as Pavitt (1984) suggested – and pursue a slow follower strategy. These technology strategies create different knowledge bases, require different types of technological capabilities and conduct to reach different stages of building technological capabilities. The Leadership strategy is characterized by maintaining a state-of-the-art R&D capability. The Fast Follower strategy is characterized by maintaining a defensive strategy of R&D or an imitative strategy, conducting R&D to effectively adapt the innovations to quickly catch up, constantly monitoring the markets and being an active learning. The Slow Follower strategy is characterized by introducing innovations when they are diffused and not conducting R&D activities.

[2]   A number of managers used the phrase 'technologically independent' which meant trying to innovate and develop technology in certain areas, leading them to the international technological frontier, while continuing to purchase equipment and technology in other areas.

called 'Vidriera Monterrey'. In 1927 the diversification process began and
two special departments were created inside the company. In 1936 'Vidriera
Monterrey' was split into several companies, according to product and
geographical approaches, and a holding company named 'Fomento de Industria
y Comercio' (FIC) was created.[3] The organizational chart of FIC for 1960 is
presented in Figure 6.1. There were ten companies: four glass container
companies referred to here as VGC, Fama and five other companies.

The organization of the technology function was decentralized to the
individual companies. Each company had a technology group with different
levels of development. Glass Containers, Glassware and Basic Industries related
companies had the most developed groups. Some of the other companies had
foreign shareholders and built up weaker in-house technological capabilities.

6.2   THE CAPABILITY BUILDING PROCESS: DEVELOPING INTERNAL INNOVATIVE TECHNOLOGICAL CAPABILITIES

Vitro-Glass Containers was the first business of the Vitro-Group, as described
in Section 5.5. The first glass container plant was established in 1909 in
Monterrey.

The project of creating a glass container plant was an entrepreneurial idea
based on the evolution of the domestic and local market. The total demand for
glass bottles was estimated at 14.4 million bottles per year and it was satisfied
mainly with imports from Germany and the US. In 1890 the first large Mexican
brewery was established in Monterrey. Some of the entrepreneurs who funded
the Cuauhtémoc brewery, as it was called, participated in the creation of the
glass container plant. Therefore this plant was primarily oriented to supply
this brewery with glass bottles.[4] The pure entrepreneurial bases of the project
is revealed by the fact that there was no sustained advantage in labor or raw
materials. The tradition of glass making in Mexico was located in Puebla, in
the center of the country, far away from Monterrey and not connected to it.
In Monterrey there were no skilled glass blowers. In addition at the beginning
of the century there were no sources of raw materials for glass making in the
country. The two main raw materials – silica sand and soda ash (sodium
carbonate) – were imported.[5]

The glass container plant was built with state-of-the-art technology under a
license from the Toledo Glass Co. in the US. As described in Section 5.2.3, in

---

[3] FIC was formally constituted on 27 August 1936 (Vitro S.A., 1998).
[4] Fernández (1993).
[5] Sada (1981).

1903 Michael Owens patented the first automatic machine to produce glass containers, which was exploited by the Toledo Glass Co. The license to VGC included designs for a plant, two automatic machines, complementary equipment and technical assistance for the construction of the plant.[6] An American engineer from the Toledo Glass Co. was engaged temporarily to oversee the building and start-up of the plant.[7]

Figure 6.1   Organizational chart of Vitro, 1960

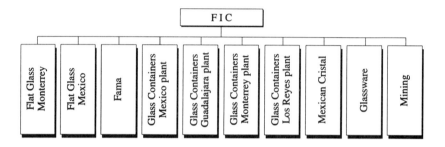

The technical knowledge to operate the equipment was basically tacit and resided in the foreign technician hired to start up the production and technical assistance provided by the licenser. In addition a number of German technicians were also engaged. Therefore the initial base of knowledge of the first plant at Monterrey relied on external sources. Even though in the early days foreign suppliers were the only source of technological upgrading, the need to build up in-house technological capabilities to adapt and improve foreign technology to suit the country- and firm-specific conditions was quickly realized. Hence VGC had to begin to develop routine production capabilities and build up innovative technological capabilities, which allowed them to progressively combine external and internal sources of knowledge.

This section examines the main events of the building up of internal technological capabilities since the earliest days. It is organized in terms of technical-functions in the following way. Section 6.2.1 describes production activities; Section 6.2.2 examines investment project management and process engineering; and Section 6.2.3 describes design engineering and capital goods supply.

---

[6]   This license had been acquired in 1905 by a group of entrepreneurs from Chihuahua and La Laguna. They later joined a group of entrepreneurs from Monterrey and created the new firm. They got rights to exploit the license for 20 years that lasted until 1925 (Fernández, 1993).

[7]   Fernández (1993).

6.2.1 Building Routine Production Capabilities and Acquiring the Knowledge to Adapt the Equipment

From 1909, when the novel Owens technology was installed, VGC gradually increased production capacity, built routine production capabilities and improved efficiency. This process was achieved by five basic activities listed below.

1. Learning by doing and using the equipment.
2. Technical assistance to acquire the basic know-how for glass container production.
3. Continuous upgrading of the machinery using the standing license.
4. Investment in additional furnaces and machines.
5. Development of minor adaptations to meet the country- and firm-specific conditions.

The expansion of production capacity of the Monterrey plant is presented in Table 6.1 below. The plant increased the number of furnaces and machines from one in 1911 to five in 1921, which allowed output to be increased from 14 million bottles per year to 49 million, respectively. The machines were upgraded over the period as revealed by the change in the machine models from AE, to AN and to AW. The increase in the number of bottles produced per year using continuously upgraded equipment gives some indication of the development of a routine production capability.

Table 6.1 Expansion of the production capacity

Year	No. of furnaces	No. of machines	Millions of bottles/year
1911	1	2 Owens machines (Model AE)	14
1912–13	3	4 Owens machines (Models AE and AN)	NA
1919	4	4 Owens machines (Models AE and AN)	15
1921	5	5 Owens machines (Model AW)	49

Source:
Based on Fernández (1993).

From the outset VGC realized that some adaptation activity was required and that this activity had to be based on internal sources of knowledge. Foreign technicians were not familiar with the country- and firm-specific conditions and were not able to offer solutions to many of the problems (see Box 6.1).

Box 6.1   The need to build internal sources of knowledge

In 1909 VGC followed the plant design provided by the Toledo Glass Co. and installed the Owens machines. However in spite of having hired a foreign technician from that company, it took two years to achieve stable production. There were three basic reasons: (i) the raw materials were of a different quality to those used in the US; (ii) the fuel was different; and (iii) the temperature in Monterrey was higher than in Toledo. VGC realized early on that foreign technicians did not know the Mexican specific conditions and it was difficult for them to find appropriate solutions, therefore it was necessary to develop internal capabilities to combine with foreign technology and assistance.

In 1919 the Board of Directors adopted a policy to set aside a portion of its annual earnings in special reserve accounts to raise equity, modernize facilities, enlarge the production capacity, and install new equipment.[8] In addition to this financial support to technical change related activities, the firm recognized that 'technology matters', and that it was necessary to learn and adapt the foreign equipment. Therefore these activities received organizational support.

Since its early years VGC had a machinery repair shop in its original plant at Monterrey. It was a small foundry to produce molds for containers and spares for the machines. The team consisted of practical technicians and a few engineers. This machinery repair team also had the task of adapting the equipment to the specific conditions whilst ensuring the continuity of the production process. In order to do this the team developed capabilities in process engineering, assembling machines and carrying out adaptations and improvements. The many changes in the technology source described in 6.3.1 put immense pressure on these activities. In addition from the 1930s VGC created new plants and continually expanded its production capacities to keep up with the growth in glass container demand. Therefore the team had also to build up skills in investment project management. Over this period the team greatly increased its expertise.

After developing the basic engineering and some design skills there were three important stages in the work of this team.

---

[8]   Ibid.

1. In 1932 the Board of Directors decided to open a small plant to produce rolling glass – a type of flat glass. The plant's layout and designs and certain equipment were designed by the engineers and technicians of VGC – the first such undertaking for them.
2. In 1934 a new glass container plant was created in Mexico City: 'Vidriera Mexico'. The plant was designed by the machinery repair team, and the design included certain individual in-house developments such as: the design of the chimney (fireplace), the design of the blending machine, the construction of the annealer and the mold machinery.[9]
3. In 1940 VGC acquired a few IS machines and designs from Hartford Empire & Co. and the team carried out reverse engineering of one of those IS machines, acquiring experience in a new activity.

The activities undertaken by the machine repair team were the basis for developing capabilities for investment project management, process engineering and design engineering as described in the following two sections.

6.2.2 The Continuous Rebuilding of Capabilities in Investment Project Management and in Process Engineering

During the first decades VGC's capabilities in investment project management and process engineering were basically located at the Monterrey plant. They were firstly nurtured through the expansion of capacities of that plant described above. From 1924 VGC started a more ambitious process of expansion based on developing its own technologies, markets and products.[10] That process became more established in the creation of new plants, the process of diversification in technology related activities and the backward integration[11] into the manufacture of equipment and raw materials. The most important of these steps are shown in Table 6.2.

Most of the new businesses were created as a split-off from the Monterrey plant. For instance the Glassware and Flat Glass businesses started their operations as special departments of the Monterrey plant; the Sodium Silicate business started using a furnace from glass container production which was reconditioned to produce sodium silicate; Fama was created based on the expertise of the machinery repair shop; etc. These businesses were later split-off as independent companies within the Vitro-Group.

---

[9] Ibid.
[10] Vitro SA (1992).
[11] In this book backward integration and vertical integration are used as interchangeable concepts.

Table 6.2 New production facilities established by VGC, 1924–70

New businesses	Year	Type of activity
Glassware	1924	Diversification in technology-related business
Flat Glass	1927	Diversification in technology-related business
Sodium Silicate	1930	Backward integration towards raw materials
Rolling Glass plant	1932	Diversification in technology-related business
Mexico plant	1934	Creation of a new glass container plant
Fama (machinery manufacturer)	1943	Backward integration towards machinery
Los Reyes plant	1944	Creation of a new glass container plant
Guadalajara plant	1951	Acquisition of a glass container plant
Monterrey's Raw Materials (silica sand)	1952	Backward integration towards raw materials
Fiberglass	1957	Diversification in technology-related business
Alcalí Industry (soda ash)	1960	Backward integration towards raw materials
Guatemala plant	1964	Creation of a new glass container plant

Source:
Compiled from Vitro S.A. (1993c) and Vitro S.A. Annual Report (various years).

Those split-off businesses from the Monterrey plant had positive consequences in terms of the knowledge accumulation. However they also meant splitting-off of knowledge from the Monterrey plant because some personnel were assigned to positions in the new plants and businesses, and this affected the growth of the stock of knowledge related to glass container technology. Whilst the capabilities in investment projects and process engineering were initially nurtured each time that a new plant or facility was created, they were weakened by the re-assignment of personnel away from the core area of accumulation in the Monterrey plant. The main splits in the knowledge base are presented in

Figure 6.2, with their relative importance roughly represented by the sizes of the sphere.

Figure 6.2   Splitting-off knowledge from the Monterrey plant, 1932–44

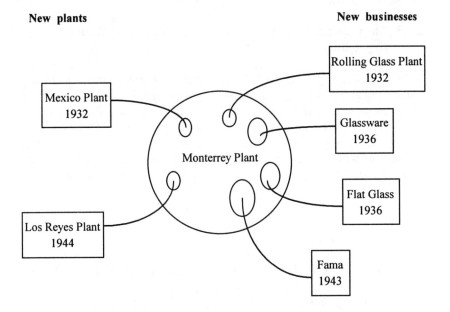

The removal of most of the machinery repair shop's team from the Monterrey plant to Fama was the most significant reduction of personnel and capabilities for investment project management and process engineering, and is analyzed later in Section 6.2.3. Some team members remained at the Monterrey plant and they began a process of rebuilding knowledge in that area. They faced two different pressures:

1. The continuing dynamic of growth of the glass container demand which required investment project capabilities to be improved.
2. The introduction of the IS machines in the 1940s which brought many process engineering problems and the need to assimilate new know-how.

Additionally in 1964 VGC participated in the creation of a new and successful company named 'Industria Centroamericana del Vidrio' (later called Empresas Comegua), located in Guatemala, and acquired 49 per cent of the shares. VGC started a process of technology transfer to that company based on its own expertise in operational know-how of a glass container facility, investment project management and the generation of improvements to the foreign equipment. This activity revealed, on the one side, the build up of innovative technological capabilities in these areas and, on the other side, the ability to transfer knowledge.

6.2.3   The Creation of Fama and the Strengthening of the Design Capabilities

In 1943 the design and engineering capabilities, concentrated in the machinery repair shop at the Monterrey plant, were split-off into a new company of the Vitro-Group. This new company was called Fama and was set up to produce machines and spares for the manufacture of glass containers. The team of the old machinery repair shop became the core of the new company. This team was merged with a small metallurgy shop which had manufactured molds and spares for the Monterrey plant. Fama remained closely related to the VGC's plants.

The creation of Fama was the result of three basic factors:

1.   The knowledge already accumulated in this area.
2.   The specific motivation of Don Adrián Sada, one of the President's sons, who wanted to found a machinery manufacturing firm to develop automatic machinery for glassware products.
3.   Certain problems in the economic environment, such as shortage of machinery and other equipment, together with the difficulties in acquiring the equipment and spares necessary to guarantee continuity of the production process during World War II.

The goal of Fama was to supply the glass container business with the best technology and to be independent from foreign equipment suppliers in the context of an unstable economy. To achieve this it was necessary to be familiar with the state-of-the-art technology and be able to adapt it to the specific Mexican and firm conditions. Fama's short-term targets were to satisfy the spare parts demand for the machines and molds for making glass containers and glassware, and to manufacture machinery.

Fama started as a small workshop with six machine-tools and 37 workers. The basic prior knowledge was made up of tacit knowledge held by the people coming from the machinery repair shop and from the foundry, designs acquired from the firm's technology sources, the assembled IS machine after reverse engineering, and the machine-tools brought in from the foundry. Due to the scarcity of skilled people it was not easy for it to expand. To deal with this problem in 1944 an apprentice school was created.

At the end of the 1940s Fama started production of Hartford-based IS machines from Hartford's designs. The first IS machines produced by Fama were one and two sections, simple cavity machines. During the first years they concentrated on developing routine production capabilities to manufacture equipment. Fama focused on using existing designs without making many changes. Very soon Fama could, and had to, make simple adaptations to the existing designs and specifications to suit local manufacturing conditions and firm-specific requirements. The design and engineering capabilities developed previously allowed Fama to be more creative.

Even though the original team from the Monterrey plant had a base of knowledge in process engineering, investment project management and less in mechanical design, its new organizational location determined a specialization in manufacturing machinery and mechanical design. The knowledge in process engineering was directed to equipment manufacture engineering and to improving the glass container production process through the adaptation and improvement of the machinery manufactured by Fama.

To strengthen Fama's knowledge in mechanical design a foreign design engineer was hired in 1948.[12] He formed a team that developed and patented the original design of a paste mold machine for glassware products in 1951 (see Box 6.2). This was the first experience of an original and formal technological development by Fama and the whole Vitro-Group. In the 1960s the machine was exported to Latin America, representing Vitro-Group's first experience of transfer of technology in this area. The design activities received a boost from this success. In addition an intensive modernization of Fama's production processes was supported by the introduction of numeric control machine-tools in the 1960s.

Since the creation of Fama the activities of adaptation, reverse engineering and improvement of foreign equipment used by VGC were developed more systematically.[13] In addition the design activities were the basis for internal developments. Therefore the technology used by VGC since Fama was created was no longer the original technology acquired, it was now an idiosyncratic combination of foreign and in-house technology.

Design capabilities were gradually strengthened during this period and some applied research activities were undertaken to support the innovation activity. However, as indicated in Section 6.3.1 below, Fama had not accumulated enough design capabilities to upgrade the original foreign technology or its own incipient developments at the pace required by the moving international technological frontier.

---

[12] Interview with the Leader of Fama's Maintenance Department at the beginning of the 1970s.
[13] Ibid.

Box 6.2   The paste mold machine for glassware products and the 'VII system'[14]

The paste mold machine was designed to produce lighting tubes, vases and other glass products. This innovation developed by Fama consisted of applying a paste in the mold to avoid joins in the products. The first model was built in 1951 and was named the 351 model. Many other models were developed in the 1950s and 1960s in order to solve problems, which basically arose from users, such as to develop the neck ring mechanism or to improve the cooling of the blank mold. The machine was exported to Uruguay, Venezuela, Australia and Germany in the 1960s. They were the basis for the 'VII system' developed in 1969 by Fama and Vitro-Glassware.

The 'VII system' was a machine to produce integral glasses without any line dividing the piece. It was a significant innovation. The machine was controlled first pneumatically and later by hydraulic controls. In the 1970s when electronic knowledge was built in the Vitro-Group, electronic controls were developed for this machine. This machine was exported to many countries.

6.3   THE CAPABILITY BUILDING PROCESS: USE OF EXTERNAL KNOWLEDGE SOURCES

Despite the building up of internal innovative technological capabilities, external sources of knowledge continued to be extremely important. The main external sources of knowledge were equipment suppliers and foreign glass container producers. This knowledge was predominantly acquired through purchasing technology and machinery, hiring personnel and visiting other companies's facilities. This section examines the use of these sources.

6.3.1   The Purchase of Technology and Equipment and the Capability in Linkage with Suppliers

After being established as a 'state-of-the-art' company in 1909, 'the Monterrey plant made it a point to adopt every technological breakthrough'.[15] Therefore it continued upgrading its equipment technology according to the trends of the

---

[14]   Based on Fama (1993) and interview with the Leader of Fama's Maintenance Department at the beginning of the 1970s.

[15]   Vitro S.A. (1997b).

technological frontier in the industry over the whole period. Technology and equipment suppliers were the main external source of knowledge.

VGC regularly changed its sources of technology and developed new links with different suppliers based on two different motivations: the shifts in the technological frontier, and specific requirements associated with its own dynamic of building up of internal capabilities and with its areas of weakness. The most relevant events are described in Table 6.3.

As described in Table 6.3, the aims of its relationships with Toledo Glass, Lynch Machinery and Hartford Empire were associated with the upgrading of equipment or changes in the equipment technology following movements in the technological frontier of the industry. For instance, VGC purchased the first automatic machines from Toledo Glass; a circular machine with a feeder based on a gravity system from Lynch Machinery; and the standing IS machines from Hartford Empire. However VGC's interest in Wheaton, Maul Bros. or Ball Brothers was associated with the need to overcome through technical assistance weaknesses in specific knowledge areas, such as operating knowhow, glass composition and furnaces. In addition in several cases it was interested in acquiring designs to support the building up of design capabilities. The several changes in the equipment suppliers presented in Table 6.3 reveal the building up of a capability for searching out new sources of knowledge.

The change of technology supplier from Lynch Machinery to Hartford Empire deserves special attention. In the 1930s VGC was using Lynch machines. The introduction of the feeder invented by Pelter, based on a gravity system, was the reason for Lynch machines taking over from the Owens machines. The Lynch machines had limitations: their circular shape took up a lot of space, they were complex and there were restrictions on increasing their production capacity by putting in more than one cavity. The technology of the IS machines, developed in the 1920s by Hartford Empire, had been substantially improved in the 1930s and offered better performance in those areas. The IS machines could use more cavities than the Lynch machine. In addition one machine section could be stopped without it affecting the other sections. For these reasons the IS machine allowed increased production capacity. These machines were the current state-of-the-art technology and have continued to be so in the 1990s. VGC had to wait to introduce this technology until its investment in the Lynch machines was recovered. In 1940 VGC purchased the designs from Hartford Empire and during the 1940s it acquired and installed some IS machines.[16] Later those machines were manufactured at Fama. In the 1960s VGC changed to Maul Bros. as the supplier of the IS machine technology.

---

[16] Fama (1993:2).

Table 6.3 Aims of the links with foreign suppliers, 1909–70

Supplier	Type of firm	Years	Main aim	Main innovations acquired
Toledo Glass Co.	Glass container and machinery manufacturer	1909–25	• Acquire the latest equipment • Acquire plant design • Obtain technical assistance	• 1909: automatic Owens machines (Model AE), the feeder was based in a vacuum system • 1911: the first upgrading of the machines by acquiring the AN machines • 1920: Owens rotated AW machines equipped with the Graham system based in a gravity flow stream feeder • 1923: new double molds
Lynch Machinery	Machinery manufacturer	1925–30s	• Change the equipment technology	• Circular machines, the feeder was based in a gravity system
Hartford Empire & Co.	Machinery manufacturer	1940s	• Acquire the latest equipment • Change the equipment technology • Acquire designs • Technical assistance	• IS machines
Wheaton	Glass container and machinery manufacturer	1950s	• Technical assistance on furnaces, formulation, molds, know-how • Acquire designs	• Inspection equipment • Improvements of the IS • Technology to produce perfume and antibiotic bottles
Maul Bros.	Machinery manufacturer	1960s	• Acquire the designs for the upgrading of the IS machine	• Improvements of the IS
Ball Brothers	Glass container and machinery manufacturer	1960s	• Acquire specialized equipment	• Sprinkling equipment • Perfume spraying equipment

Source:
Several interviews, Fernández (1993) and Sada (1981).

The relationship established with Hartford Empire, and the later change to Maul Bros. as the source of technology, reveal several issues related to the accumulation of routine production capabilities and innovative technological capabilities by VGC, which are described below.

1. *The need to acquire machinery designs to nurture the process of building up design capabilities.* After acquiring the first IS machines and the design made by Hartford Empire, VGC carried out reverse engineering of the IS machine. This new activity, the decision to create Fama in 1943 and the support to build up design capabilities revealed a change in the target of the technology purchase. Indeed VGC started to be interested in the manufacture, adaptation and subsequent development of machinery instead of the pure acquisition or manufacture. Therefore from the 1940s access to machinery designs was a key element in the purchase.

2. *The lack of in-house capabilities to upgrade the IS machine to keep pace with the technological frontier.* Once Fama was able to demonstrate its manufacturing capabilities and some emergent design capabilities, Hartford Empire made the decision not to sell the improvements in its design to VGC and Fama. Unfortunately Fama did not have strong enough design capabilities to develop improvements internally at the pace of the frontier. Therefore it had to turn to another technology supplier in order to be able to continually upgrade its equipment. In the 1960s VGC acquired the IS machines and designs made by Maul Bros. This company had carried out reverse engineering of the Hartford Empire machines. Using Maul Bros. as its supplier VGC could always keep up-to-date with improvements to the IS machines.[17]

3. *The development of operational know-how on glass containers production.* Once VGC had built up the routine production capabilities to operate the IS machines it was keen to increase the efficiency of the whole production process. In the 1950s the assistance given by Hartford Empire was becoming more and more inadequate for two reasons. First, Hartford Empire produced machinery and not bottles, so its knowledge about the whole operation of the production process was scant and it had to subcontract other glass container companies to give the necessary

---

[17] Interviews with the Leader of Fama's Maintenance Department at the beginning of the 1970s, a firm's employee engaged in 1930, who was Upkeep from 1950 to 1980, and a Department Leader of the Monterrey plant in the 1950s and 1960s and later Director of Dirtec in the 1970s and 1980s. For a definition of Upkeep see note 26.

after-sales assistance. Second, VGC's employees were increasing their tacit knowledge through experience and developing expertise to the extent that its demands exceeded Hartford Empire's operational knowledge on glass container production.[18]

The relationship established in the 1960s with Maul Bros., another machinery manufacturing firm, revealed a similar problem: an imbalance between internal knowledge in different areas and what equipment suppliers could offer. This was one of the factors that explains the signing in 1974 of a Technical Agreement with Owens-Illinois, a glass containers and machinery manufacturing firm, as described in 7.2.1.

The result of the several changes in the technology source and equipment suppliers was a diversity of the equipment in operation, both between plants and within a single plant. For example in the 1950s VGC had mainly Lynch circular machines and a few Hartford Empire IS machines and it began to introduce Fama IS machines based on Hartford's designs. In the 1960s it still had some Lynch rotary machines, along with IS machines from different suppliers such as Hartford, Fama and Maul. The concept of all the IS machines was the same but the specific characteristics of the construction, the mechanisms, and several improvements introduced by each supplier were specific. That diversity had important consequences on the type of knowledge VGC had to acquire. It had to continually modify the routine operation of the equipment and build up a broad maintenance capability associated with the lack of standardization. In addition VGC had to build a capability to adapt equipment not only to the usual country- and firm-specific conditions but to the idiosyncratic combination of equipment technology it had installed.

6.3.2 Other Mechanisms to Learn from External Sources of Knowledge

Visits to foreign glass container makers

Visits to foreign glass container makers were an important source of information about new equipment technology and a mechanism to acquire knowledge to solve operational problems. This mechanism was used as early as 1913–15 when one manager went to work in an American glass container company to learn about the technological problems in the industry and to acquire experience in the operation of furnaces and machinery. During 1919–21 the son of one of Vitro-Group's founders was sent to the US to study glass engineering in the

---

[18]   Interview with a firm's employee engaged in 1930, who was Upkeep from 1950 to 1980.

Toledo Glass Co. – VGC's technology leader – and worked in its glass container plants to acquire practical experience.[19] Since the 1950s VGC's personnel have made frequent visits to Wheaton and Ball Brothers, who were glass container producers and VGC's main equipment suppliers at that time. From these visits the firm obtained a regular technology benchmark and realized that, in spite of the effort to upgrade the equipment, it was still far from achieving the prevailing state-of-the-art. The main problem was the technological lag, therefore personnel had to be able to identify upgrading and new equipment existing at foreign plants in order to ask the suppliers to provide them.[20] VGC also still had some operational problems and personnel had to learn how to solve them.

Hiring experienced personnel from outside

VGC used both permanent and temporary hiring of foreign technicians to acquire knowledge in areas of weakness, such as managerial skills and technical knowledge. For instance in 1909 German technicians were engaged in the new plant.[21] That year, as mentioned before, an American engineer from the Toledo Glass Co. was hired on a temporary basis to install the original Owens machines at the Monterrey plant. He played a key technical role in leading the construction of the plant. In 1911 when VGC was trying to overcome technical problems and make a product of reasonable quality, the general manager travelled to the US and contracted technical assistance from Michael Owens, the inventor of the machines they were using.[22] In the 1920s, in order to develop the plan of diversifying into glassware products, VGC hired a European technician in glass blowing to train Mexican workers in a new skill. In 1948 an American engineer was engaged by Fama to lead the development of design activities. These foreign technicians had an important impact on the process of building up the most essential knowledge base in operating know-how, engineering and mechanical design. Whilst VGC hired foreign technicians mainly to overcome weaknesses in these essential knowledge areas, these hired-in technicians also occupied key managerial roles. This facilitated the implementation of their knowledge to solve specific problems and contributed to increasing the knowledge at organizational level.

---

[19] Fernández (1993:179).
[20] Interview with a firm's employee engaged in 1930, who was Upkeep from 1950 to 1980.
[21] This group of German technicians was hired for a first failed attempt to create a glass container firm in 1903 (Fernández, 1993).
[22] Fernández (1993).

6.4　EFFORTS TO MANAGE THE USE OF EXISTING KNOWLEDGE

By the 1950s there was an accumulation of different types and stocks of knowledge in the organizational units. For instance Fama had concentrated the mechanical design and engineering capabilities of VGC and had strengthened the design activities. Plants had built operational know-how and adaptation skills. However Fama and the plants were quite isolated.[23] Also learning occurred mainly at the individual level and there was limited sharing of knowledge developed internally from experience in VGC's plants, or acquired by personnel from visits to competitors's facilities.

The recognition of those problems and the need to overcome them contribute to explaining the establishment in the 1950s of several organizational arrangements to facilitate the process of sharing the existing knowledge across organizational units and knowledge areas. In addition some efforts were concentrated on codifying the most basic pieces of tacit knowledge in order to facilitate the sharing of knowledge. This section describes the main arrangements.

6.4.1　Mechanisms to Improve the Sharing of Knowledge

Technical and Operational Meetings

Over the whole of this period the Glass Containers operations had no central unit to coordinate technical activities. Each plant had its own technical department concerned mainly with machinery engineering. These departments were not formally integrated at divisional level and there was little interaction between departments. Fama was located in a separate organizational unit. Plants interacted with Fama as an equipment supplier, and Fama was called in when the machinery presented any problem, but there was no formal technical linkage.[24] Two types of meetings were set up as the main mechanism to interact and share knowledge, as described in Table 6.4.

Technical meetings were the main mechanism for interaction between the plants themselves, and between the plants and Fama. They were directed to addressing the principal concern which was the operation of the equipment. These meetings were the source of many improvements. Even though Fama frequently incorporated the identified improvements in the design of the new machinery, no formal feedback mechanism was established from Fama to the

---

[23] Interview with a Department Leader of the Monterrey plant in the 1950s and 1960s and later Director of Dirtec in the 1970s and 1980s.
[24] Ibid.

plants. Therefore these meetings were more a source of knowledge for Fama than a mechanism to increase the knowledge in the whole organization. Operational meetings were held by each plant. There was no interaction between plants in this knowledge area.[25] Plants had developed their own ways of doing things and they did not share them.

Table 6.4   Meetings to share knowledge carried out from the 1950s

Type of meeting	Objective	Participants		Level
		Fama	Plants	
Technical meetings	• Sharing of knowledge related to machinery and molding	• Managers and technical staff	• Machinery managers • IS machine leaders • Upkeeps[26]	• Between plants and Fama
Operational meetings within plants	• Trouble-shooting		• IS machine leaders • Upkeeps	• Within individual plants

Source:
Interview with the Director of Dirtec in the 1970s and 1980s.

Other mechanisms not explicitly designed for sharing knowledge

To support the process of creating new plants or diversifying towards other business undertaken by VGC, technical staff as well as lower- and middle-level management were moved from established plants to new facilities. This practice was intended to ensure the dissemination of the values, ways of doing things and best practices throughout VGC related businesses. This has had a positive impact on the sharing of knowledge within the company overall. In addition due to the size of the company, its family nature and the fact that the organizational boundaries were not yet profoundly rooted, personal contacts were an efficient way of sharing knowledge.

---

[25] Ibid.
[26] This is the name used in the industry for the technician in charge of fixing the machine's problems. The Upkeep is responsible for the whole glass forming process.

6.4.2 Codification of the Most Basic Knowledge

One of the main difficulties in the process of knowledge sharing was the poor documentation of codifiable tacit knowledge. Personnel learned from experience and observation, and transmitted their knowledge verbally. Documentation of the most basic operating procedures emerged as a necessity to increase efficiency. The main experiences of documenting are described below.

The job history records

In the 1950s VGC started recording a type of job history. It was a very elementary documentation of the characteristics of each production run of bottles. When a higher efficiency was achieved they filled in the details of the main modifications to the machine mechanisms, and recorded the speed, gob weight, heat, etc.[27] However these records were neither used to plan the same type of production run nor written into operating procedures. The Upkeeps continued to rely on their own tacit knowledge more than on the written documents and most of the codifiable tacit knowledge remained non-codified. They were familiar with the Lynch machines still in operation and could achieve 95 per cent of efficiency without following accurate operating procedures.[28] The compiling of an organizational memory had started but the personnel had no routine to access it or to update it. In spite of this informality it was an important first step in the documentation process.

In the 1960s and 1970s, when the new and complex Hartford Empire based IS machines were widely introduced into the company, efficiency dropped to 70 per cent. The know-how was not controlled and some problems with the adjustment of the machines were experienced. In addition the available documentation was limited and the tacit knowledge acquired through experience by the Upkeeps was not sufficient to deal with the new, complex technology. VGC faced difficulties in maintaining stability of efficiency. Therefore new tacit knowledge, accurate operating procedures and job history records were required to optimize the equipment (see Box 6.3).

The introduction of the standard

In 1964–5 VGC introduced a 'standard' indicator to try to control costs and reach a more stable level of efficiency. This 'standard' was an indicator of efficiency by product and monitored weight/capacity/product family/machine

---

[27] Interview with a firm's employee engaged in 1930, who was Upkeep from 1950 to 1980.
[28] Interview with a Department Leader of the Monterrey plant in the 1950s and 1960s and later Director of Dirtec in the 1970s and 1980s.

types. The operating procedures were set up to reach that 'standard', and also the minimum efficiency that had to be reached for each production run of containers was defined. VGC was then able to compare real data from a production run against the 'standard' to upgrade the operating procedures when necessary. The productivity in each plant could be measured against time, the efficiencies could be compared between plants together with the increase in productivity.[29] The introduction of the 'standard' and the operating procedures to implement it reduced the power of the operators and Upkeeps, which was based on keeping tacit, codifiable tacit knowledge. In practice, this allowed a more reasonable balance between non-codifiable and codifiable tacit knowledge, and also between tacit and codified knowledge related to the operation. This resulted in increased efficiency.

Box 6.3 The need to codify tacit knowledge about the operation [30]

Efficiency reached in the production process depended on: the type of machine, the experience of the operator and the Upkeep, and the machine controls. VGC's knowledge about the internal functioning of the IS machines was still weak in the 1960s. The control of the machines was mechanical, so they were manually manipulated by the operators and Upkeeps. Therefore efficiency was very dependent on the operators's and Upkeeps's abilities to overcome mechanical failures. These people only transmitted their experience verbally. When these people made changes to the mechanical controls of the machine to try to increase its efficiency nobody was informed and it was not documented. They adjusted the timing by manually moving some buttons. Thus the exact conditions under which they could get a higher efficiency in one type of production run remained tacit at the individual level, and it was not possible to maintain levels of efficiency. The documentation of the job history, the use of accurate operating procedures, as well as the access to them became an important issue.

6.5   AN ASSESSMENT OF THE DEPTH OF THE KNOWLEDGE BASE

Over the whole of this period VGC was building the minimum essential knowledge base. From building routine production capabilities, it was able to gradually build innovative technological capabilities and so undertake a few

---

[29]   Ibid.
[30]   Ibid.

innovation activities. External sources of knowledge were very important from the earliest days, but VGC was able to build up internal capabilities and then combine external and internal sources of knowledge. The main problems observed by VGC at that time were similar to those that can be found in the DCL when analyzing how firms learn and move from operating to innovating capabilities and build the minimum essential knowledge base (vertical movements up the y-axis in Figure 2.2 of Chapter 2). However the characteristics of the process at VGC illuminate some issues that have to be taken into account to analyze the learning processes.

1. The depth of the knowledge accumulated by technical-function was uneven. According to the framework presented by Bell and Pavitt (1995), based on Lall (1992), basic innovative technological capabilities were essentially reached in production activities, product centered, as well as in linkage activities with suppliers. The type of investment activities and process centered activities undertaken corresponded to an intermediate stage in the process of building up technological capabilities. The development of a few original designs of plant and equipment by Fama reveals an intermediate level also in capital goods activities. The experience in technology transfer since 1964 reveals more advanced capabilities in linkages with other glass container firms. However some other technical-functions were very weak, such as the linkages with customers and with the Science and Technology System.

2. Even though there was a gradual change in the type of activities undertaken by technical-function, the sequence of stages is not clear. For instance, it is difficult to identify the jump from routine production capabilities to basic innovative technological capabilities in production centered activities, because it was necessary to develop minor adaptations from the outset. In relation to linkage activities, from the earliest days in order to upgrade its technology, VGC actively searched for new information from current and new suppliers, so the jump is also not clear in this technical-function.

3. The development of innovative technological capabilities took place at different speeds across organizational units. The Monterrey plant was the seed of VGC in terms of businesses, personnel and knowledge. However as new businesses were split-off so was knowledge. This later affected the process of increasing the knowledge by that plant and then by VGC. Even though the new businesses or plants shared the same basic knowledge base and way of doing things, these new units later followed their own dynamic of learning. For example Fama emerged as a vertical disintegration from VGC and specialized in knowledge related to the machinery. Soon after Fama overcame VGC in terms of

learning capabilities. Plants also learned at different speeds and the effort to share knowledge within plants was scarce. When the type of innovation activities undertaken required a greater integration of knowledge, more effort was put on setting mechanisms for sharing knowledge.

4.   One of the main weaknesses that slowed the process of accumulation was the difficulty in codifying the codifiable tacit knowledge and in making effective use of any codified knowledge.

The process of building the minimum essential knowledge base was a slow one, particularly from 1909 to the 1950s. The meager support provided by the State for industrial development pressured VGC to assume functions that exceeded the role of a private firm, such as attention to basic education, housing and health. The weaknesses of industrial development motivated the company to internalize several activities in order to assure a regular supply of inputs of a constant quality. These factors affected the efficiency of the accumulation process. In addition the protected market exerted no pressure for a quicker pace.

After 60 years there was still a gap in using and operating the equipment and in machinery production in relation to the technological frontier. VGC had 70 per cent of operational efficiency by 1970, while Owens-Illinois – one of the technology leaders – had 80 per cent.[31] In terms of equipment technology, VGC followed the frontier quite closely, particularly from the 1950s. By the 1960s Fama mastered independent design and innovation, but still lagged behind the major international players because of the difficulties to upgrade both the original foreign technology and its own incipient developments at the pace demanded by the technological frontier.

---

31   Interview with the Director of Dirtec.

7   Starting a Transition Process Towards Building up Strategic Capabilities, 1970–90

7.1   INTRODUCTION

Vitro-Glass Containers started a Transition Process by 1970, but this was never completed and has continued until the present day. The Transition Process is the stage of accumulation from having the minimum essential knowledge base to building strategic capabilities. In principle this stage is characterized by: (i) the accumulation of routine production capabilities, together with basic and intermediate technological capabilities in some technical-functions and advanced innovative technological capabilities in others; and (ii) the emergence of embryonic strategic capabilities in a few technical-functions, technical areas or knowledge fields.

The main purpose of this chapter is to describe the characteristics of the Transition Process between 1970 and 1990. During this period VGC built upon the minimum essential knowledge base previously established, undertook more technologically complex activities, implemented new ways of doing things and raised some areas of knowledge specialization. The importance of internal sources of knowledge increased, particularly R&D activities – including some mainly applied research, product and process development, and minor improvement activities. These new activities required the integration of knowledge located in different organizational units. VGC also continued to learn from competitors and external technology sources, and continued its more traditional innovation activities oriented to adapting and assimilating foreign equipment. This was a period of moving forward in the process of knowledge accumulation. However the learning processes combined the gradual undertaking of more innovative activities in certain technical-functions based on R&D and the gradual integration of more complex knowledge bases, with a low innovative profile in other areas.

During this period VGC built up a number of embryonic strategic capabilities, such as in electronic control systems, glass composition, investment project management and engineering processes. However they did not develop to become strategic capabilities. This chapter examines how this was related to several issues such as the uneven depth of the knowledge accumulated by technical-function, technical area and knowledge field; the different speed of the learning processes across the organizational units; the inconsistent organizational support for undertaking development projects; and the limited efforts to share and codify knowledge. All these features affected the process of building innovative technological capabilities and contributed to why the embryonic strategic capabilities did not become strategic capabilities and the Transition Process remained incomplete.

This introductory section includes a brief description of the context, the technology strategy and the organizational structure of the Vitro-Group and VGC in the period analyzed. Section 7.2 describes the main events in the fast follower technology strategy. Section 7.3 examines the main events and characteristics of the process of strengthening the company's internal innovative technological capabilities, highlighting the effect of the dual technology strategy in this process. Section 7.4 examines the outcomes of the capability building process and the main directions of accumulation. Section 7.5 describes some of the attempts that were made to manage knowledge, to make effective use of existing knowledge and to strengthen the knowledge creation process. Finally Section 7.6 presents an overall assessment of this period.

The context and the technology strategy

The Transition Process has evolved in the context of a redefinition of the company's business strategy. After several decades of intense expansion of production capacities, the growth of the domestic market in the 1970s was insufficient to keep up with the rate of the firm's growth. VGC started looking to the US market to further its expansion plans. This strategy was reconfirmed in the 1980s with the contraction of the domestic market associated with the economic crisis of 1982, and the change towards an open and competitive market in Mexico from the end of the 1980s. A market-oriented strategy was directed to increasing exports and specifically to penetrating the US market. Such a strategy brought pressure to upgrade and improve equipment technology and increase operational efficiency.[1]

During this period the company pursued two distinctive parallel technology strategies. One was to be a fast follower of the technology leaders, and the central event that supported this strategy was the signing of a Technical Agreement with Owens-Illinois. The second strategy was to continue aiming

---

[1]   Nichols, N (1993), Interview with E. Martens, Vitro-Group's CEO from 1985 to 1993.

to be 'technologically independent',[2] and the main event in this strategy was the organization of the technology function at the group level and the creation of Vitro-Tec. These two strategies could have been developed jointly, but in fact were not. There was a dual and unrelated technology strategy. Certainly the development activities were more concentrated in some areas, however there was no clear strategy about 'what to buy and what to develop internally'.

The balance between these two strategies changed during the Transition Process. Initially from 1970 to 1990 the target of technological development was relatively more favored and the firm progressed towards completion of this stage, as analyzed in this chapter. However in the 1990s the fast follower strategy was given relatively more support and the firm regressed in some aspects, as analyzed in Chapter 8.

The organizational structure

The organizational structure of the Vitro-Group also changed in this period. In 1976 FIC became 'Vitro SA' and the companies became divisions.[3] Vitro-Group adopted the M-form organizational structure with six product-divisions, as illustrated in Figure 7.1. The organization of the technology function changed following the intense organizational change in the Group as a whole. Technology was defined as a corporate function. Vitro-Tec, the central R&D unit, was set up at group level and was located in the Basic Industries Division. Technology centers were created at divisional level. Dirtec, the technology center of VGC, was located organizationally in the operation area of this Glass Container Division.

7.2   THE CAPABILITY BUILDING PROCESS: FAST FOLLOWER AND EXTERNAL KNOWLEDGE SOURCES

At the beginning of the 1970s VGC still faced two major technological problems. On the one hand, the IS machines produced by Fama still experienced technical problems and lagged behind the technological frontier. Despite Fama's capabilities to produce, adapt, improve and develop equipment, it had not been able to keep pace with the moving technological frontier. On the other hand,

---

[2]   As referred to in footnote 2 of Chapter 6, this meant trying to innovate and develop technology in certain areas, leading them to the international technological frontier, while continuing to purchase equipment and technology in other areas.

[3]   Vitro SA was constituted and listed in the Mexican Stock Market on 5 January 1976 (Vitro SA, 1998).

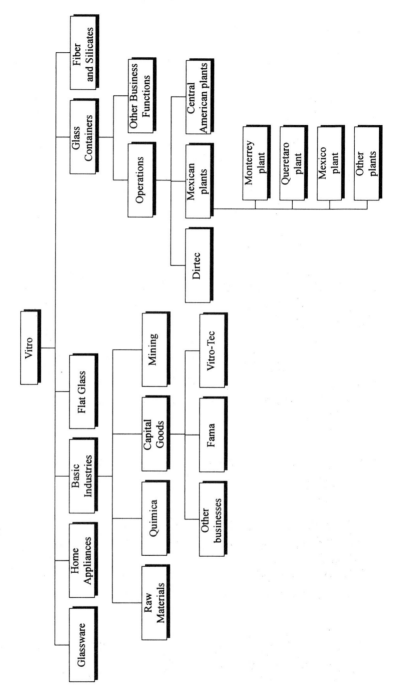

Figure 7.1 Organizational chart of Vitro, 1987

VGC had its own problems over being able to effectively operate its machines, and its equipment suppliers were unable to offer solutions, as described in Section 6.3.1. These two issues supported the arguments of certain high-level managers that the company should look outside to draw more effectively on external sources to acquire technology.

The firm was under particular pressure to solve these problems promptly because it had started more systematic export activity to the US, a more demanding market. In addition Owens-Illinois, being the first in the US market, was expanding its influence to Latin American countries. VGC was participating in the Mexican and Central American markets and was concerned with the increase in the competition in those markets.

In this context the argument that VGC should pursue a fast follower technology strategy was strengthened. This argument was based on the new market oriented strategy, the need to overcome technical problems in the equipment that Fama had not been able to solve and the urgent need to increase operational efficiency in the short term.[4] The main event that supported such a strategy was the signing of a Technical Agreement with Owens-Illinois – the world technology leader – in 1974. The conclusion of this agreement is examined in Section 7.2.1.

However, the firm also had concerns about being dependent on a unique technology source and falling behind the frontier, so it established links and purchased technology from different suppliers. These links are described in Section 7.2.2.

7.2.1 The Technical Agreement with Owens-Illinois

In 1974 VGC signed a ten-year Technical Agreement with Owens-Illinois. It was renewed in 1984 for another 10 years and in 1994 it was signed for a further five years.[5] The licensee group was made up of Vitro-Group's subsidiaries, including those located abroad. The license gave Fama the right to manufacture equipment based on technical information and licensed inventions and sell it to the Vitro-Group. Fama was also allowed to sell equipment to third parties in specific countries where Owens-Illinois had no subsidiaries or joint ventures. The Technical Agreement offered two types of knowledge:

1. Engineering and know-how to manufacture equipment, which included both product technology (equipment designs) and

---

[4] Interview with the Director of Vitro-Tec during 1977–87.
[5] The change in the number of years was related to the adjustment of the date of the Technical Agreement of VGC and Anchor Glass Containers Corporation, which got the Technical Agreement in 1989 when it was acquired.

manufacturing process technology (upgrading and technical assistance for equipment production).

2. Process engineering, know-how and training to use the technology in producing glass containers using Owens-Illinois technology.

The former was used to support Fama's operation and the latter was used by VGC.

The Technical Agreement allowed VGC to implement Owens-Illinois technology, solved certain problems related to the machinery, increased the speed of the IS machines and made for greater operational efficiency. It also offered access to Owens-Illinois's facilities thus opening up a means of learning from Owens-Illinois. Even more important was the ability to continually update its equipment designs at the pace of the world technology leaders.

There were three types of problem related to the introduction of the Owens-Illinois technology. First, there was an important stock of equipment in operation that had been acquired from other technology sources, so the introduction was paced by the timing of the effective life of that equipment. Therefore it was necessary to couple Owens-Illinois's technology with the equipment technologies already in operation. Second, Owens-Illinois technology had to be adapted to VGC-specific conditions. These two factors demanded the development of internal innovative technological capabilities to carry out successful operation of the Owens-Illinois technology. Third, VGC had already accumulated knowledge and a routine for carrying out adaptations, therefore Owens-Illinois technology was combined with already developed adaptations and improvements. Hence the technology transferred from Owens-Illinois to VGC promptly became an idiosyncratic Vitro/Owens-Illinois technology, which continually demanded in-house innovative technological capabilities to keep it in operation.

7.2.2 Links with other Equipment Suppliers

In spite of the open access to Owens-Illinois technology through the signing of the Technical Agreement, VGC still attached high priority to keeping up-to-date with the latest equipment technology in the international market. Therefore it continued to look for information about and acquire equipment from any other alternative supplier that offered innovative equipment, as in the case of the electronic control for the IS machine from Ball Corp., or from suppliers who could bring about a potential breakthrough in the industry, as was the case in the acquisition of a new type of hydraulic rotary machine from Lynch Machinery. VGC was also aware of the advantages of diversifying its technology sources to reduce the dependence on one technology supplier, which explains the acquisition of equipment from Emhart Hartford in 1980. The main links established during this period are described in Table 7.1.

All these purchases reveal that the capability for developing linkages with suppliers continued to be relevant and also that Owens-Illinois technology was the main but not the unique foreign technology used in this period.

Both the Technical Agreement and the links with other equipment suppliers were oriented to following the technological frontier by acquiring

Table 7.1   Aims of the links with foreign suppliers, 1970–90

Supplier	Type of firm	Years	Main target	Main innovations acquired
Owens-Illinois	Glass container and machinery manufacturer	From 1974 on	• Technical assistance on process engineering • Change the equipment technology • Acquire designs • Agreement to protect the market	• IS machines Owens-Illinois based
Ball Corp.	Glass container and machinery manufacturer	1975	• Acquire the latest equipment	• Electronic control for the IS machine
Lynch Machinery	Machinery manufacturer	1970s	• Acquire the latest equipment	• Hydraulic rotary machine
Emhart Hartford	Machinery manufacturer	1980	• Complement an order of machines supplied by Fama • Diversification of the technology source	• IS machines Emhart based

Source:
Several interviews.

the best technical solutions from outside. The use of these external sources of knowledge was to acquire technology for use, as opposed to developing in-house technology. However the need to adapt to the country- and firm-specific conditions and the actual way of doing things in the company demanded that specific efforts be made towards learning from outside and supporting the fast follower strategy.

7.3   THE CAPABILITY BUILDING PROCESS: STRENGTHENING INTERNAL INNOVATIVE CAPABILITIES

Between 1909 and 1970 VGC built up its minimum essential knowledge base. In the late 1970s the Vitro-Group moved beyond this stage by creating a new organizational structure that was more explicitly committed to innovation. This involved two related steps of organizational restructuring of the technological activities. On the one hand, incipient R&D activities were brought together in Vitro-Tec – a central unit serving the whole group and specializing in basic and applied research and development activities. At the same time divisional technology centers were set up to work more closely on the production function and be more oriented towards minor improvements and adaptations. Dirtec was the technology center for VGC – the Glass Container Division.

The knowledge specialization process, the creation of a central R&D unit and the strengthening of the R&D activities at group and divisional levels increased the knowledge of process technology and allowed the firm to develop more complex innovation projects. However both the more formal organization of the technology function and the new innovation activities brought new learning problems, such as the integration of different knowledge fields and organizational units. At the same time VGC strengthened its capabilities in investment project management and process engineering based on different types of innovation activities.

Section 7.3 examines the strengthening of the process of building internal innovative technological capabilities, which was supported by the strategy of becoming 'technologically independent'. This process included both in-house developments and also the use of external sources to support the process of knowledge creation.

The creation of Vitro-Tec at the Vitro-Group level is reviewed in Section 7.3.1. At the glass container divisional level (VGC), two main units are examined: in 7.3.2 the creation of Dirtec and the strengthening of applied research and development in VGC, and in 7.3.3 the strengthening of design capabilities at Fama – the machine manufacturer.

7.3.1 The Creation of Vitro-Tec: A Central R&D Unit

The Vitro-Group established an R&D unit in 1977, according to the strategy of 'technological independence' conceived in the 1940s and the in-house capabilities already built up. It was called Vitro-Tec and was oriented to supporting the accumulation of technological capabilities in the long term.[6]

The approval to create Vitro-Tec came after the success of the development of the 'VII system', a machine to produce integral glasses designed by Fama, which allowed Vitro-Glassware to be technologically independent in relation to this equipment, as described in Box 6.2. This success strengthened the confidence of Vitro-Group's President and CEO that they could develop their own technology.

Vitro-Tec was defined as the Vitro-Group's central R&D unit and was located at Vitro-Basic Industries organizationally. The R&D capabilities initially built up at Vitro-Glassware and Fama were transferred to this unit. Vitro-Tec was mainly oriented to strategic projects within the established divisions, for instance exploring the introduction of new technologies to manufacture the current product mix. The improvement of machinery was considered as one of the main targets. In addition there were some specific problems in the operational areas that had to be solved.[7] According to the new organization of the technology function, 80 per cent of Vitro-Tec's time was assigned to developing major improvements. At the divisional level technology centers were set up and they were more oriented to requirements at plant level. They had to assign only 20 per cent of their time to major improvements, as described in Table 7.2.

Table 7.2 Organization of the technology function, 1977–90

Unit	Target	Distribution of time by activities
Vitro-Tec: a central unit at corporate level	Strategic projects	• 80% major improvements • 20% continuos improvements
Technology centers at divisional level (e.g. Dirtec in VGC)	Plants's requirements	• 20% major improvements • 80% continuos improvements

Source:
Adapted from interviews with the ex-Directors of Vitro-Tec.

[6] Interview with the Director of Vitro-Tec during 1977–87.
[7] Ibid.

Vitro-Tec was organized into three departments defined by the most significant knowledge areas for the Vitro-Group: materials, electronics and mechanical design. Three types of project were undertaken: (i) disciplinary projects developed by each individual department, (ii) joint projects between these departments to integrate different knowledge areas, and (iii) projects of interaction with the divisions, where multi-disciplinary teamwork was organized using people from Vitro-Tec, Dirtec and the plants.[8]

In the early years certain very specific problems that the plants had been unable to solve, such as reducing losses from 5 per cent to 1 per cent by improving the features of the arm of the push-out mechanism, were identified and tackled. Several ideas which had originated in the plants but which the plants had not had the time or the resources to further by themselves were developed, for example the quadruple cavity machine to produce vials instead of the more familiar machines with two cavities.

By 1980 Vitro-Tec had taken on a more strategic focus and started to use a technology planning approach, based on the identification of opportunities, the examination of the technological position of the divisions in the international industry and the analysis of their competitors' products. Formal exercises to support the R&D activities were carried out. These allowed identification of the technological fronts or main areas of knowledge of each Vitro-Group division, for instance returnable and non-returnable bottles for VGC, and glass forming machines for Vitro-Basic Industries. From all the divisions 87 possible areas of knowledge were identified, and 16 more strategic areas were selected. The relevant technological parameters in each front (for instance bottle thickness, machine speed or energy expenditure) were identified and analyzed for their impact on the cost structure. The parameters were obtained by technical analysis of competitors' products, and VGC's comparative position was assessed. Positioning included: (i) where VGC was currently, (ii) where consultants might lead VGC, (iii) the best practice, and (iv) the level reached by the science.[9]

The divisional Presidents, the CEO and Vitro-Tec's Director met each month in the 'war room', had discussions on their strengths and took strategic decisions based on positioning exercises, such as where they wanted to be in each parameter and in what parameter they wanted to base their advantages. Vitro-Tec provided support to the divisions to reach their desired position. Vitro-Tec was clearly enthusiastic about the technology strategy of being 'technologically independent' and supported it.

The plan to collaborate in a technology development project with Heye Glas, described in Box 7.1 below, is an example of a new way of working established by Vitro-Tec. This project illustrates, firstly, a different type of

---

[8]   Ibid.
[9]   Ibid.

external linkage based on collaborating in technology development. The aim of this project was to strengthen the firm's innovative capabilities, associated with the technology strategy of being 'technologically independent', instead of acquiring ready made technology as in the past, related to the fast follower technology strategy. Secondly, it shows that Vitro-Tec and VGC were looking for a new technology to radically reduce container thickness and to move beyond the technological frontier in the industry, so they were planing to build a strategic capability to compete on this basis. Therefore this project illustrates some attempts by the company to start using technology as a strategic tool to compete at the international frontier. However the non-completion of the project reveals that the embryonic strategic capability built was not taken further to become a strategic capability.

More formal and systematic activities of information search were established in Vitro-Tec. They were oriented to supervising the Vitro-Group's patenting interests, watching competitors' patenting trends and supporting positioning and R&D activities.

7.3.2 Strengthening Divisional Capabilities: The Creation of Dirtec at VGC

As part of the reorganization of the technology function by the Vitro-Group, divisional technology centers were created in the divisions. Dirtec was a divisional technology center created at VGC. It was geographically located at Monterrey, close to 'Vidriera Monterrey' (the oldest plant), Fama (the machinery manufacturing firm), and the Corporate building. Dirtec was mainly oriented to short term projects using traditional approaches and sources of knowledge. As described in Table 7.2, 80 per cent of the time of its personnel was assigned to continuous improvements and only 20 per cent to major improvements. It was a structure for interaction between VGC, Fama and Vitro-Tec. Even more important, it became a technical link between VGC's dozen plants in Mexico and Latin America and facilitated the sharing of tacit knowledge between them. The organizational structure of Dirtec itself changed during this period. The final organizational structure and the main activities of each department are outlined in Table 7.3.

The specialization of Dirtec's departments reveals in some sense their stage of development and the problems they had to deal with. For instance the creation of a Transfer of Technology Department is related to the fact that transfer of technology was a special concern, particularly in this period, and it was related to the transfer of both in-house developments and Owens-Illinois technology. The setting up of an Electronic Technology Department reveals the importance of this knowledge field in VGC, as described in Section 7.4.1.2.

Box 7.1 The project with Heye Glas: an example of positioning in bottle thickness

Weight reduction results from reducing the bottles thickness. Lightening is an important parameter of the bottles, particularly of the non-returnable ones. This was one of Vitro-Tec's targets in relation to VGC at the end of the 1970s. A development project was set up in 1978. The team responsible for the project gathered information and identified the comparative position of VGC in that parameter. The result was: VGC, 1.9 mm; Saint Gobain, 1.7 mm; and Toyo Glass, 1.7 mm. Therefore, VGC's bottles were thicker than others.

The team also conducted a literature review and located another scientist working on the same problem. He was contacted and through him they discovered that a German company, Heye Glas, had also got in touch with him. Heye was also interested in reducing the thickness of its bottles. Vitro-Tec's Manager contacted Heye Glas and in the early 1980s they had three meetings, exchanged documents and interacted. They were working together at the frontier and ahead of the market, which did not yet require a lower weight. On this their knowledge was at an equal level. In other areas VGC was ahead. For instance it had a higher machine speed. By 1982 Heye Glas proposed that VGC should join with it and together they should develop a lighter bottle technology, i.e. the NNPB process, to change the existing process technology and be ahead of the state-of-the-art. This new process technology was oriented to radically reduce the bottle weight and increase productivity. Both companies analyzed the possibility of signing a joint venture to develop that technology.

Even though Vitro-Tec had created knowledge, interacted with Heye Glas and actually an embryonic strategic capability had been built in relation to weight reduction, the joint venture did not develop further. Top management did not recognize the potential of this embryonic strategic capability to become the base for building a strategic capability.

This issue will be analyzed in Box 10.2.

Dirtec contributed to the strengthening of VGC's capabilities in process engineering and investment project management which had been built up before 1970. These areas of knowledge specialization were different from but complementary to Vitro-Tec's and Fama's.

However VGC's Divisional President took the view that the technological position of the division must be that of a fast follower of Owens-Illinois. This view determined a different direction for the learning activities. Dirtec focused on projects basically oriented to assuring effective transfer of Owens-Illinois

Table 7.3   Organizational structure of Dirtec and main activities, 1990

Departments	Main activities
Transfer of technology	• technological audit and service to plants • elaboration of a system of information and updating of the plants's equipment • adaptation of Owens-Illinois engineering • development and transfer of Vitro technology • documentation of development, engineering and improvements made by plants • reception of machinery and equipment at the plants • training
Process engineering	• technical assistance in the operation of the whole production process • support to projects for increasing productivity and reducing costs • support to mold design engineering • technical audit of equipment and operations • transfer of technology to continuos improvement • training in new processes
Electronic technology	• identification of the needs of automation in the production area • control of projects that incorporate new electronic technology • documentation of the projects to assure the transfer of technology to plants • monitoring electronic technology • looking for support to develop technology in universities and research centers
Advanced engineering	• R&D to assure the achievement of 'technological independence' • selection, evaluation and acquisition of technology • technological monitoring and benchmarking in machinery and equipment, glass composition, etc. • development of new products, processes and formulas • promotion of alliances with suppliers and support for this activity • analysis of changes and improvements in Owens-Illinois technology • training
Engineering services	• elaboration of projects of large investment, modifications, actualization and maintenance of the existing installations; and managing the implementation process • building and reconstruction of furnaces and feeders • offering technical support to describe the technical specifications and select the equipment and suppliers • technical audit of equipment and installations
New products	• undertaking projects of optimization of the product design • supervision of the central design areas, under the marketing function, to assure time reduction for product development and continuous improvement in design and molding • acting as a bridge between technology and marketing, and between operation and logistic • monitoring and control of the quality system • identification of future requirements of design, finishing and packaging of containers
Finished product and packaging	• providing technical assistance in the handling of the products • managing the technical specifications of the product according to customer requirement • acting as a bridge between Dirtec and the Direction of Quality
Technology management	• coordination of the exchange of technology between VGC and other firms • developing channels of communication and systematize information flows between plants • standardizing performance indicators • selection of personnel

Source:
Adapted from the description of the job positions of Dirtec's technical staff (Vitro SA, 1996b).

technology, to supporting the reduction of all costs and to increasing operational efficiency. It was less interested in technology development activities. Most of the projects had a shorter horizon than had been envisaged by the organization of the technology function. Overall Dirtec's technical staff assigned less than 20 per cent of their time to development activities.[10] The difference in the emphasis of the technology strategy and in the learning strategies made it difficult to coordinate Dirtec, Fama and Vitro-Tec in process engineering and investment-related activities. Some characteristics of the knowledge created in these areas are described in Section 7.4.2. The differences in the targets will be analyzed in Section 9.4.

The Advanced Engineering Department did undertake a limited range of R&D activities. One of the most significant projects was related to glass composition. This activity had its roots in 1967 when a Glass Laboratory was established at the Monterrey plant. The need to build knowledge in this area was a requirement for controlling the basic production process due to the particular requirements of the Mexican market and VGC specific conditions, such as: (i) VGC having to supply a smaller market with a different specialization than its technology suppliers, requiring the glass formula to be different; (ii) the application of foreign glass formulas in different situations generated unknown problems for its technology suppliers who had no solution to offer.[11]

The Glass Laboratory was directed to undertake testing of glass, identify defects and develop new formulas. This technological capability remained at VGC and was not relocated to Vitro-Tec because of its direct importance for cost reduction. The target of developing new formulas through R&D activities was strengthened when Dirtec was established in 1977. Since then the Glass Laboratory was directed to the long-term objective of being independent in knowledge concerned with glass composition, along with other short-term activities. A further reason why internal knowledge was critical was that Owens-Illinois was far from being the technology leader in glass composition at the world level. The development of a new formula by 1985 was the main achievement. It allowed the cost of the glass to be reduced. The description of this project is presented later in Box 7.2.

7.3.3 Strengthening the Design Capabilities at Fama

Based on the knowledge already accumulated, new and more precise strategic objectives were laid out for Fama following the new organization of the technology function. These objectives included: (i) incorporating already

---

[10] Interviews with the two Directors of Vitro-Tec.
[11] Interview with the Leader of the Glass Laboratory.

developed improvements in the machines, (ii) developing both new improvements and selected in-house equipment technology, and later on (iii) selling machines and technology in the international market. These objectives were supported by investments to modernize and expand the facilities, and by increasing reverse engineering, adaptation and R&D activities.

In the 1970s and 1980s Fama was technologically upgraded. By 1980 Fama had introduced CNC technology, CAD/CAM and FMS. It was upgraded following the Vitro-Group's and VGC's tradition to be state-of-the-art. By 1980 Fama's technology-related activities were reorganized following the creation of Vitro-Tec. The Unit of Technological Research (UIT) was created to coordinate the R&D activities carried out on site. With the creation of the UIT Fama focused more on development than on continuous improvement, showing a more long-term innovation focus than Dirtec and VGC's plants. Many developments in different types of equipment were made in this period, some of which were patented. They incorporated the operational experience of the plants, the manufacturing capabilities developed by Fama and the R&D activities developed at the UIT and Vitro-Tec. They revealed a considerable strengthening of design capabilities.

Fama and Vitro-Tec interacted intensively in this period. Fama supported the construction of prototypes. Even though the patents were generally assigned to Vitro-Tec, the development work was done jointly. Fama and Vitro-Tec were located in the same division and in nearby buildings, which facilitated the communication and flow of information. Also their interest in long-term projects, learning strategies and level of capabilities were convergent, whilst there were differences with VGC on these issues.[12]

As a result of greater involvement in the international market, foreign customers became a source of knowledge. Fama learned from these experiences and accumulated a stock of technological knowledge useful for VGC.[13]

At the same time that Fama was increasing its knowledge base through R&D activities. It was obliged to start the manufacture of the Owens-Illinois based equipment according to the signing of the Technical Agreement and the fast follower strategy. This required major efforts in order to understand the mechanical and design principles of the new machines, to manufacture the equipment and to adapt the Owens-Illinois engineering to the already installed idiosyncratic equipment.[14] Fama introduced many improvements and made adaptations to the Owens-Illinois based equipment, which became Vitro/Owens-Illinois technology. These changes were based on Owens-Illinois engineering,

---

[12] Interviews with Fama's and Dirtec's personnel.
[13] Interview with the Director of Fama in the 1980s.
[14] Ibid.

Fama's in-house developments and improvements made by plants and Dirtec. However such efforts meant that the time that could be dedicated to in-house developments to achieve 'technological independence' was greatly reduced. The manufacture and adaptation of the Owens-Illinois equipment required a different type of internal capability. The coexistence of two technology strategies making demands in different directions affected Fama's process of building up innovative technological capabilities, as will be analyzed in more detail later in Section 10.3.2.

To sum up, the organization of the technology function strengthened the accumulation of internal innovative technological capabilities by the Vitro-Group and VGC. One of Vitro-Group's strategies was to give autonomy to the divisions, therefore each division independently defined its strategic objectives. However Vitro-Tec was a 'space' in which to interact and share knowledge, align technology strategies, generate synergy and accumulate innovative technological capabilities at group level. Vitro-Tec's technical staff interacted with Dirtec, Fama and the plants. For instance the technological fronts committees had two leaders, one from the plant and one from Vitro-Tec. Members of the committee related to glass container activities included plant employees from operation, engineering and maintenance, technical staff of Dirtec and Fama, as well as engineers and designers from Vitro-Tec. This interaction allowed ideas to flourish.[15]

Vitro-Tec was an organizational space specializing in undertaking new and more complex innovation activities. R&D activities were systematically carried out, new knowledge bases were built such as in electronics and glass composition, and new sources of external knowledge were used to support in-house technological capabilities. The results in terms of the technological achievements are presented in Section 7.4. However at the group, division and even organizational unit levels there were different learning strategies and they set several distinct targets. For instance Vitro-Tec was interested in strategic developments while the plants and Dirtec, from the VGC Division, were more concerned with the operational side and were seeking small improvements.[16] Some units were more positive about the fast follower technology strategy and others were more enthusiastic about becoming 'technologically independent'. For this reason they built different internal capabilities and accumulated an uneven depth of knowledge. These differences affected the interaction between them, generated misunderstandings and limited the integration and creation of knowledge. These issues will be analyzed in more detail in Chapters 9 and 10.

---

[15] Interview with the Director of Vitro-Tec during 1987–9.
[16] Interview with the Director of Vitro-Tec during 1977–87.

7.4 THE DIRECTIONS OF THE KNOWLEDGE ACCUMULATION AND THE EMERGENCE OF EMBRYONIC STRATEGIC CAPABILITIES

This section examines the directions of the knowledge accumulation during this period in terms of the specific knowledge fields, technical-functions and technical areas. Special attention is given to the nature of the knowledge base and the role of organizational issues in the process of knowledge creation. The section also describes the progress of the Transition Process in terms of building embryonic strategic capabilities or strategic capabilities.

The type of innovation activities undertaken required the combination of: different knowledge bases (mechanical engineering, electronics and glass composition) and knowledge from different organizational units (Vitro-Tec, Fama, Dirtec and the plants). The difficulties that emerged in this process limited the scope of the embryonic strategic capabilities to become strategic capabilities.

Section 7.4.1 examines the creation of knowledge in the fields of electronics and glass composition based on R&D activities. Section 7.4.2 examines the strengthening of the innovative technological capabilities in process engineering and investment project management. Detailed descriptions of individual projects will be used to illustrate the type of learning problems they had to deal with while building up embryonic strategic capabilities.

7.4.1 Creating Knowledge by R&D Activities: Electronic Control Systems and Glass Composition

The new organization of the technology function and the strategy to carry out R&D activities allowed VGC, Fama and Vitro-Tec to undertake projects with a higher degree of innovativeness. They created and accumulated knowledge, and embryonic strategic capabilities were established as a result of this process. Sections 7.4.1.2 and 7.4.1.3 examine the process of building embryonic strategic capabilities in electronic control systems and glass composition respectively. However the company's patenting in the US is examined first in Section 7.4.1.1 to assess the technological progress achieved by the Vitro-Group in glass container related activities.

7.4.1.1 The Vitro-Group's patenting activity [17]

Patenting activity in the whole Vitro-Group had its roots in the 1950s when one model of the paste mold machine for glassware products was patented in

---

[17] The evolution of the whole patenting activity period, including the 1990s, is analyzed in this section because this activity was much more intense during this period.

the US. The patent granted in 1978 for the electronic control system of the IS machine was the first event of a new era. As a result of the establishment of Vitro-Tec, more systematic patenting activity was developed in the 1980s. In 1995 the Vitro-Group had 55 active patents in the US and 19 applied for.[18] Most of the company's patents protected developments made during the late 1970s and the 1980s.

Thirty-four of the 55 active patents of the Vitro-Group in the US in 1995 were related to the glass container areas.[19] Most of these patents were granted between 1982 and 1987, as can be observed in Figure 7.2. This was the period when Vitro-Tec was flourishing.

Figure 7.2 Evolution of the Vitro-Group's patents granted in the US in glass container by area, 1975–95

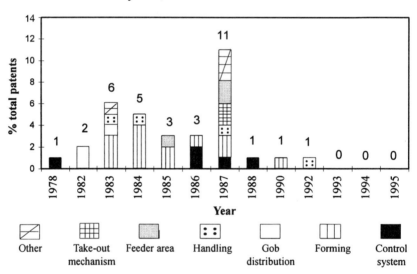

Source:
Ditac (1995).

The Vitro-Group had at least one patent in most of the knowledge areas in glass containers. Half of the 34 active patents in 1995 were in glass forming and control systems areas, as shown in Table 7.4 below. This suggests a particular effort in the R&D activities in these areas. Glass forming is an important area where all companies have many patents. Patents are basically

---

18 By 1995 Vitro-Group also had 53 active patents and 25 applied for in Mexico.
19 Patents in glass container areas were granted by Vitro-Tec, Fama and Vidriera Monterrey. Following Ditac (1995), the analysis refers to all of them as the Vitro-Group's patents.

oriented to developing small improvements in the many mechanisms of the IS machine.[20] As Table 7.4 illustrates, the Vitro-Group had in the glass forming area 37 per cent of the 34 US active patents in glass containers, Owens-Illinois had 17 per cent from 348, and Emhart Glass had 34 per cent from 318 active patents. The Vitro-Group had in the control systems area 15 per cent of all its US active patents in glass containers, while Owens-Illinois and Emhart Glass had only 5 per cent of their patents in this area, suggesting this was an area of higher specialization in the Vitro-Group.

Table 7.4 Areas of patenting related to glass container: the Vitro-Group and its major competitors, 1995

	Structure of all US patents active in 1995		
Areas of patenting	*Vitro-Group*	Owens-Illinois	Emhart-Glass
Glass forming	37%	17%	34%
Electronic control systems	15%	5%	5%
Other areas	48%	78%	61%
Total	100%	100%	100%
Total number of patents in glass container	(34)	(348)	(318)

Note:
The numbers between () refer to the total US patents of each firm in glass container related areas, which were active in 1995.
Source:
Ditac (1995).

Figure 7.2 also shows by area the year when patents were granted. In some areas the development of one or two patents in the same year suggests that patents were the product of a specific project, as in the case of the take-out mechanism in 1987. However the number of patents and spread of patenting activity in the control system and glass forming areas suggest more concentrated R&D in these areas.

The case of the knowledge in the control system area is particularly important in terms of the creation of knowledge. Firstly, the Vitro-Group's first patent of an electronic control was close to the first patent in this area. Ball Corporation was granted its patent of the C300 in 1970, Owens-Illinois was granted its first patent of the Soc-Box in 1973 and the Vitro-Group was granted its patent

---

[20] Interview with staff from Ditac's Patents Department and a manager of the Advanced Machinery area from Dirtec's Advanced Engineering Department.

in 1978. Secondly, in the 1980s other patents related to electronic knowledge were granted. Some of them were improvements to the original patent (they are included in the control system area in Figure 7.2), but others involved the application of this knowledge to develop electronic controls for specific machine mechanisms, such as the electronic gob distributor and the electronic control system for the feeder (they are not included in the control system area in Figure 7.2).

Considering only the glass container areas, the Vitro-Group ranks fourth in number of active patents in the US. It concentrated 5 per cent of the total actives patent in glass container areas in 1995. However it had a much smaller number of patents than the two technology leaders, representing only 10 per cent of their patents.

Even though patents show some output of the research activities, they neither reveal the intensity of the technology-related activities nor the impact of the innovations they protect. For instance Heye Glas – the technology leader in the NNPB process, a highly diffused technology today – has only 16 patents, less than VGC, but one of those 16 has had a major impact on the industry.

Neither does patenting activity reveal knowledge created in areas arising as embryonic strategic capability, such as glass composition. There are only a few patents by Owens-Illinois in glass composition. German companies, which are very competent in this area, have not been granted patents in the US. Patents are not a proper means by which to protect knowledge from imitation in this area.[21]

In the case of the machine area, only major or significant innovations have been patented by the technology leaders, for instance a new machine (e.g. the rotary machine) or a new process (e.g. the NNPB). The technology leaders and other companies do not usually patent machine-related knowledge because of the ease with which it can be copied.[22] Fama and Dirtec have developed many improvements and adaptations which have not been patented.

7.4.1.2 Knowledge creation in electronic control systems

The creation of knowledge in electronics is associated with the project to develop an electronic control system for the IS machine. This project was one of the main technological achievements in this period and it was the route to building up an embryonic strategic capability.

The change from a mechanical timing drum to an electronic timing drum to control the functioning of the machine's mechanisms was associated with the need to increase the machine speed. This change was taking place in the

---

[21] Interview with the Leader of the Glass Laboratory.
[22] Interview with a manager of the Advanced Machinery area from the Dirtec's Advanced Engineering Department.

industry in the middle of the 1970s. Ball Corporation was the first to patent an electronic control system for the IS machine in 1970 and market it in 1974. VGC introduced Ball's 'C300' control in 1975. At the same time a project to develop its own electronic control system was being undertaken by Fama.[23]

Vitro's electronic control system was a product development for Fama, who designed the new equipment for the IS machine. It represented a process innovation for VGC associated with the introduction of a different system of control in the IS machine. The in-house knowledge consisted of: (i) the design of the printed circuit board, although the components including the printed circuit and the manufacture of the board were purchased abroad; and (ii) the strategy of control focused on the glass forming process.

Ball Corporation focused its control system on the functioning of the machine's mechanisms. This control system constituted a change from a mechanical sequence to an electronic sequence, being basically an electronic timing drum. The project developed by Fama and Vitro-Tec was focused on the control of the glass forming process, which was a broader focus than the control of the mechanisms. One of the main differences was in the use of the pass-gob sensor – an electronic trigger. The pass-gob sensor gives the time of the gob's fall. It is connected with two other sensors that help to synchronize loads: the cut sensor and the gob distributor sensor. The pass-gob sensor contributes to increasing the quality of the containers, being an additional feature to the electronic timing drum.[24]

The development of the project presented below illustrates the process of building an embryonic strategic capability, the problems that must be dealt with in the process and the difficulties encountered in converting an embryonic strategic capability into a strategic capability. Certain problems in the knowledge creation process were related to the lack of reliability in Fama's and Vitro-Tec's capabilities compared with the technology licenser, receiving inconsistent organizational support during the development of the project, the existence of different learning strategies in the organizational units and the need to integrate knowledge across uneven units.

The development of an electronic control system for the IS machine [25]

By 1972 Fama was introducing numeric control machine-tools and engaged an electronic engineer to provide maintenance for the new electronic machines.

---

[23] Interview with the project leader.

[24] Ibid.

[25] Interview with the project leader, Fama's Maintenance Leader at the beginning of the 1970s, the present Manager of the Dirtec's Electronic Technology Department, the Electronic Maintenance Leader of the Monterrey plant and other personnel from the plants, Dirtec and Fama who participated in the project.

He was interested in applying the knowledge he had acquired during his Masters studies in electronics to develop a control system for the IS machine. He became the leader of a project, which followed the main stages described below.

1. The project started during bootleg time with the support of the Maintenance Leader. The first stage was to develop a prototype of a centralized console for the molding machines to facilitate the maintenance, giving an output useful for the sponsor. A PLC (programmable logical controller) was bought in the US and adapted to an old machine with pneumatic control. The test was successful and they were able to reduce the downtime associated with maintenance. Fama's Director ordered this innovation to be installed on all the molding machines.

2. After this success the project leader and the Maintenance Department Leader submitted a project to Fama's Director in 1974 to develop electronic controls for the IS machine. However Fama's Director instead offered support for the development of an electronic control for the 'VII System' of Vitro-Glassware. The 'VII system' had been developed by Fama and promoted by Fama's Director. This control system was developed and the project to develop the control system for the IS machine continued as a by-product.

3. In 1978 the project leader was relocated from Fama to Vitro-Tec's Electronics Department. He was officially assigned to work on developing controls for the IS machines and a formal team of four members was constituted. That year they were granted the first patent. However at that point the project required more funding. The divisions of Vitro-Group were reluctant to fund new ideas which were not immediately useful to them, even though they might further Vitro-Group's goals. By 1979 the Monterrey plant decided to sponsor the next stage: a control panel for sections of the machine. From the machine users's point of view, it was easier to control the machines by sections instead of having a control for the whole machine. This development was called 'Vitro I'. The first prototype was tested in 1984 in the 61 line at the Monterrey plant with the support of Dirtec.

4. By 1981–2 the project was again without sponsors and it was funded by Fama's UIT as a hidden project. After some financial restrictions the project to develop the 'Vitro II' model was restarted in 1984. The team tried to overcome some of the problems identified by the plant's personnel in the former prototype. The prototype of 'Vitro II' was built and in 1986 it was tested in the 21 line at the Monterrey plant.

5. Throughout the experience of developing the electronic control system for the 'VII System', it had been realized that a control oriented to the glass forming process was better than the electronic timing drum

diffused throughout the industry. The team decided to work towards giving the new model that focus. Due to its strategic focus Vitro-Tec decided to support the project to build the prototype of the 'Vitro III' model. This model was oriented to measuring the time it took for mechanisms to be moved into different positions to control the glass forming process. Sensors were included for this function. This model was more precise than the previous ones. By 1987–8 three prototypes of the 'Vitro III' with sensors were installed, the first in the 63 line at the Monterrey plant, and the other two with a number of improvements in the 12 line at the Guadalajara plant and in the 34 line at the Querétaro plant.

6.   By 1988–9 the team was working on the design of the final product, which was called 'Vitro III-A'. At the same time another team from the Vitro-Tec's Mechanical Engineering Department was undertaking a project to develop a 90 degree push-out mechanism for the IS machine. Both projects were integrated and a new feature was added to the 'Vitro III-A' version: to handle a 90 degree push-out mechanism. In 1990 Fama started manufacture of the 'Vitro III-A' electronic control, which was installed in the 93 line at the Monterrey plant. Fama also started manufacture of the 'Vitro II-A' version because of plants preferences for one or the other model.

From 1978 the project was located at the Electronics Department of Vitro-Tec, but it required the integration of knowledge across disciplines and organizational units. There was an Advisory Committee made up of the Production Manager from the Monterrey plant, Dirtec's Director, the Manager of Fama's UIT and other Vitro-Tec managers. The team also interacted with personnel from the Monterrey plant and Dirtec. Teamwork contributed to solving several problems related to the integration between electronics and mechanical engineering knowledge.

There were many changes to the models and versions to improve the prototypes. The source of the changes were the plants, Fama and the original team. The importance and nature of these sources were changing. Initially the plants had problems with the operation of the controls and some requirements reflected more the need for training than new ideas. Later as they were learning by doing they could identify certain aspects that required improvement. However users could not be very active in the improvement of the electronic controls, they had to present the problem and an electronics expert was required to change the software. This affected the speed with which improvements could be made and reduced the satisfaction of plants. At the same time the Owens-Illinois's 'Soc-Box' control was introduced in several plants. The performance of both the 'Soc-Box' and several of Vitro's prototypes was compared, which reduced the confidence on Vitro's developments when they were at an early stage.

By a far from straightforward process, characterized by inconsistent support, this project allowed the creation of knowledge in electronics at Vitro-Group. A family of products was created, which included the Vitro II-A, the Vitro III-A, an electronic push-out, an electronic distributor and a cooling system. Later this knowledge was applied to improving other equipment, such as the furnace controls, the feeder controls, and the control of the decorator's and annealer's furnaces.

In 1990, after 15 years of learning in this field, the company's knowledge base in electronic control systems had reached the stage of an embryonic strategic capability. The idea and the background knowledge necessary to develop a different type of control system were the result of designing a control system for glassware production. The knowledge was related to the specific conditions and business that the Vitro-Group had, and the directions of the searching activities they carried out. Built on the company's distinctive knowledge, this embryonic strategic capability could have been the basis for moving on to build a strategic capability. However the knowledge was not developed and never used as a strategic capability to create a competitive advantage.

In 1990 there were changes in the technology strategy which affected more deeply the support for this project, the creation of knowledge in this area and the building of a strategic capability from the embryonic strategic capability already built. This issue is analyzed in Section 9.6 and particularly in Box 9.5.

7.4.1.3 Knowledge creation in glass composition

VGC's knowledge in glass composition was related to the creation of the Glass Laboratory, described in Section 7.3.2. The project to develop a glass formula was the most important achievement of the Glass Laboratory and was the means by which knowledge in this area was built.

The project started in the 1970s and was oriented to developing a new glass formula more appropriate to the VGC requirements for glass. A different combination of raw materials was used to melt it in the furnace, which meant a process innovation for the plants. After this VGC was able to be independent from Owens-Illinois in this knowledge area and glass composition became an embryonic strategic capability.

The development of this project, summarized in Box 7.2 below, illustrates the process of building an embryonic strategic capability in glass composition, how the work was done and the several problems that VGC had to overcome while undertaking innovation activities. As in the case of the electronic control system, one of the problems was the lack of credibility in in-house developments when they were compared with the same development from a technology supplier.

Box 7.2 The change in the glass formula [26]

At the end of the 1970s a team was organized in the Glass Laboratory to improve the glass formula used by VGC. The team started by gathering information and doing a literature review. One of the first activities was to analyze competitors' products and establish their comparative positions. A laboratory analysis was made using bottles with the same type of glass, according to viscosity, produced by Owens-Illinois, European companies and VGC plants. The team measured the RMS (Range of Machine Speed) parameter and identified the relative positions of the companies. It realized that Owens-Illinois – VGC's technology supplier – occupied 11th position. German companies were ahead, followed by French companies. Thus by the end of the 1970s Owens-Illinois was out of date on this aspect. The Guadalajara plant was in 17th position. Rockware – a British firm that also used Owens-Illinois technology – was ahead of the VGC plants.

The team began work on improving the RMS parameter. Before the analysis, which revealed the positioning of firms, there had been a prevailing view in the company that Owens-Illinois and American companies in general were the most advanced in the world. However after this benchmarking they felt more confident in undertaking in-house developments. The team looked for support from the Alfred University in the US. They also interacted with some local universities such as the University of Nuevo León and the Technological Institute of High Studies of Monterrey (ITESM). By 1984–5 a new formula had been developed, which allowed a reduction in the cost of the glass. No patents were sought for this development as this is not a useful way of protecting knowledge in this area.

There were some internal problems when VGC decided to introduce the new formula, which required certain raw materials that were not produced by Vitro-Basic Industries – the internal supplier of raw materials. The decision to use the new formula affected one of the main features of the Vitro-Group: the vertical integration. Also there was a lack of confidence that their own formula was superior to that provided by Owens-Illinois. After long discussions the new formula was introduced. This decision had many consequences: (i) the in-house knowledge created in glass composition was recognized by the Vitro-Group; (ii) VGC did not depend on Owens-Illinois for glass composition; (iii) VGC reduced its dependence on Vitro-Basic Industries in relation to raw materials; and (iv) Vitro-Basic Industries had to look for other customers for some of its products.

By the mid-1980s knowledge about glass composition had therefore been accumulated as an embryonic strategic capability. It was located in the Glass Laboratory of VGC. Vitro-Tec as well as other divisions also had created some knowledge in this area, but there was a different depth of knowledge and interaction between them was weak, as was the case with the internal supplier of raw materials.

---

[26] Interview with the Leader of the Glass Laboratory.

This project facilitated the creation of knowledge in glass composition at VGC. A base of knowledge was created and the formula was used by VGC. The process of knowledge creation received support from VGC's high-level management because of its direct impact on cost reduction. However once the formula was introduced, the organizational support for this project was reduced, personnel were assigned to other functions after 1985, the formal process of knowledge creation was stopped and little effort was put into nurturing the knowledge base. Even though the glass formula was distinctive knowledge, it was used only to reduce costs and not to distinguish the firm competitively. Therefore, the embryonic strategic capability did not progress to become a strategic capability.

In 1990 there were changes in the technology strategy which affected even more deeply the support of the creation of knowledge in this area, and the possibility of building a strategic capability based on the embryonic strategic capability already built. This issue is analyzed in Section 9.6.

To sum up, the description of the projects and patents granted in electronic control systems and glass composition presented in this section showed that VGC, Vitro-Tec and Fama created knowledge in this period based on R&D activities. These activities allowed them to strengthen their innovative technological capabilities and to carry out innovation activities of a different nature in comparison with the former period. The result was the building up of embryonic strategic capabilities in these areas. However, there were several difficulties in this process, three of which were especially important. First, there were differences in the learning strategies pursued by the organizational units and they devoted different resources to this activity and learned in different directions. As a result they accumulated different types and depths of knowledge by knowledge field and by technical area. Second, there were changes in the organizational support for R&D projects over this period that reduced the effort on creating knowledge and building up innovative technological capabilities in one direction. Third, a sort of internal benchmark with the Owens-Illinois technology was established in such a way that it reduced the credibility of in-house developments, mainly whilst they were still at an experimental stage. These difficulties reveal some of the types of problems encountered by a firm passing through the Transition Process from building the minimum essential knowledge base to building strategic capabilities. They are further analyzed in Chapter 9.

7.4.2 The Strengthening of the Capabilities in Process Engineering and Investment Project Management

The innovative technological capabilities in investment project management and process engineering were also strengthened in this period and became embryonic strategic capabilities. They were an important part of the knowledge base for increasing operational efficiency and expanding the investment in Mexico and Central America. The knowledge base in these areas was founded on the empirical experience in operating and adapting the equipment, and in undertaking investment projects. Being based less on formal R&D, the links with Vitro-Tec and Fama were weaker than in the case of the electronic control systems. These activities required intense interaction between Dirtec and plants.

7.4.2.1 Process engineering

The dynamics of keeping pace with the technological frontier obliged Dirtec and the plants to maintain an intensive adaptation activity to combine different equipment technologies, and also to strengthen their knowledge in process engineering to achieve efficient operation of their idiosyncratic equipment. The incorporation of VGC's own original designs, as a result of the R&D activities, also contributed to that diversity and increased the effort to make efficient use of that equipment. In addition the signing of the Technical Agreement with Owens-Illinois and the technology strategy of being a fast follower committed VGC to ensuring a good transfer of Owens-Illinois technology and prompt achievement of the required performance of the continually improved equipment. All these issues challenged the in-house capabilities in process engineering and pressured VGC to increase its knowledge base in this technical area. The changes in the IS machines used to produce Coke bottles and the machines for producing Gerber containers, plus the evolution of performance, illustrate the strengthening of these capabilities.

Changes in the equipment and machine capacity: the Coke bottles [27]

The IS machines to produce Coke bottles were manufactured by Fama using a mixture of equipment technologies, such as Emhart, Owens-Illinois and Vitro. They were incorporated in the glass container plants. As described in Table 7.5, the characteristics of the machines (type of transmission, control and process), the number of cavities and the number of sections continually changed. At the same time VGC was able to increase its production capacity from 15 to 450 bottles/minute using the NNPB technology.

The changes in equipment, that resulted in increased productivity, were different in different periods. In some periods increased performance occurred when new basic characteristics were incorporated in the machines. For instance from 1962 to 1976 the basic characteristics were changed (e.g. the mechanical transmission was changed to electrical, and the mechanical drum was changed

---

[27] Interview with the Manager of Dirtec's Process Engineering Department

to an electronically controlled one). In this period production capacity increased from 50 to 60 bottles/minute. From 1984 to 1993 a new process technology was introduced in the machine: the NNPB technology which combined with an increase in the number of cavities allowed capacity to be raised from 100 to 450 bottles/minute.

Table 7.5   Evolution of the machines to produce Coke bottles, 1946–96

Year	Basic characteristics	No. of cavities	No. of sections	Bottles/ minute*
1946	• mechanical transmission • mechanical drum	single	2	15
1950–2	• mechanical transmission • mechanical drum	single	4	25
1956–8	• mechanical transmission • mechanical drum	single	5	40
1958–62	• mechanical transmission • mechanical drum	single	6	50
1974–6	• electrical transmission • electronic control	single	6	60
1980–2	• electrical transmission • electronic control	single	8	80
1984	• electrical transmission • electronic control	double	10	100
1993	• electrical transmission • electronic control • NNPB	triple	10	450
1996	• electrical transmission • electronic control • NNPB	triple	10	500

Note:
* No. of bottles/minute = No. of cuttings/minute x No. of sections.
Source:
Own analysis based on Fama (1993) and charts of Dirtec's Process Engineering Department.

In other cases the change consisted only of expanding production capacity by increasing the number of cavities or sections. For instance, between 1976 and 1982, having mastered operation of the equipment incorporating new characteristics introduced earlier, new sections were added resulting in increased performance.

All these modifications to the IS machine put pressure on the Process Engineering Department to get to grips with the changes to the equipment and be able to tackle the new problems that arose and they also put pressure on the plants to maintain operation and increase the productivity level. Hence the increased performance was also the result of learning by doing and improved process engineering,[28] revealing a strengthening of the company's capabilities in this area.

Changes in the equipment and operational efficiency: the Gerber containers [29]

Gerber was a major customer of VGC. The equipment to produce containers for Gerber baby food has been upgraded over a period of years, as illustrated in Table 7.6 below. The process engineering effort was directed to improving operational efficiency,[30] which increased from 80–85 per cent in 1974 to 92–94 per cent in 1996. Production capacity increased from 60 to 170 bottles/minute in the same period. There was one main change in the technology from the IS machine to the '41 process'. In 1978 VGC carried out a test of the '41 process' and in 1980 it was introduced at the Querétaro plant.

The increase in operational efficiency and productivity at the Monterrey plant was achieved by the introduction of cold glass in the IS machine, with Owens-Illinois's assistance.[31] The introduction of new equipment technology – the '41 process' – in the Querétaro plant meant an initial drop in the operational efficiency of the production of Gerber containers from 85–90 per cent using IS machines in 1976 to 70 per cent in 1980 using this new equipment. Dirtec's technical staff were not knowledgeable about the new technology and there was a general lack of experience in plant personnel (this plant had been created in 1979). The later increase in the operational efficiency from 70 per cent in 1980 to 92–94 per cent in 1996 was associated with both process engineering activities and learning by doing.[32]

The several changes in the equipment to produce Coke bottles and Gerber containers and the continuous increase of efficiency suggest the strengthening

---

28 Ibid.
29 Ibid.
30 See footnote to Table 7.6.
31 Interview with the Manager of Dirtec's Process Engineering Department.
32 Ibid.

of process engineering capabilities. In addition, the increase in the 'pack to melt' indicator[33] at divisional level from 70 per cent in 1970 to 81.3 per cent in 1989 also reveals both a general increase in the operating efficiency of the IS technology, and the introduction of improvements in the equipment designed to raise efficiency. This suggests that an embryonic strategic capability was built in process engineering, which was used to increase efficiency. However VGC still had some problems with the operation, and was still operating the equipment with a 'pack to melt' ratio which was closer to the technology leader than before but still lagging. Hence the embryonic strategic capability in this technical area had not yet become a strategic capability.

Table 7.6   Evolution of the machines and efficiency to produce Gerber containers, 1974–96

Year	Plant	Improvements	Operational efficiency[a]	Productivity gob cuttings/ section	bottles/ minute[b]
1974	Monterrey	IS machine, double cavity, 6 sections	80–5%	10	60
1976	Monterrey	IS machine, double cavity, 8 sections, with cold glass	85–90%	11	90
1980	Querétaro	'41 process', double cavity, 8 sections	70%	NA	NA
1990	Querétaro	'41 process', double cavity, 8 sections	90%	NA	NA
1996	Querétaro	'41 process', triple cavity, 10 sections	92–4%	17	170

Note:
a. Indicator of overall productivity provided by VGC. It is based on several parameters, such as weight, capacity and type of container produced by each machine.
b. No. of bottles/minute = No. of cuttings/minute x No. of sections.
Source:
Own elaboration based on Dirtec's Process Engineering Department.

[33] This indicator is one of the main measures of operational efficiency in the industry. It measures the weight of molten glass in relation to the weight of packed glass.

7.4.2.2 Investment project management

A further development of capabilities for managing investment projects by Dirtec, and also in process engineering, was associated with the expansion of the production capacities in Mexico and Central America. Four large projects to create new plants were implemented, as described in Table 7.7. At the same time many projects to expand the existing plants (e.g. to add new furnaces and lines) and also to maintain their production capacities (e.g. rebuilding furnaces) were carried out.

Table 7.7 New production facilities established by VGC, 1970–89

Year	Firm	Place	Products
1978	Centroamericana plant	Costa Rica	Glass containers
1978	Borosilicate plant	Mexico	Ampoules, flasks and vials
1979	Querétaro plant	Mexico	Glass containers
1986	Toluca plant	Mexico	Glass containers

The technical staff of the Engineering Services Department consisted of 10 engineers, each one specializing in a particular area. For each project these technical staff organized a team of people from plants and from external sources. Basic and detailed engineering were carried out by the technical staff using VGC's own plant technology. Civil engineering was contracted out locally under the supervision of this Department, because the frequency of the projects did not economically justify the development of in-house capabilities in this area. The department usually contracted external experts for the administration of the projects, however it kept overall control.[34]

The Engineering Services Department of Dirtec gradually learned from the investment projects. Even though large investment projects were sporadic, there were usually three to four small furnace rebuilding projects each year. These projects involved the same activities as the larger projects. There was an organizational arrangement in the Engineering Services Department to rotate the direction of the small projects between the technical staff. This practice allowed all the technical staff to gain experience in the management of projects,[35] and constituted a learning mechanism in this technical-function.

---

[34] Interview with the former Manager of Dirtec's Engineering Services Department.
[35] Ibid.

The ability to manage the investment projects was strengthened during this period as suggested by the following facts. [36]

1. The technical staff learned how to keep better control of projects.
2. They gained the ability to implement more complex projects within the same time scale. For instance they spent 15 months creating the Centroamerica plant at Costa Rica (one furnace with four lines) and only 16 months on a much larger, more complex and more modern plant at Querétaro (three furnaces and 11 lines).
3. The selection of the equipment and the process control systems were improved during this period.
4. They learned to prolong furnace life before having to do a major reconstruction. For instance in the Guatemala plant created in 1964 the life of the furnace was six to eight years, in the Costa Rica plant created in 1978 it was 10 to 12 years and in the Querétaro plant created in 1979 it was 13 years. This was associated with both improved materials used for building the furnaces and the improved capability for managing investment projects.
5. They learned to increase the total production obtained from a furnace. Fifteen years ago the life of the furnaces allowed the generation of 450 tons/square foot through the whole life. By the end of the 1980s the Engineering Services Department was able to extend this production capacity to 850 tons/square foot.

This is evidence that VGC had strengthened its innovative technological capabilities in investment project management built in the former period. It in fact built an embryonic strategic capability in this technical-function based on the very applied work of the Engineering Services Department.

To sum up, the evidence presented in Section 7.4.2 reveals an increase in the innovative technological capabilities in process engineering and investment project management. It shows that VGC created knowledge in these areas based more on experience and adaptation activities than on formal R&D. In this sense the nature of the knowledge base was different from that of the electronic control systems and glass composition described above. The organizational units and actors were also different. Even though the knowledge in process engineering and investment project management requires inputs from the other knowledge bases and also from R&D activities, the interviews revealed that they were seen as unrelated areas of knowledge and activities. There were few attempts to coordinate the learning activities undertaken by Dirtec, Vitro-Tec and Fama, or to integrate their knowledge in these areas. The type of interaction

---

[36] Ibid.

between Dirtec, Vitro-Tec and Fama was not oriented to strengthening these embryonic strategic capabilities with R&D based activities and thus build strategic capabilities.

7.4.3 Incipient Knowledge Management

During this period VGC carried out an incipient management of the company's knowledge in order both to make effective use of existing knowledge – by utilizing, sharing, integrating and adapting it – and to facilitate the creation of new knowledge. The effort was concentrated in two main directions: (i) managing internal knowledge, and (ii) using external knowledge. The stress in each direction towards making effective use of existing knowledge or creating new knowledge was related to the targets of each technology strategy.

Sections 7.4.3.1 and 7.4.3.2 describe how VGC began to set up mechanisms to manage internal knowledge by extending the processes of knowledge sharing and knowledge codification. Section 7.4.3.3 examines the attempts to manage external knowledge and linkages to the internal innovative process. In both cases special attention is put on the effectiveness of the knowledge management.

7.4.3.1 Managing internal resources: Looking for knowledge sharing

In the pre-1970 period there were few organizational arrangements to increase the sharing of knowledge within VGC and across the whole Vitro-Group. The new structure of the technology function established at the end of the 1970s favored a greater interaction between personnel and organizational units in technology related activities and facilitated their sharing of the knowledge. As previously mentioned, Vitro-Tec was the vehicle for interaction between the divisions, in the same way that Dirtec acted between plants within VGC. New organizational arrangements were set up during this period and gradually new ways of doing things were established by these units. The main mechanisms used during this period are summarized in Table 7.8 and examined below.

Meetings to analyze experience

The technical and operational meetings established earlier (see Section 6.4.1) continued, but there were some changes in these activities. As the general operation of the IS machines became better understood the technical meetings about IS machines became more sporadic, being held only once a year and became more focused on specific problems. Lack of feedback continued to be one of the limitations to any impact these meetings might have had. Increasing operational efficiency still being a matter of concern, therefore operational meetings were systematically organized amongst plants. One of the targets of these meetings was to get ideas for continuous improvement projects.

Table 7.8 Mechanisms to share knowledge, 1970s and 1980s

Some mechanisms	Objective	1970s–80s relative to the 1960s
Technical meetings	• sharing of knowledge about machines and molding related issues • increasing knowledge	• less frequent and more focused
Operational meetings	• troubleshooting and continuous improvements	• between plants and not only at the plant level
Training	• increasing the number of technicians • developing new technical skills • increasing the number of engineers	• more technical focus rather than former general education focus • train-up existing personnel instead of recruiting
Teamwork	• sharing of knowledge and increasing the knowledge base	• new practice

Source:
Several interviews.

Training

Training acquired a singular importance during this period. Different organizational arrangements and activities were established such as a training program at a divisional level named 'Catve' and training courses at plant level. Scholarships at the group level continued to be awarded to support the training of technicians and engineers.

Catve – the technical training program of VGC – was established by 1983. The program was oriented to focusing the general technical training provided by technical schools to the special requirements of the glass industry. It was an integral program that looked to combining technical assistance, training and technical audit to plants. However the main objective was to encourage people to learn.[37] Training was developed during production time so it could take place simultaneously with problem-solving on the line and auditing of the equipment. Teachers were recruited from diverse sources – retired employees, active employees from technology and operational areas, suppliers, technology licensers and academics for very specific topics.[38]

Catve also provided an effective channel for sharing existing knowledge within VGC, and making effective use of external knowledge to support the fast follower technology strategy.

Teamwork

Teamwork was established as a new way of organizing the work by Vitro-Tec. Staff worked in cross-functional and cross-divisional teams for product and process developments, as described in the case of the Vitro's electronic control (see Section 7.4.1.2). The objective was to share knowledge, integrate knowledge from different fields and technical areas located in different organizational units, look for synergy and increase the knowledge base. This mechanism was tightly related to the technology strategy of being 'technologically independent' and the efforts to create knowledge. Even though this was a powerful mechanism to achieve these objectives broadly analyzed in the strategic management literature, the results at VGC were less successful than those described in Section 3.3. There were very few instances of teamwork and those that did occur were not sufficient to spread this practice within the company. This issue along with other limitations to the success of teamwork will be analyzed in Section 9.5.

Although the processes of sharing knowledge extended during this period, the new practices were not dispersed widely across the organization, and generally the old ways of doing things continued. For instance some of the limitations that had been observed before 1970 were not overcome, such as the lack of establishing feedback mechanisms. Learning still remained basically at individual or group level and there was no significant change in the effectiveness of the conversion of individual into organizational learning. This issue is analyzed in Section 9.3.

7.4.3.2 Managing internal resources: Efforts to increase the codification of knowledge

There was a greater concern than before over the documenting of knowledge, which was associated with the new type of innovation activities undertaken.

---

[37] Interview with the present and former Leaders of Catve.
[38] Ibid.

The main experiences of documenting are presented in Table 7.9 and described below.

Table 7.9   New mechanisms of knowledge codification

Some mechanisms	Purpose	Responsible
Patents	• Protect the company's proprietary knowledge	• Vitro-Tec
Bulletins	• Explicit: share of information and knowledge • By-product: document some experiences	• Vitro-Tec
Manuals, course modules, and videos by Catve	• Explicit: support training courses • By-product: document tacit knowledge and convert foreign documents in manuals and other types of codified knowledge	• Dirtec

Source:
Several interviews.

Patents and bulletins

Following the strengthening of the knowledge creation process, an effort was made to document and protect by patents the knowledge developed in the Vitro-Group. Vitro-Tec also played an important role in formalizing and documenting adaptations and improvements developed in the divisions. The effort to codify knowledge was more oriented towards protecting knowledge with patents than creating an organizational memory that could be accessed at any time by anyone. Therefore in spite of filing of patents little effort was put into documenting in log-books development projects as a whole. Vitro-Tec regularly edited bulletins oriented to sharing information within the Vitro-Group which was another way of documenting some of the company's experience. However this was not done in a systematic way.

Training as a way of codifying knowledge

Catve was explicitly designed to train personnel however, as a by-product, it was a crucial factor in the process of nurturing the organizational memory of

VGC. Catve has documented technical activities in manuals. There is a Catve manual for each area of technical knowledge. The company claims that approximately 90 per cent of the basic technical knowledge is set out in a Catve manual.[39] In addition other data were expanded to support training courses, such as programs, guides, working notebooks, videos and other documents. In particular a technical library was created in the Human Resources area of each plant in which to locate the course modules.

Even though the codification of knowledge acquired other dimensions with the patents, bulletins and manuals, this activity was still incomplete. Vitro-Tec, Dirtec and Fama did not carry out complete documentation of the most important innovations. Much of the codifiable tacit knowledge remained non-codified, which persisted as a weakness in the accumulation process. At the plant level VGC continued to have insufficient documentation of the operating procedures in this period.[40] The limited knowledge codification and the imbalances across organizational units are examined in more detail in Section 9.3.

7.4.3.3 Ways of managing the use of external sources of knowledge

Part of the VGC strategy in building innovative technological capabilities was to change the type of external linkages and develop technological collaboration with foreign companies. This was pursued at the level of major projects, as described in Box 7.1 about the project with Heye Glas. It was also pursued at a lower level in connection with all the mechanisms used for learning from external sources. However the effectiveness of these different mechanisms in facilitating learning from external sources to strengthen the innovative capabilities varied. Literature reviews, patents and information searches, reverse engineering and the analysis of competitors' products were used quite successfully to complement the R&D activities directed to creating knowledge. On the other hand, there were great difficulties in sharing external knowledge acquired as a result of visits to foreign glass container makers and hired technicians, and in using it to strengthen the innovative capabilities to support the fast follower technology strategy or the knowledge creation process. This was basically individual knowledge that had to be integrated with an increasing amount of in-house knowledge and with the existing ways of doing things, deeply rooted in the company. As analyzed later in Section 9.3, VGC experienced difficulties in converting individual into organizational learning.

---

[39] Interview with the present and former Leaders of Catve and the current Leader of the Monterrey Plant's Training Center.
[40] Interview with the Monterrey plant's Molding Leader and Dirtec staff.

Literature reviews and patent and information searches

As the R&D activities were more formally carried out at Vitro-Tec, Fama's UIT and the VGC's Glass Laboratory, these units were concerned with the scientific and technological frontiers. Therefore literature reviews and patents and information searches became important as a way to learn from science development and the industry's technology leaders. The project with Heye Glas, the development of an electronic control system and the creation of a new glass formula (see Box 7.1 and 7.2, and Section 7.4.1.2) reveal the use of these mechanisms.

Reverse engineering and the analysis of competitors' products

The reverse engineering activity had its root in the 1940s when the Monterrey Plant carried out reverse engineering of an IS Hartford Empire machine. This activity was reinforced when Fama was created and since then became more formally developed. It was the base for many improvements incorporated in the equipment and for increasing the understanding of the functioning of that equipment.[41] Analysis of competitors' products and benchmarking exercises were particularly carried out in this period to support the first stages of the R&D activities by Vitro-Tec and the Glass Laboratory. For instance the creation of a new glass formula started with the analysis of the bottles made by a set of international players, as described earlier in Box 7.2.

Visits to foreign glass container makers

Visits to foreign facilities continued to be a very important learning mechanism and were oriented to acquiring information and tacit knowledge from technology sources and other glass container makers. Bormioli and Toyo were the most often visited companies in this period along with Owens-Illinois, as described in Table 7.10.

However during this period there was a change in the aims of the visits. VGC considered it was near to the technological frontier and that it could update through Owens-Illinois and its own developments. Therefore visits were geared towards identifying the latest improvements in the machines introduced by Owens-Illinois and observing new ways of doing things. This contrasted with the earlier patterns when visits were often undertaken to detect new equipment technologies, with a view to changing the company's technology source. VGC was well informed about the technologies in operation but it did

---

[41] Interviews with a manager of the Advanced Machinery area from Dirtec's Advanced Engineering Department.

not routinely receive the latest developments made by Owens-Illinois.[42] These visits were a complement to a more efficient use of the Technical Agreement with Owens-Illinois and effectively supported the fast follower technology strategy.

Table 7.10   Characteristics of the visits to foreign glass container makers

Visited firms	Objective	Participants	Duration
Owens-Illinois	• identify the latest improvements in machines • observe new ways of doing things	• technical staff from Dirtec • IS machine and production leaders from plants • Upkeeps	• mainly from one week to a month
Bormioli	• acquire know-how in the production of perfume containers • learn from its expertise in combining different equipment technologies	• technical staff • managers • Upkeeps	• short stays
Toyo	• observe new ways of doing things • learn about the operation of the machines	• technical staff • managers	• from one week to a month

Source:
Several interviews.

However the impact of what was learned through these visits at organizational level was uneven. VGC quickly assimilated the information about the latest improvements made by Owens-Illinois and requested them.[43] Therefore this individual learning was shared at organizational level. However learning how

---

[42] Interviews with a manager of the Advanced Machinery area from Dirtec's Advanced Engineering Department and the Director of Dirtec.

[43] Interview with a manager of the Advanced Machinery area from Dirtec's Advanced Engineering Department.

to combine different equipment technologies, as was intended to be gained from the visits to Bormioli, took time to be internalized. This required the development of understanding the more complex problems of the equipment and later applying this knowledge to a different combination of the equipment.[44] Sharing and implementing new ways of doing things learned from Owens-Illinois and Toyo Glass required, on the one side, attention to combining what was learned with in-house practices and, on the other, the organizational support to do this. Learning how to combine different equipment technologies and learning new ways of doing things both require a longer time horizon than does learning how to operate the equipment. In addition deliberate management attention and a specific learning strategy are needed. This type of learning from external sources was less fruitful and remained basically at the individual level. Therefore it was less successful in supporting the fast follower technology strategy and contributed even less to the knowledge creation process. This issue will be further analyzed in Section 9.3.

Hiring experienced personnel from outside

In this period VGC hired experienced people as a way of quickly accessing new knowledge. However the role of the hired foreign people changed. It became more technical and less managerial. As VGC personnel were gaining in experience and tacit knowledge, and were developing managerial skills, VGC requirements were becoming very specific in technical areas. For instance a specialist in IS machines was recruited from Bormioli to enhance the knowledge in equipment for the glass forming process; a specialist in fabrication and operation of furnaces was also recruited from Bormioli to strengthen the knowledge on furnaces; and a couple of German scientists were hired to contribute to the knowledge in glass composition. This mechanism was successful in terms of solving specific technical problems. However the managerial role of the hired people was smaller than had been the case of people hired-in in the past and this reduced their power to share their knowledge and ultimately change the actual practices in VGC. The knowledge possessed by the hired technicians increased the organizational knowledge by adding individual knowledge. But there were difficulties in integrating that external knowledge with internal knowledge in order to create new knowledge. Therefore the conversion of individual into organizational learning was limited.

To sum up, the management of knowledge utilization and creation was still incipient, both in terms of managing internal and external sources of knowledge. Even though a number of mechanisms and organizational arrangements

---

[44] Ibid.

were set up and new practices began to be established, their scope was still limited. They covered specific aspects and they were not articulated to ensure an effective use of existing knowledge or to contribute to the creation of knowledge, as will be analyzed in more detail later in Section 10.2.1.

7.5   AN ASSESSMENT OF THE DEPTH OF THE KNOWLEDGE BASE

Based on the minimum essential knowledge base already built, from 1970 VGC went further in the process of knowledge accumulation and started a Transition Process towards building strategic capabilities. During the evolution of this Transition Process VGC was able to gradually undertake activities with a higher degree of innovativeness (vertical movements up the y-axis over the minimum levels in Figure 2.2 of Chapter 2), combining different knowledge bases and seeking to build more complex ones (incipient horizontal movements along the x-axis in Figure 2.2) as described by the strategic management literature. It was able to build up embryonic strategic capabilities in electronic control systems, glass composition, process engineering and investment project management. However at the same time it continued its more essential accumulation in other areas, learning to move from operating to building the minimum essential knowledge base (vertical movements up the y-axis in Figure 2.2), as described by the developing countries literature.

Two different technology strategies were pursued in parallel: 'fast follower' and 'technologically independent' strategies. These technology strategies set different targets and pushed the innovation activities in different directions. Actually only the 'technologically independent' strategy was directed towards completing the Transition Process. The perception of the fast follower technology strategy pushed aside the Transition Process back, or at least made this process more difficult.

The description presented so far has shown that by 1990 the Transition Process had not been completed because the embryonic strategic capabilities built by the company did not go progress to the stage of becoming strategic capabilities. The knowledge created was not used to distinguish the firm competitively. The characteristics of the Transition Process at VGC illuminate some issues that must be taken into account to analyze the learning processes in this stage.

1. The depth of knowledge built by technical-function was still uneven. According to the framework presented by Bell and Pavitt (1995), based on Lall (1992), intermediate technological capabilities can be defined in product related activities, and were maintained and also strengthened

in the case of investment activities. Linkage with suppliers combined very basic activities of searching information with some attempts to undertake collaborative research. Linkages with customers and the Science and Technology System have remained weak. The creation of knowledge and the building of an embryonic strategic capability in glass composition reveals a higher level in this process related activity, as the electronic control systems do in the case of the capital goods supply. Whilst in some technical-functions the type of learning problems were still those that can be found in the developing countries literature, in others problems of a different nature emerged. In addition to the uneven stages reached between technical-functions, the sequence of stages by technical-function continued to be unclear. For instance the embryonic strategic capability built to support investment activities was reached without undertaking R&D activities.

2. The building up of embryonic strategic capabilities required the integration of knowledge across fields (e.g. chemical, mechanical engineering and electronics). The more formal organization of the technology function set up in this period favored the undertaking of those innovation activities, but the need arose also to integrate knowledge across organizational units. The type of learning problems associated with the building of embryonic strategic capabilities were similar to those presented in the strategic management literature about the largest companies in the world, as described earlier in Sections 2.3, 3.2 and 3.3.

3. The signing of the Technical Agreement with Owens-Illinois – associated with the fast follower technology strategy – and the setting up of Vitro-Tec – related to the 'technologically independent' strategy – reveal the type of problems experienced by a firm in a Transition Process. Both technology strategies were pursued in parallel but they were disconnected and pulled the firm in different directions. For instance the Technical Agreement urged that attention be concentrated on adapting the equipment, while Vitro-Tec exerted pressure to increase the R&D activities to create new knowledge. The situation of being a company in transition led it to take decisions in both directions. This contributes to explaining the differences observed in the learning strategies pursued by different units, particularly by plants and Dirtec in contrast to Fama and Vitro-Tec. That resulted in a different type and depth of knowledge being accumulated across organizational units. The dual technology strategy reduced the effort to create knowledge and to convert the embryonic strategic capabilities into strategic capabilities.

4. In addition VGC had a traditional view of technology strategy, it followed a sort of 'hardware' technology strategy in treating technology

as equipment and not as knowledge. It sought out the best machines and has continued upgrading the equipment to keep pace with the technological frontier, without considering the underlying knowledge accumulation and learning activities associated with such continuous technological upgrading. One of the most dramatic results of this view has been the pressure that such idiosyncratic equipment put on the adaptation activities.

5. New practices to share and codify the company's knowledge were set up, and new types of links were established with external sources of knowledge either to make effective use of existing knowledge or to contribute to the knowledge creation process. The efforts to manage the knowledge were still incipient, and the new practices were isolated and coexisted with other old practices deeply rooted in other less innovative activities also undertaken, resulting in a low effectiveness of the knowledge management.

8 The Fragility of the Transition Process in the 1990s

8.1 INTRODUCTION

The Transition Process from building the minimum essential knowledge base towards building strategic capabilities, which had started in the 1970s, had not been completed by the 1990s. Even though some aspects of the Transition Process progressed, others regressed.

The 1990s was a period of turbulence in all businesses associated with changes in the competition conditions and the economic environment. Vitro-Glass Containers business strategy, technology strategy and organizational structure were being continually adjusted to meet these changing conditions. VGC was still undergoing a Transition Process, which is a fragile process. The company was under a lot of pressure and took business and technology related decisions that altered the speed and direction of the knowledge accumulation process.

The fragility of the Transition Process is associated with the fact that it occurs between two poles and is pulled in different directions. It becomes even more fragile when there are critical changes in context. At this stage the firm is vulnerable, should it move forward towards building strategic capabilities or backward to keeping the minimum essential knowledge base to survive in the market. Actually the existence of a dual technology strategy is closely related to this situation.

As in the earlier period, the central characteristics of the Transition Process were the existence of differences in learning strategies, speed of learning and depth of knowledge between VGC and other divisions, between plants, between different business-functions, and even between departments within the technology function. The duality of the technology strategy also continued to be a characteristic during this period.

However this was a different phase in the Transition Process. It was different because: (i) the emphasis was mainly directed towards improving day-to-day running to raise operational efficiency and product quality; (ii) the R&D activities were reduced; (iii) the fast follower technology strategy received greater support; (iv) there was an increased instability in the technology strategy, particularly in that strategy oriented towards 'technological independence';[1] (v) there were changes in the management of knowledge; (vi) some of the embryonic strategic capabilities built earlier were weakened, such as capabilities in the areas of glass composition and electronic control systems; and (vii) new embryonic strategic capabilities began to be built up, such as the Job Changes activity, and the linkages with customers and suppliers, which required different combinations of knowledge bases.

During the 1990s the Transition Process oscillated. Some embryonic strategic capabilities that had been accumulated were weakened and others were maintained; new embryonic strategic capabilities were also built. However all in all the embryonic strategic capabilities did not develop into strategic capabilities that distinguished the firm competitively, therefore the Transition Process remained incomplete. The main purpose of this chapter is to describe the characteristics of the Transition Process during the 1990s and some of the new learning problems that emerged in this different context.

This introduction includes a brief description of the context, the technology strategy and the organizational structure of the Vitro-Group and VGC in the period analyzed, which is presented below. Section 8.2 describes several events that contributed to the strengthening of the fast follower strategy, particularly the changes in the organization of the technology function and the new focus on day-to-day activities. Section 8.3 examines the modifications in the direction of knowledge accumulation. Section 8.4 examines the strengthening of the 'technologically independent' strategy after 1994 by changing the aims of knowledge management. Section 8.5 presents an assessment of the period while Section 8.6 summarizes the whole process of building technological capabilities from the earliest days.

The context and the technology strategy

This was a difficult period of adaptation to a new economic and technological environment. The process of opening up the economy was furthered and the regional market was established through the signing of the NAFTA agreement in 1993. At the same time the industry was being threatened by containers made from other materials, such as plastic and aluminum, which generated increasing pressures to look for cost reduction, quality increase and product innovation. New entrants in the US market set up a change in competitive conditions. The result of this was an increase in the level of competition both

---

[1]   As referred to in footnote 2 of Chapter 6, this meant trying to innovate and develop technology in certain areas, leading them to the international technological frontier, while continuing to purchase equipment and technology in other areas.

in Mexico and the US. In addition, in December 1994 there was a new crisis in the Mexican economy which reduced domestic demand.

VGC was well positioned in both the Mexican and the US markets. It dominated all the product markets in Mexico excluding beer bottles, having a monopolistic position in many of them. Its position in the US was based on the acquisition of Anchor Glass Containers Corporation (AGCC) in December 1989[2] and 10 years's experience of exporting to that country.

The acquisition of AGCC illustrates some of the pressures that VGC has had to deal with since the late 1980s. The opening up of the economy, which started in 1987, immediately threatened some of Vitro-Group's business. For instance Vitro-Glassware had lost 50 per cent of the Mexican market at the end of the 1980s. The Group was afraid it would also lose the domestic glass container market if US players decided to enter. Therefore it was decided to go ahead in the US market and not wait for its US competitors to enter Mexico. An opportunity arose when AGCC – the second largest producer in the US – went on sale. In December 1989 Vitro-Group acquired AGCC by a hostile corporate take-over and it also acquired the Latchford Glass Co. – another small company. These acquisitions pursued the objectives of protecting its domestic market and expanding its presence internationally.[3]

However the acquisition of AGCC had both positive and negative consequences for the business position of VGC and the Vitro-Group. In the late 1980s the Vitro-Group was evaluating two strategies, either to expand the glass container business or to diversify into packaging and become a packaging company.[4] The decision taken was to make the Group stronger in glass containers by acquiring AGCC. With that acquisition VGC became the third largest player internationally, jumping from the sixth place it occupied in the 1980s, and the second largest in the US. However the Vitro-Group had decided to expand in an industry that was being threatened by containers made from other materials. In addition there was a decline in sales in the US market where the substitution was more aggressive. From this point of view the acquisition of AGCC was a risky strategic decision. Moreover AGCC was 500 million dollars in debt before the purchase and for this reason the previous owners had not invested in any machinery or furnaces to upgrade their installations. Although AGCC was the second largest producer, it was not one

---

[2] Vitro-Group held shares in AGCC from 1983. In August 1989 the Group implemented a strategy to take control of the firm buying up a large portion of stock at 20 dollars per share, more than twice its market value. AGCC's Board of Directors was firmly opposed to Vitro's take-over bid and tried to block it. After two months of legal wrangles, Vitro agreed to pay 21.5 dollars and to withdraw the suit it had filed against the AGCC's chief executive (Pozas, 1993:49).

[3] Vitro SA (1989).

[4] Interview with the Divisional President of VGC and the two Directors of Vitro-Tec.

of the lowest cost producers. Due to the evolution of the US glass container market, the acquisition of AGCC had a negative impact on the financial health of the overall Vitro-Group in the 1990s and generated pressures to look for cost reductions and to raise operational efficiency.

Because VGC was forced to align itself with the changes in the economic and technological context, this was a period of continuous redefinition of its business and technology strategies. One of the main technology related decisions was whether to continue being a fast follower of Owens-Illinois, or whether to continue to undertake its own developments in order to become 'technologically independent'. Even though the fast follower strategy was significantly more favored in this period, the company continued as before to pursue both strategies.

Particularly in the early 1990s VGC pursued a short-term version of the fast follower strategy, focusing on assimilating Owens-Illinois technology and increasing operational efficiency rather than on promoting R&D activities to catch up quickly. This was not the result of a serious discussion based on a long term view. On the contrary, strategic planning exercises were weak in this period.[5] The decision was made based on the changes in the company's context imposed by the threats mentioned earlier; the pressures associated with the acquisition of AGCC; and a change of power inside the Vitro-Group which favored the promoters of a fast follower strategy for VGC. In addition in a period of looking for cost reduction and efficiency increase, the argument that they were paying two million dollars annually to Owens-Illinois as royalties without taking advantages of all the opportunities that the Technical Agreement offered was very persuasive.[6] Two main events supported the strategy. One was the introduction of the Owens-Illinois's NNPB technology combined with the company's explicit prohibition on adaptation through in-house improvements.[7] The other was the decentralization of Vitro-Tec towards the divisions and the discouraging of technology development and improvement activities.

Even though the 'technologically independent' strategy was weak at the beginning of the 1990s, by 1994 it had again been reinforced. Indeed considerable organizational effort was put into identifying 'what to buy and what to develop' and in trying to strengthen the in-house technological capabilities in those areas where they wanted 'to develop'. However from 1994 on this strategy was driven more by the rationality imposed by the fast follower strategy, the pressures induced by the financial constraints and the weaknesses associated with the reduction in R&D activities. Over the whole 1990s this technology strategy was basically unstable.

---

[5]   Interview with personnel from the technology planning area of Ditac.
[6]   Interviews with the Divisional President of VGC and the Director of Dirtec.
[7]   Interviews with several managers and technical staff of Dirtec, Vitro-Tec and Fama.

The organizational structure

Since the late 1980s the Vitro-Group has made several organizational changes directed towards integrating related businesses and streamlining its activities to meet the changes in its context. In particular the organizational location of the activities that provide the raw materials and capital goods underwent many changes, which suggests that the Vitro-Group was redefining its vertical integration strategy, but without any long-term view. For instance, in 1989 Fama became a division, in 1991 it was integrated into the new Vitro-Capital Goods Division, in 1994 it was integrated into the Vitro-Packaging Division, and in 1996 into the new Vitro-Chemical, Fibers and Packaging Division.

At the same time the Vitro-Group looked for different organizational structures to manage its glass container operations. In 1991 the glass container operations of Mexico, the US and Central America were integrated into one new division named Vitro Glass Containers of North America. The integration was purely a formality. In real terms there were two organizational structures – each with a full range of business-functions –, one was Mexico and Central America and the other was AGCC in the US. In 1994 these two structures separated. In 1995 all the glass container operations were again formally integrated and Vitro's Chairman announced that in 1996 they were going to consolidate functions across AGCC, Glass Containers in Mexico and Vitro Packaging (Mexican glass container's trading company in the US). The objective of this operational streamlining was to create cross-cultural management teams to increase efficiency in administration, production and purchasing, and reduce expenses.[8] The integration of both divisions began in January 1996, but in August the Vitro-Group announced that AGCC was to be sold. This was completed in February 1997. The organizational structure presented in Figure 8.1 corresponds to 1995.

The organization of the technology function had been radically changed in 1989. Vitro-Tec – the central R&D unit – was decentralized into the divisions and disappeared. The technology activities were concentrated in the divisional technology centers, such as Dirtec in VGC. A Direction of Technology (Ditac) and a 'Technology Intelligence Center' were established at Group level.

8.2 THE CAPABILITY BUILDING PROCESS: STRENGTHENING THE FAST FOLLOWER STRATEGY AND THE FOCUS ON DAY-TO-DAY ACTIVITIES

The strengthening of the fast follower strategy and the emphasis on day-to-day activities to increase operational efficiency and quality affected the

---

[8] Message from the Chairman of Vitro SA (1995).

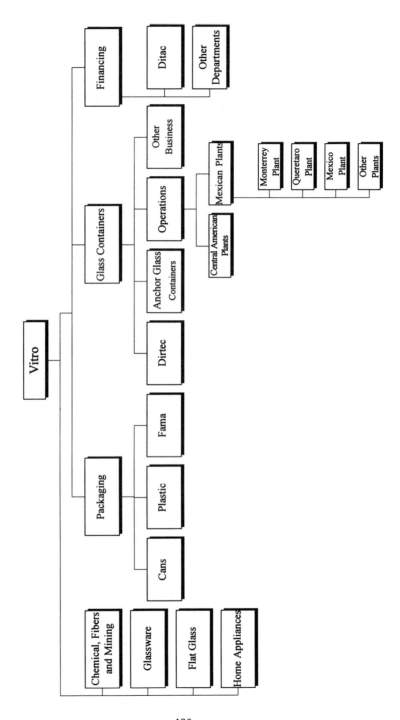

Figure 8.1   Organizational chart of Vitro, 1995

capability building process in the 1990s. The decentralization of Vitro-Tec towards the divisions and the discouraging of technology development and improvement activities, the introduction of the NNPB Owens-Illinois technology with the explicit prohibition on adapting it through in-house improvements, the increased short-term focus of Dirtec, and the new orientation of Fama towards manufacture and the adaptation of Owens-Illinois equipment are the most relevant events, which are examined in this section.

8.2.1 The Decentralization of Vitro-Tec and the Discouragement of R&D Activities

In 1989 there was a change in the organization of the technology function of the Vitro-Group. Vitro-Tec was decentralized into divisional technology centers. Dirtec, as the technology center of VGC, assumed an even more important role in all the technological activities related to glass containers. The change was justified by the intention of closing the gap between the business-functions of technology and production.[9]

However the characteristics of the decentralization reveal that it was seen primarily as a way of reducing the scale of R&D activities and changing the direction of accumulation, rather than as a measure to locate R&D capabilities closer to production. The three following facts illustrate this point. Firstly, even though several Vitro-Tec personnel were relocated to the divisions, the criterion was not to move whole teams. Instead, personnel were almost randomly assigned to different divisions and departments. Some teams disappeared, others were fragmented, and only a few survived. For instance the electronic team members were almost entirely relocated to Dirtec, but in different departments. However the mechanical team was disbanded and most of the personnel were laid off.[10] Secondly, the technology centers, such as Dirtec, were explicitly oriented to giving technical assistance to plants and supporting their search for continuous improvements, while R&D activities were explicitly discouraged. Thirdly, even though the patent department was kept at the Vitro-Group level, it was more oriented to supervising VGC patenting interests than to supporting the use of patents as a source of information about competitors.

8.2.2 The Focus on Owens-Illinois as a Technology Source

Despite the signing of the Technical Agreement with Owens-Illinois in 1974, VGC had continued to use different technology sources and was aware of the

---

9 Interview with the Director of Vitro-Tec during 1987–9.
10 Interviews with technical staff and managers of Dirtec and Vitro-Tec.

latest technology in the market. At the end of the 1980s the NNPB technology was a novelty in the international glass container market. Heye Glas and Owens-Illinois had developed the NNPB technology to produce lightweight bottles.[11] The use of IS machines with the NNPB process enabled production of a more uniform and thinner bottle wall, as described earlier in Section 5.2.2. Therefore containers were of higher quality and were cheaper due to the smaller amount of glass.

By 1987–8 VGC licensed the NNPB technology for IS machines with double cavity from Toyo Glass. Toyo Glass had a license from Owens-Illinois, thus its machines were the first models of the Owens-Illinois NNPB technology with the addition of several improvements made by Toyo Glass. VGC was closely following the technological frontier of the industry but also trying to diversify the technology sources. Therefore the Toyo Glass NNPB technology was introduced to produce lightweight bottles for beer and soft-drinks. As was usual during the introduction of a new equipment technology, a few IS machines with the new process, five plunger mechanisms that were an essential part of the new equipment, and also the machine's designs were purchased. The results were not good due to failures in the Toyo Glass designs, which were partially corrected by Dirtec.

By 1989 the changes in the context described above, in particular the process of opening up the economy, and the substitution of plastic and aluminum for glass in the container market, increasingly forced the search for cost reductions and increased efficiency. In addition, in that year the Vitro-Group acquired AGCC in the US, where the substitution process was swifter than in the Mexican market. Therefore VGC became very concerned about the performance of its equipment and the quality of the containers.

By 1989 Owens-Illinois had launched the NNPB triple cavity technology, which provided the means for higher productivity and quality. It was very suitable for some of the Mexican plants that used long runs and for most of AGCC's plants. VGC was able to acquire the technology easily through the Technical Agreement. In 1989 VGC made the decision to introduce the Owens-Illinois NNPB triple cavity technology for IS machines. This decision was accompanied by the VGC management's order to replicate Owens-Illinois technology and not introduce any in-house improvements into those machines.[12]

This decision was also related to the change in technology strategy that was taking place at VGC. The introduction of the Owens-Illinois NNPB technology

---

[11] The antecedent of this project was the attempt to carry on collaborative research between Heye Glas and VGC at the beginning of the 1980s, as described in Box 7.1. Several characteristics of the collaboration between Heye Glas and Owens-Illinois are described in Box 10.2.

[12] Interviews with technical staff and managers of Dirtec and Vitro-Tec.

was one way to push the organization in the direction of being a fast follower instead of developing its own technology and becoming 'technologically independent'. The NNPB technology was very complex. By accelerating the introduction and assimilation of this technology VGC was forced to concentrate its technology-related activities on being a fast follower of Owens-Illinois.

The introduction of the Owens-Illinois NNPB technology was the first action to strengthen a fast follower strategy linked to Owens-Illinois. In addition there was a strong recommendation to gradually change the overall equipment to an Owens-Illinois technology base.

The 1990s has been a period of learning about the routine operation and basic maintenance of this new complex process to ensure a high operational efficiency. Probably due to its strategic character, the introduction of this technology has received more organizational support than any other. Managers from Dirtec and the plants implemented certain actions to internalize external tacit knowledge to accelerate the assimilation. Some plants sent large numbers of their personnel to receive training at Owens-Illinois's facilities even before they acquired the equipment. For instance the Production Manager of the Querétaro plant spent two years in Owens-Illinois's plants and the Job Changes Manager of the Monterrey plant spent one month in Owens-Illinois's plants. The Monterrey plant had still not introduced the NNPB machines by 1996. In contrast less effort was put into carrying out R&D activities to maintain a defensive R&D strategy to catch up quickly in the future. The main concern was catching up with the present technology.

The introduction of the Owens-Illinois NNPB technology had two main impacts. First, the process was accompanied by a change in the behavior towards learning to be fast followers and quickly increasing operational efficiency instead of learning to undertake in-house developments. However this change in behavior was not widely and quickly diffused within VGC because the triple cavity machines were not required in all plants and lines. For instance until 1991 only three machines were installed at AGCC, and one at the Querétaro plant in Mexico, representing less than 3 per cent of the total number of machines in both countries. In 1996 still only seven machines were installed at the Querétaro plant, representing 9 per cent of the 79 machines installed in Mexico.[13] It is difficult to change the way of doing things over a short period of time and even more difficult when there is low impact of the strategy. Dirtec, Fama and the plants continued as before in relation to almost all the machines, except for the NNPB triple cavity technology. They continued making corrections to some of Owens-Illinois's designs, coupling Owens-Illinois technology with in-house developments, and combining it with selected

---

[13]   Interviews with technical staff of Dirtec's Technology Management Department.

mechanisms from other technologies. Therefore the process of adopting the fast follower strategy was slow.

Second, the introduction of the NNPB technology concentrated a great effort on manufacturing and machine operation, and that effort affected the time assigned by Dirtec and Fama to more formal technology development activities oriented to different purposes, as described in the following sections.

8.2.3 The Increased Short-term Focus of Dirtec

Dirtec had a very short-term orientation since it was created at the end of the 1970s. Technical assistance to plants and continuous improvements were its main activities during the time when Vitro-Tec existed, and according to the organization of the technology function. Even though the knowledge in glass composition was based on R&D activities, those activities were undertaken by one small team out of the whole technical staff. Once Vitro-Tec was eliminated as a unit, Dirtec was only concerned with the plants, hence there was a greater bias towards short-term technical assistance and continuous improvements.[14] Even though some of the Vitro-Tec technical staff were relocated to Dirtec, they were absorbed into short-term activities. The reduction of the number of patents granted in the US from 31 during the 1980s to two during the early 1990s reflects these changes (see Figure 7.2 in Chapter 7)

In the 1990s great effort was put into understanding and operating the IS machines using the new Owens-Illinois NNPB technology. But an even more massive effort was put into raising the operational efficiency of all plants's equipment and the container quality produced by any process. The attention of plants and Dirtec was concentrated on increasing the indicators of efficiency such as the 'pack to melt' ratio, and in fulfilling the requirements to obtain the ISO-9001 international quality control norm.[15] To reach those targets, significant effort was put into supporting projects of continuous improvement, being close to customers and suppliers, and documenting the operating procedures.

The projects of technological upgrading implemented by Dirtec during 1991–6 illustrate the new focus of this unit. According to Dirtec, projects of technology upgrading are oriented to integrate external or internal improvements in a planned way to assure better operation and greater efficiency of the whole production process.[16] In the 1990s Dirtec had six main projects of technology upgrading. The goals were to increase efficiency and satisfy customer

---

[14] Interview with the Manager of Dirtec's Transfer of Technology Department.
[15] Interviews with the Director of Dirtec, Dirtec's technical staff and the Monterrey plant personnel.
[16] Dirtec, internal document, 1996.

requirements. There were 15 significant improvements made during 1991–6, most of which were related to more than one project of technological upgrading. All of them were directly related to raise efficiency and eight were also to satisfy customer requirements. These projects are listed in Table 8.1 below.

Ten of the 15 improvements were oriented to increasing machine speed. Seven improvements were related to the Job Changes project to reduce downtime associated with the change in variable equipment. In addition the five improvements oriented to product weight reduction (lightening) had an impact on the machine speed. These projects also highlighted the VGC shift towards customers and the importance they were putting on the introduction of the NNPB technology. Half of the improvements were associated with the NNPB technology, which underlines the effort undertaken by Dirtec to learn about that process and equipment and adapt other stages of the production process to the new technology. All these improvements were in some sense a response to the need to raise efficiency, according to the new Dirtec focus.

The acquisition of the Anchor Glass Containers Corporation in the US also affected Dirtec's technological activities. Following this acquisition, great effort was made to upgrade the equipment technology and improve the operation. Even though AGCC was initially managed as an independent division, VGC and particularly Dirtec actively participated in the modernization of its installations. Vitro/Owens-Illinois technology was gradually introduced into AGCC. During the first years, activities related to the demand for machines were the main form of interaction between AGCC, and both Fama and Dirtec. They worked together to adjust the specifications of the machines. This activity was very time consuming because AGCC had very diversified equipment.[17] In 1990 only 8 per cent of AGCC's equipment had been converted to Vitro/Owens-Illinois technology. In addition the secular trend to substitute other materials for glass, and the more aggressive competition conditions in the US in the 1990s pushed even more for a focus on operational efficiency to reduce costs. Dirtec gave AGCC technical assistance to improve some activities that had a direct impact on costs, such as the Job Changes (see Section 8.3.1). Therefore the supply of equipment to AGCC and the effort to make it more efficient increased the pressure on Dirtec and Fama to reduce technology development activities.

Thus the stress on the fast follower technology strategy linked to Owens-Illinois, the discouraging of technology development activities, the emphasis on raising efficiency and quality, and the modernization of AGCC all pushed Dirtec to become more oriented towards short-term technical

---

[17]   Interview with the Director of Fama.

Table 8.1 Projects of technological upgrading, 1991–6

Goals / Improvements	Improve customer orientation		Raise efficiency		Improve customer orientation & raise efficiency	Reduce inventory
	NNPB	Samurai[18]	Job change	Speed increase	Lightening	Equipment standardization
Cooling process 3 projects	xx			xxx	x	x
Electronic control 3 projects	x		xx	xxx		xxx
Feeding system 2 projects	x		x	x	x	
Mould operation 1 project				x		x
Other mechanisms 2 projects			x	xx		x
Plunger mechanism 4 projects	xxx	x	xxx		xxx	
Total: 15 projects	7	1	7	10	5	6

Source:
Dirtec, internal document, 1996.

---

18 'Samurai' is a project established by Dirtec to introduce a new technology to interact with customers in the design of the containers. (See Section 8.3.1).

assistance and continuous improvement. New areas of attention became relevant and the effort to increase knowledge in the directions that had emerged earlier was diminished. The new directions of accumulation are described in Section 8.3.

8.2.4 The New Orientation of Fama: From R&D to Design Replication

Initially Fama was not affected by the change in the organization of the technology function. However this was also a period of redefinition of the vertical integration within the Vitro-Group. There were many organizational changes in the divisions that provided raw materials and equipment. In particular Fama was moved to a different location in the organizational structure and this period of instability affected its learning strategy, as will be analyzed in more detail in Section 10.3.2. Two decisions had a strong effect on Fama's horizon: (i) it was once more reoriented from the international market towards the Vitro-Group, this time to supply VGC and also AGCC; and (ii) in 1994 its design capabilities, comprising four engineers and 16 designers, were relocated to Dirtec.[19]

In 1990, following the decision to introduce the Owens-Illinois NNPB technology, Fama started the manufacture of the new IS machines for the Mexican plants and AGCC. The machines were IS machines of 10 sections with triple cavity, they were equipped with Com-soc electronic control systems, also from Owens-Illinois. The 1990s therefore was a new period of learning for Fama, which was focused on the manufacture of the NNPB machines. The NNPB machine was a new complex product for Fama and its personnel had to replicate the design and specifications given by Owens-Illinois. This activity required much effort and was time consuming.[20]

At the same time that Fama received the order to replicate the Owens-Illinois technology, it was having to be innovative in other activities. Fama began the manufacture of Vitro's electronic control systems (see Section 7.4.1.2), which resulted from R&D activities of the Vitro-Group undertaken previously. This activity was also time consuming because new problems associated with the manufacture of the electronic controls had to be solved. Also Fama had to supply AGCC with equipment other than the NNPB. AGCC had a different combination of equipment technologies from the Mexican plants. AGCC wanted to use its spares inventory and it ordered very specific machines which combined up to seven different technologies, such as AGCC, Emhart Glass, Maul, Jeff, Quantum, Owens-Illinois and Fama.[21] Fama

---

[19] Interview with the Manager of Marketing at Fama.
[20] Interview with the Manager of Fama's Production Engineering Department.
[21] Interview with the Director of Fama.

and Dirtec had to deal with these orders and be creative in order to couple different technologies.

The Vitro-Group's decision to introduce the original Owens-Illinois technology, the effort to manufacture the new complex NNPB machines, the manufacture and coupling of quite specific equipment for AGCC and later the relocation of its engineering capabilities forced a reduction of the technology development activity by Fama and affected its capacity to undertake innovations. Fama's UIT, created at the beginning of the 1980s to undertake more formal R&D activities, was eliminated.

To sum up, the evidence presented so far reveals that in the 1990s the fast follower technology strategy received great support. VGC pursued a particular version of that strategy with a short-term focus, as opposed to the knowledge building version based on R&D to learn quickly from external sources.[22] This is revealed by the elimination of Vitro-Tec, the discouraging of R&D activities, the increase of Dirtec's focus on short-term technological activities and the main message to Fama to be oriented to replicate Owens-Illinois designs. However although less supported the strategy to develop technology persisted and it was reinforced from 1994, as described later in Section 8.4.

8.3   THE CHANGING DIRECTIONS OF KNOWLEDGE ACCUMULATION

The strength of the technology strategy focused on being a fast follower of Owens-Illinois and the decisions that supported that strategy had important consequences for the direction of knowledge accumulation. The urgency to increase operational efficiency and product quality moved Dirtec to pay attention to new areas of knowledge accumulation, while using the existing knowledge base, as described in Section 8.3.1 below. The effort to build up new knowledge in the electronic control systems and glass composition was reduced, as described in Section 8.3.2. VGC did not continue the gradual process of accumulation that could be seen in earlier years, and the innovation activities in those areas were of a different nature, with a different focus and different actors. In contrast the capabilities for managing investment projects and process engineering were directly related to the new focus of the technology strategy and so they were strengthened. Finally Section 8.3.3 provides some evidence of the increase in operational efficiency and product quality as a result of the new directions of knowledge accumulation.

---

[22]   For a characterization of each type of strategy see footnote 1 of Chapter 6.

8.3.1 The Emergence of New Directions of Accumulation

There were two basic new areas of knowledge accumulation, one concerned with improving Job Changes activity and the other with increasing the linkages with customers and suppliers. Instead of focusing on knowledge fields such as glass composition or electronic control systems, the new areas of accumulation had a more practical focus. They were oriented to increasing operational efficiency and product quality, according to the new emphasis of the technology strategy. The building of embryonic strategic capabilities in these areas required knowledge in mechanical engineering, glass composition and electronics to control the whole production process, apart from capabilities in process engineering. This knowledge had been built up earlier and was used to support these areas under the new strategic emphasis in this period.

Improving the 'Job Changes' activity

Job Changes are the activity of changing the variable equipment of the IS machine. This activity can be required for: (i) changing the blanks and molds in the same large order, because molds have a short life; (ii) changing isolated spares of the equipment; or (iii) changing the molding and other variable equipment to produce containers with different specifications. Job Changes are a basic technical activity required to maintain the continuity of the production process, it is a task with a very practical focus. Each Job Change invokes a stop in the production line, thus the speed in completing Job Changes affect the efficiency of the line and therefore of the plant.[23]

Job Changes have always been an important activity at VGC. Due to the small size of the Mexican market, plants have had to fill small orders of different shapes, therefore they have had to make frequent changes in the molding, which has had an impact on their operational efficiency. In contrast the glass container plants in the US have traditionally run one color and one bottle type for five or six years to meet the needs of their major customers,[24] as highlighted in Sections 5.3 and 5.4. Job Changes in VGC became a critical activity in the 1990s when operational efficiency became a key target.

This activity was not facilitated by the choice of technology. The Owens-Illinois technology used by VGC was designed for the long runs of the American plants. The Owens-Illinois IS machine is a robust machine with very thick irons. This robustness allows increased machine speed but leaves little space to facilitate adjustment of the variable equipment, so it is not friendly to Job

---

[23] Interview with the Job Changes Manager at the Monterrey plant.
[24] Nichols (1993:169), Interview with E. Martens, the Vitro-Group's CEO from 1985 to 1993.

Changes.[25] Mexican plants produce shorter runs than Owens-Illinois technology is designed for, which has increased the difficulty of this activity. In the US market – oriented to long runs – the Job Changes activity has had a minor impact on efficiency. Recently due to the increase in flexibility this activity has increased in importance in the US.

The operation of equipment, designed for long runs, when used in short runs brought the need to solve several problems, which was the origin of an embryonic strategic capability in Job Changes. The description of this activity in the 1990s, presented below, illustrates the type of problems that concerned VGC in this period, the relationship between Job Changes and the level of efficiency, how this technical area was made stronger, the relative expertise in relation to AGCC and the embryonic nature of this potential strategic capability.

The stress on increasing operational efficiency in the 1990s has stimulated the development of routines that allow fast changes in equipment.[26] Even though Job Changes are undertaken on line by plant personnel, they have been supported by a more formal activity carried out by Dirtec. This technical area was made stronger by three means: (i) by learning by doing while undertaking this activity; (ii) by development activities undertaken by Dirtec (in fact one of the Dirtec's technological upgrading projects listed in Table 8.1 focused on this activity, and seven of the 15 improvements have been targeted to reduce downtime for mold changes); and (iii) by the technical assistance that the Monterrey plant received during 1993–4 from Vetropack – a Swiss packaging company that was the leader in Job Changes at the international level.

The importance of this activity is uneven within plants because they have a different product mix, which generates a different frequency of undertaking Job Changes. For instance the Querétaro plant produces long runs with the NNPB technology, so it carried out 70 Job Changes between January and April 1996, whereas the Monterrey plant which supplies small orders had to undertake 217 Job Changes in the same period, as illustrated in Table 8.2 below. Therefore the effort expended on this activity differs between plants as does the experience and knowledge of their personnel.

Table 8.2 below contains the number of Job Changes by plant and the level of the efficiency approached by the 'pack to melt' indicator. Even though the level of efficiency depends on many factors, the fact that the three plants with the lowest level of efficiency also undertook a large number of Job Changes suggests that this activity affects the level of efficiency. However the small differences in performance also suggest that, in spite of the complexity of the

---

[25] Interviews with the Job Changes Manager of the Monterrey plant and the Maintenance Leader of the Mexico II plant.

[26] Interview with the Job Changes Manager of the Monterrey plant.

activity, the plants have developed a certain expertise so that it does not significantly affect their global performance. The Mexico II plant presents high levels of both efficiency and number of Job Changes. This plant put a great effort into adapting the IS machine to reduce its robustness and to facilitate the Job Changes activity even more, which resulted in an improvement in its level of efficiency.[27]

Table 8.2 Job Changes and efficiency at the plant level, January–April 1996

Plants	Pack to melt ratio (%)	Number of Job Changes
Toluca	93.2	48
Mexico II	92.6	287
Mexico	92.1	97
Querétaro	90.6	70
Mexicali	89.2	47
Guadalajara	87.0	157
Monterrey	86.0	217
Los Reyes	85.7	279
At divisional level	88.5	1236

Source:
Own elaboration based on charts of Dirtec's Technology Management Department.

The interaction with AGCC was one important factor in identifying Job Changes as an embryonic strategic capability of VGC. AGCC produces fairly long runs in most of its plants, however for some of its plants Job Changes were an important activity. In addition due to the increase in flexibility in the 1990s, plants have to be prepared to supply smaller orders more efficiently than before. On average Job Changes at AGCC required double the time taken in VGC's plants,[28] revealing either AGCC's weaknesses in this activity or VGC's strengths. VGC has transferred knowledge to AGCC to try to improve the undertaking of Job Changes.[29]

The activity of Job Changes uses knowledge built previously. It is based on mechanical engineering and electronics knowledge oriented to improving the equipment to facilitate the change of variable equipment and on capabilities in

---

[27] Interview with the Maintenance Leader of the Mexico II plant.
[28] Interview with the Director of AGCC's 'Center of Excellence'.
[29] Interviews with technical staff and managers of Dirtec and AGCC's Technical Center.

process engineering. In a mature industry, as glass containers are, the mastery of this activity allows to differentiate the firm. It is quite a practical embryonic strategic capability of VGC that directly affects operational efficiency by reducing downtime. It has an important tacit component and relies mainly on internal sources. This knowledge has been documented in the operating procedures of the Job Changes Department at the Monterrey and other plants.

Job Changes capability can be considered to be an embryonic strategic capability but it does not look like a strategic capability. First, VGC perceived weaknesses in this area and contracted foreign technical assistance. Second, VGC was able to identify its capabilities in this technical area when supporting AGCC's activities. Finally, VGC has not managed the Job Changes capability as a strategic capability which would distinguish the firm competitively.

Strengthening capabilities for linking with customers and suppliers

In the 1990s VGC has been preoccupied with increasing flows of information with customers and suppliers to raise efficiency and increase quality. This behavior is related to changes in the company's context and the arrangements to achieve the international quality control norm ISO-9001 by many VGC's plants. Some customers and suppliers were also interested in enhancing their relationship looking for the same quality certification. Some characteristics of the links are described below.

Customers

In the past VGC had only commercial relationships with its customers. It sold its products and was not very concerned with customer's requirements, the commercial relationship was driven by VGC as supplier. There was no interaction in innovation related activities. The quasi-monopolistic conditions of the closed economy facilitated VGC in pacing the introduction of product innovations in the domestic market.[30] The conditions of the market have changed in two directions, there has been an increase in the competition and a new focus on product differentiation. Both changes have meant that interaction with customers is crucial. Some actions VGC has taken in that direction are described below.

1. VGC has been oriented towards searching for new information from customers and absorbing it. Such behavior has been quite successful in identifying customer needs. However it has been less successful in

---

[30] Interviews with Catve's Leader and the Manager of Dirtec's Finished Product and Packaging Department.

acquiring knowledge from its customers. Some of VGC's larger customers have also been interested in deepening their relationship with VGC to assure their own ISO-9001 certification.[31] They have done some quality testing at VGC sites, but have still not been interested in interacting in joint projects.

2. VGC has established a new technology to interact with customers in the design of containers. The project – named 'Samurai' – focuses on product innovations. Samurai facilitates side-by-side working with customers to design containers using computers. There are three customer sites: Monterrey, Mexico City and Dallas-Texas. The first two sites were created in 1993–4. The project aims to reduce the new-product cycle initially from 16 to 12 weeks and later to 4/6 weeks.[32] It requires perfect coordination between the sites where the design is drawn up, Fama who makes the molds and plants who manufacture the containers. Developing that coordination has been a task during this period. In 1996 Samurai was at the stage of having the infrastructure and skills to interact with customer on the sites, but the coordination was not sufficiently developed to enable the molds and containers to be made in the planned time if there were multiple orders. One of the six technological upgrading projects of Dirtec listed in Table 8.1 was oriented to improving the operation of the Samurai system. This is an area where VGC is still building an embryonic strategic capability. In spite of VGC's efforts to improve the implementation of Samurai from the supplier side, there is a shortage on the customer side. Customers did not go to the sites, therefore VGC has had to stimulate customers to increase interaction and flows of information.

3. A new mechanism for interaction with customers has been implemented initially by AGCC in the US. It consists of signing long-term alliances with customers. It has acted as a protection in a more competitive market.

Suppliers

VGC has internal, domestic and foreign suppliers. Links with them have assumed a different nature and intensity over time.

1. Linkages with foreign suppliers of equipment have been very strong over time. VGC has interacted with its suppliers to adapt foreign equipment to the firm- and country-specific conditions. However it has been less active in developing joint innovative projects.

---

[31] Interview with the Manager of Dirtec's Finished Product and Packaging Department.
[32] Vitro SA (1996a).

2. The interaction with Fama – its main machine supplier – has been intense, but its nature has changed over time. It has mostly consisted of transfer of technology rather than efforts to develop joint innovative projects, due to the differences in learning strategies, as analyzed in detail in Section 10.3.2.

3. Because of the degree of vertical integration in the Group, the main suppliers of the raw materials have usually been companies from other divisions inside the Vitro-Group. VGC has led the relationship but there has been little interaction to develop innovations with them. Like other glass container companies, VGC has defined its glass formula and ordered the raw materials to be included, according to the chemical composition. When VGC developed the new glass formula it looked for suppliers outside the Vitro-Group that could supply different raw materials. However rather than cooperating to develop new materials it has steered towards other already known and commonly used raw materials.[33] Neither Vitro-Tec nor the vertical integration of the Vitro-Group has facilitated the establishment of better interactivity. Recently there have been moves within the Vitro-Group to seek to develop a new formula that could reduce costs, based on the interaction to identify innovative raw materials.[34]

4. VGC's and Fama's suppliers of components are small and usually domestic companies. VGC and Fama have transferred technology to them to assure their quality standards.[35]

In the 1990s there has been a greater concern to increase flows of information with customers and suppliers. In the case of customers the target has been related to knowing about the technical requirements rather than to developing joint innovation projects. Interactions with suppliers has had a more innovative content, even before the 1990s. However there have been few experiences of joint innovative projects. Therefore the capability for developing linkages with customers and suppliers is still weak, and it does not look like an embryonic strategic capability. However there have been efforts to increase relationships and build up different types of links in the 1990s. In particular the Samurai project looks to be the basis for building at least an embryonic strategic capability, but it is still too early to be evaluated.[36]

---

[33] Interview with the Technology Director of Vitro-Chemical, Fibers and Mining.
[34] Interviews with the Technology Director of Vitro-Chemical, Fibers and Mining and the Glass Laboratory Leader.
[35] Interviews with technical staff of Dirtec's Advanced Engineering Department and the Manager of Fama's Process Engineering Department.
[36] VGC is working in another project oriented to improving the final product called 'Enhanced value finisher'. However this is a recent project that was not analyzed in this book.

8.3.2   The Evolution of the Old Knowledge Bases

In the 1990s the knowledge bases built up earlier received differing attention and were managed in different ways according to the changes in technology strategy. This was evident in the main areas of accumulation during the 1970s and 1980s such as: (i) capabilities in process engineering and investment project management, and (ii) knowledge of glass composition and electronic control systems.

Strengthening capabilities in investment project management and process engineering

The capabilities for managing investment projects and process engineering were directly related to the focus on increasing operational efficiency and the target of transferring technology to Latin America. Therefore in the 1990s there has been a special concern to strengthen the knowledge bases that support these capabilities.

Most of the technological upgrading projects implemented by Dirtec in the 1990s, described in Table 8.1, support process engineering-related activities to assure better operation and efficiency of the production process. Tables 7.5 and 7.6, presented in Chapter 7, show some of the output from this effort, such as the increase in the operational efficiency to produce Coke bottles and Gerber containers in the 1990s, as a result of the strengthening of the capabilities in process engineering.

The capability to manage investment projects has also been nurtured in the 1990s. AGCC was the main acquisition in this period, as described in Section 8.1. However it was managed separately and AGCC kept its own technical area for investment projects. Therefore this was not a factor that contributed to the strengthening of VGC's capabilities in this technical-function. This capability was basically nurtured by the expansion of capacities in Mexico and the penetration of the South American market. The three larger projects are described in Table 8.3 below.

The investment project to create the Mexicali plant was the main event in the strengthening of the capability for managing investment projects. This was a new plant which incorporated the experience accumulated by the Engineering Services Department and the latest technology in the world. It is a model plant which was awarded ISO-9001 quality certification within four years.[37]

Special concern to support this technical-function also derived from the strategy of transferring technology to Latin America. In the 1990s and

---

[37]   Interview with the former Manager of Dirtec's Engineering Services Department and the Director of Dirtec.

particularly since 1994 VGC has redefined its strategy towards Latin American markets. These have been seen as emerging markets by international investors with growth potential. As they are smaller than the US market, VGC's experience of short production runs and supplying a market niche could be to its advantage. Two strategies have been followed: (i) new acquisitions, as described in Table 8.3, and (ii) sale of technical assistance contracts. Contracts were signed for transferring technology and know-how, specifying the equipment and supporting large investments (which included layout design, and design and construction of furnaces).

Table 8.3   New facilities and subsidiaries in Latin America, 1990–6

Year	Firm	Activity	Place	Product
1992	Mexicali plant	Creation	Mexico	Glass containers
1994	Compañía Manufacturera de Vidrio del Perú	Participation (30% shares)[38]	Peru	Glass containers
1995	Vitro-Lux	Acquisition	Bolivia	Glass containers

In spite of the fact that the embryonic strategic capabilities in process engineering and investment project management were strengthened in the 1990s, they did not reach the stage of a strategic capability. They continued to be largely based on experience as in the 1970s and 1980s, which was one of their weaknesses. Even though several projects of technological upgrading implemented by Dirtec in the 1990s supported these capabilities, these projects had a short time horizon. Therefore these capabilities continued to receive little support from more basic and long-term oriented R&D activities. As before there was little effort made to integrate knowledge across fields and organizational units to nurture the knowledge bases of these capabilities. All this reduced the potential of these embryonic strategic capabilities to become a strategic capability.

The weakness in glass composition and electronics knowledge

During 1970–90 VGC had accumulated knowledge in glass composition and electronic control systems, which was a basis on which embryonic strategic

---

[38]   In 1995 and 1996 the participation was 23 per cent.

capabilities were built. In the 1990s the development projects were stopped and these knowledge bases were neglected. The knowledge had been based on R&D activities, which were run down during this period. In addition the stress on the day-to-day running of the company also contributed to explain what happened in the accumulation process of these knowledge bases.

In the case of the electronics knowledge, even though most of the team members were moved from Vitro-Tec to the Electronic Technology Department of Dirtec, this Department was not focused on R&D activities.[39] This team, interacting with Fama, developed small improvements in the Vitro III-A electronic control system. These improvements were essential upgrading geared to avoid obsolescence of the control systems and to introduce some plant's requirements. The improvements consisted of new programs incorporated into existing equipment, such as an automatic rejecter of hot bottles that Dirtec had bought in, and programs to freeze the finish, the preform and the bottles.[40] R&D activities in glass composition were also stopped and no more positioning exercises were undertaken.[41]

Therefore during the 1990s VGC continued to rely on the knowledge base in glass composition and electronic control systems built up much earlier. It put a stop to any further accumulation of knowledge in these two critical fields, as analyzed in more detail in Section 10.3.4. The knowledge creation process was replaced by activities directed to just avoiding obsolescence of existing knowledge. Hence instead of a strengthening of these embryonic strategic capabilities to develop strategic capabilities, they were weakened. It can be argued that as far as these capabilities were concerned VGC went into reverse.

8.3.3 Measuring Technological Advance: The Increase in Operational Efficiency and Product Quality

An evaluation of the effort that Dirtec and the plants put into increasing operational efficiency and product quality in the 1990s can be assessed by the improvement of two performance indicators: (i) the 'pack to melt' ratio, and (ii) the internal reject rate.

The 'pack to melt' ratio

This indicator measures the weight of packed glass in relation to the molten glass. It is an indicator broadly used in the industry. Figure 8.2 shows the level

---

[39] Interviews with the Managers of Dirtec's Electronic Technology and Transfer of Technology Departments.

[40] Ibid.

[41] Interview with the Leader of the Glass Laboratory.

of 'pack to melt' ratio reached at divisional level. The evolution of the indicator since the 1970s shows an increase in the efficiency of IS technology operation from 70 per cent to 81.3 per cent in 1989, and to 88.5 per cent 1996. This performance is associated with learning by doing, strengthening of the process engineering capabilities and incorporation of certain improvements to raise efficiency, as already analyzed.

Figure 8.2   Indicator of performance: pack to melt ratio (%), divisional data

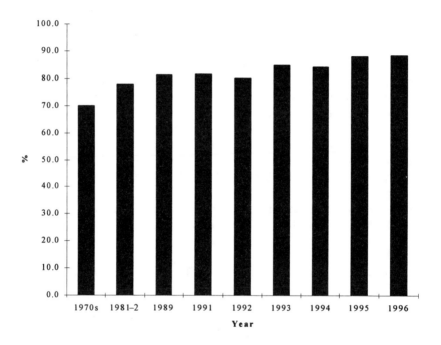

Source:
Own elaboration based on Dirtec's Technology Management Department.

In 1995 the AGCC performance of this indicator was 86 per cent, 2 per cent lower than the 88 per cent observed by VGC in the same year. Owens-Illinois reported the same 88 per cent. The comparison with the international technology leader indicates that VGC had reached a good level of performance.

The 'internal reject' rate

Another indicator of efficiency related to quality is the 'internal reject' rate. Divisional data presented in Figure 8.3 show a significant reduction in the internal rejects between 1989 and 1995 from 9.6 per cent to 2 per cent. This reveals an improvement in the different stages of the production process. The pressure to reduce internal rejects has been associated with the process of obtaining the international quality control norm ISO-9001, as well as a specific effort to reduce costs.[42]

Figure 8.3 Indicator of performance: internal reject (%), divisional data

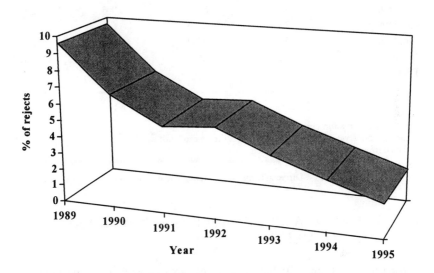

Source:
Own elaboration based on Dirtec's Technology Management Department.

At plant level, Table 8.4 shows how each Mexican plant reported an increase in its performance in the 1990s, measured by both the 'pack to melt' ratio and the 'internal reject' rate. This reveals the success of the effort to improve operational efficiency and product quality.

However Table 8.4 also shows that wide differences in performance between plants persisted, particularly in the 'pack to melt' ratio. As described in Section 8.3.1 and Table 8.2, plants have different equipment and product mix, carry out different numbers of Job Changes and do things in different ways. These differences affect operational efficiency. In spite of these differences, these indicators show the progress of VGC's performance.

---

[42] Interviews with several of Dirtec's technical staff.

Table 8.4   Indicators of performance at the plant level

Plants	Pack to melt (%)		% of Internal rejects	
	1989	1996[c]	1989	1995
Toluca	90.7	93.2	1.2	0.0
Mexico II[a]	79.3	92.6	NA	NA
Mexico	73.8	92.1	20.8	0.8
Querétaro	83.5	90.6	4.4	1.3
Mexicali[b]	71.4	89.2	29.6	3.0
Guadalajara	85.1	87.0	6.9	4.1
Monterrey	79.8	86.0	9.4	2.2
Los Reyes	79.5	85.7	5.5	3.8
Division	81.3	88.5	9.6	2.0

Notes:
a. the first observation corresponds to 1993.
b. the first observation corresponds to 1992, the year of start up.
c. data corresponds to the 1st semester.

Source:
Own elaboration based on Dirtec's Technology Management Department.

8.4   TOWARDS A MORE EXPLICIT KNOWLEDGE MANAGEMENT

During the 1970s and 1980s there was incipient knowledge management. A number of organizational arrangements and mechanisms were explicitly set up to use, adapt, integrate and change existing knowledge and to contribute to creating new knowledge, as described in Section 7.4.3. There was an increase in the knowledge sharing within the firm and also in knowledge codification. However the organizational arrangements and mechanisms tackled only isolated aspects of the company's innovation activities and they were not articulated.

At the beginning of the 1990s there was a change in the focus of knowledge management, following the emphasis of the technology strategy on increasing operational efficiency in the day-to-day running of the business. The management of knowledge was deliberately directed to raising efficiency. However there was only an implicit method of assessing what was needed for that purpose and what was not, with no clear and consistent set of decisions to support the strategy. Only a few new practices were established, such as continuous improvement activities. VGC's knowledge management centered basically on using existing knowledge. At the same time the firm decided to redirect the knowledge accumulation process, reduce the previous effort on knowledge creation and practically ignore the knowledge accumulated through R&D activities. Thus the main emphasis of the company's knowledge management in the early 1990s was essentially negative. It centered on limiting, reorienting or abandoning certain knowledge bases that had been built in the past.

From 1994 the orientation of knowledge management changed to a more positive view about using, adapting, integrating and changing the base of knowledge already built and facilitating the process of creating and renewing knowledge. This change in knowledge management was related to the renaissance of the 'technologically independent' strategy. There was a new emphasis on this strategy and some attempts were made to: (i) strategically define 'what to buy and what to develop' and to precisely define the areas in which they wanted to develop technology, based on the knowledge base already built; and (ii) change the way of doing things by promoting the sharing of existing knowledge, increasing knowledge codification and integrating knowledge across organizational boundaries, or in other words, looking for more consistent knowledge management. The main event incorporated in this strategy was the identification of areas of strength and potential synergy at the Vitro-Group level. This event is described below in Section 8.4.1.

However this strategy did not go very far because it received only intermittent support from the top management. While in the 1970s and 1980s the two technology strategies had moved in parallel, at this time the strategy of being a fast follower with the focus on operational efficiency and quality led all the technology related activities. The main impact of the renaissance of the 'technologically independent' strategy was on the strengthening of the knowledge management oriented to using and integrating existing knowledge and facilitating the creation of new knowledge. The setting up in 1994 of a number of organizational arrangements explicitly oriented to managing knowledge was the main contribution to that target. However the new directions of knowledge accumulation in the 1990s, described in Section 8.3, remained basically the same.

8.4.1 Explicit Efforts to Define 'What to Buy and What to Develop'

In February 1996 Ditac – the Direction of Technology of the Vitro-Group from 1990 – with the support of top management worked up an 18 month plan that included the re-organization of strategic technological activities at the group level. The Vitro-Group had begun to concentrate again on strategic planning,[43] and Ditac was in charge of leading the technology planning

---

[43] Vitro SA (1996a).

exercise. This covered the business units, the divisions and the group itself. Ditac elaborated on the basic information, such as the identification of new trends in the industry and the technology profile of competitors based on patent data. Divisional technology centers interacted to identify weaknesses and strengths in the main technologies used by each division.[44]

Ditac had analyzed the technology and business strategies of a Japanese firm which were based on its core technologies. Ditac sought to reproduce this model at the Vitro-Group.[45] Therefore the idea of developing core capabilities on the basis of areas of strength was explicitly leading this exercise.

Vitro-Group's experts from different knowledge areas participated in the exercise. The Divisional Technology Managers realized that the capabilities developed by Vitro-Group were dispersed across different divisions and business units. Together they identified certain areas of common knowledge, areas of expertise and strategic targets. They found several areas of potential synergy between VGC; Vitro-Glassware; Vitro-Chemical, Fibers and Mining; and Vitro-Flat Glass in:[46]

1.   melting (furnace design and maintenance)
2.   chemical composition of glass
3.   glass forming
4.   decoration
5.   electronic process control

They exchanged information and identified where the knowledge was located across different organizational units. They found that the depth of knowledge in each area varied from division to division. For instance VGC was strong in glass composition, decoration and electronic control systems. Vitro-Glassware and Vitro-Flat had developed strong capabilities in melting (furnace design and maintenance). A shared view that synergy between the divisions would help to increase the knowledge base of the Vitro-Group as a whole was emerging.[47]

At the same time certain areas of knowledge specialization were identified as strategic for different reasons. Melting was considered strategic because most of the divisions used a furnace to melt the raw materials to produce glass. The importance of decoration was associated with the fact that there is no competition in this area and Latin American markets still used returnable bottles with a label. Glass composition was seen as strategic because within Vitro-

---

[44]   Interview with the Directors of Ditac and Dirtec.
[45]   Interview with the Director of Ditac.
[46]   Interview with the Directors of Ditac and Dirtec.
[47]   Interview with the Director of Ditac and the Technology Director of Vitro-Chemical, Fibers and Mining.

Group the knowledge was held in many divisions, which could use domestic raw materials and thus reduce costs.[48] It was decided to centralize the core technologies at corporate level, and decentralized at divisional and business unit levels leave other more specific technologies and capabilities.[49] This exercise opened the discussion about the need to organize teamwork at the Vitro-Group level related to the knowledge fields where potential synergy could be developed. One of the first actions was the establishment of a cross-division team in glass composition which met every month. The strategic planning exercise was the basis to establish several strategic projects in 1997.

The identification of areas of strength and potential synergy project was oriented to strategically define 'what to buy and what to develop'. The idea was to build upon the knowledge base accumulated in the past and to define which specific areas of strength to develop, while deciding to buy technology in areas of weakness. This project required a more efficient use of the existing knowledge and the establishment of new practices to facilitate the process of knowledge creation. However there were difficulties in implementing this project and changing the existing way of doing things. These difficulties were exacerbated by the instability of the dual technology strategy, as analyzed in detail in Section 10.3.

8.4.2 Explicit Efforts to Increase the Sharing and Codification of Knowledge

Since 1994 Dirtec had been particularly concerned with increasing the sharing of knowledge within and between plants, between plants and Dirtec, and between Dirtec and Fama. There were three targets: (i) to support the raising of operational efficiency; (ii) to look for standardization; and (iii) to facilitate the increase of knowledge in the areas where they had decided to develop technology instead of buying in. Some organizational arrangements were explicitly designed to promote the sharing of individual knowledge at the organizational level and to increase the documentation of knowledge. The main organizational arrangements that were established or further supported in this period are presented in Table 8.5.

In this period special emphasis was put on the sharing of knowledge between VGC and AGCC. AGCC was a very large company with a different managerial culture, a different national culture, different employee backgrounds and ways of doing things. It might be a source of technological learning. During the first years following its acquisition, activities related to the demand for machines

---

[48] Interviews with the Divisional President of VGC, the Director of Ditac, the Director of Dirtec and the Technology Director of Vitro-Chemical, Fibers and Mining Division.

[49] Interview with the Director of Ditac.

were the main form of interaction between AGCC and both Fama and Dirtec. They worked together to adjust the specifications of the machines. Later, due to the attempts to manage knowledge across organizational boundaries, a great effort was put into knowledge sharing. AGCC's personnel increasingly participated in the technical meetings in Mexico, visits to plants were organized in both directions, and bulletins were issued in both Spanish and English to diffuse experiences.[50] At the level of the Vitro-Group, workshops which included AGCC's personnel were organized to transfer the best practices related to the management model.

Table 8.5   Main organizational arrangements to increase the sharing and codification of knowledge, 1994 onwards

Organizational arrangement	Objective	1994–6 relative to before
Technical meetings	• Sharing of knowledge • Looking for standardization	• New emphasis on setting standards
Teamwork	• Sharing of knowledge	• Mainly oriented to continuous improvement at plant level, rather than only for product development
Written reports about visits to foreign facilities	• Sharing of knowledge	• New mechanism
Log-books	• Recording the development of projects • Sharing of knowledge	• New mechanism
Bulletins	• Diffusing information and sharing of knowledge	• New version of Vitro-Tec's bulletins
Manuals on operating procedures	• Filling in the ISO-9001 formats	• A more formal activity

Source:
Several interviews.

---

[50] Interview with the Director of Dirtec.

All these organizational arrangements were designed to change the way of doing things and to increase the sharing and codification of knowledge. For instance the filling in of log-books or writing reports about visits were designed to overcome limitations of the learning mechanisms in the 1970s and 1980s such as the emphasis on individual rather than organizational learning. However the instability of the dual technology strategy has made the establishment and diffusion of the new practices difficult. The day-to-day focus reduced the time available to undertake the new activities such as completing log-books, editing bulletins or reading written reports. At the same time there was pressure to codify the operational procedures associated with the preparations for the ISO-9001 quality certification. There were different attitudes towards sharing and codifying of knowledge across organizational units and between personnel, which resulted in a limited conversion of individual learning into organizational learning. The degree to which each organizational arrangement worked is analyzed in detail in Section 9.3, and the reasons for that result are analyzed in Sections 10.2.1 and 10.3.1.

8.5 AN ASSESSMENT OF THE TRANSITION PROCESS DURING THE 1990s

This was a period of turbulence for VGC. There were many changes in the economic and technological environment which threatened the company and forced it to focus on increasing operational efficiency and improving the day-to-day running of the business. This pressure came when the firm was passing through a fragile stage of accumulation. Being in a Transition Process, the firm was able to move between two poles, either forward to build strategic capabilities and complete the Transition Process or backward to reinforce the minimum essential knowledge base. In fact Vitro-Glass Containers went forward in terms of building new embryonic strategic capabilities (e.g. in the area of Job Changes), keeping some empirically based embryonic strategic capabilities (e.g. process engineering and investment project management); improving performance; and actively managing knowledge from 1994. However the firm went into reverse in terms of knowledge accumulation in the R&D-based embryonic strategic capabilities which had been built in the 1970s and 1980s (e.g. glass composition and electronic control systems), as well as in the R&D bases of the empirically based embryonic strategic capabilities.

During the 1990s VGC continued to follow a dual technology strategy. However the fast follower strategy predominated and all the technology related activities were influenced by the target of increasing the firm's operational performance. In addition the instability of the technology strategy was greater than before, particularly the support of the 'technologically independent' strategy, and so the building of strategic capabilities became even more unstable. These characteristics altered the direction of knowledge accumulation.

The Transition Process was still not completed because neither the embryonic strategic capabilities built in the past nor the new embryonic strategic capabilities were being developed into strategic capabilities. A strategic capability is based on an innovative technological capability which is used to distinguish the firm competitively, to compete on the base of knowledge. In the 1990s VGC's embryonic strategic capabilities were not used in this way. Some characteristics of the Transition Process during the 1990s are summarized below.

1. In the 1990s VGC decided to concentrate its efforts on being an efficient fast follower of Owens-Illinois. Taking the Transition Process up to the point of being an active fast follower can be efficient, but this strategy must be supported by R&D activities to ensure a quick assimilation of the upgrading introduced by the technology leader. However VGC reduced its R&D activities in this period and related the fast follower strategy to the target of increasing operational efficiency. This combination of events resulted in a particularly short-term version of the fast follower strategy and not the knowledge building version based on a defensive R&D strategy. This affected perceptions about the usefulness of R&D activities as will be analyzed in Section 10.2.3, the target of knowledge management, the type of existing knowledge that needed to be shared and codified, and the need for creating knowledge. VGC has also pursued a particular version of the 'technologically independent' strategy over time. Under this heading the firm looked towards leadership in some areas but was a follower in others. The 'technologically independent' strategy really acquired meaning after 1994, when VGC started identifying 'what to buy and what to develop'. Hence the firm had no clear definition of any of its technology strategies and did not pursue a consistent or stable technology strategy, as will be analyzed in detail in Section 10.3.

2. In the 1990s, as in the 1970s and 1980s, the depth of knowledge accumulated by technical-function, technical area and knowledge field was highly uneven. VGC did not build company-wide the common basic knowledge required to interact across disciplinary and organizational boundaries and support further accumulation in certain areas.[51] In addition in the 1990s there was a change in the direction of the knowledge accumulation which affected the level of innovative tech-

---

[51]   The type, level and evolution of the unevenness is a symptom of the Transition Process and is analyzed in more detail in Section 9.2.

nological capabilities already built. According to the framework presented by Bell and Pavitt (1995), based on Lall (1992), in terms of the most advanced innovative technological capabilities revealed in the earlier period, such as the R&D activities related to production, VGC seems to have reduced its level of accumulation. The decentralization of Vitro-Tec towards the divisions was in fact a contraction of the company's R&D activities. In addition the content of the technology-related activities changed towards more continuous improvement. In fact the process of creation of new knowledge in electronics or glass composition was halted, and these embryonic strategic capabilities were therefore weakened. The advanced innovative technological capabilities in investment activities were maintained, and they were still based largely on experience. Even with no R&D activities, the transfer of technology to Latin America reveals the level of expertise reached in this technical-function. New types of linkages were established with some suppliers based on collaboration in technology development and transfer of technology. However these activities were still incipient. Although linkages with customers were strengthened, this remains a relatively weak activity. The focus on continuous improvement and day-to-day running allowed the development of other capabilities related to the operation, such as Job Changes, besides the strengthening of process engineering. They were the focus of some development activity over the 1990s.

3. The origin and emergence of embryonic strategic capabilities vary between different types of capabilities. On the one hand, certain embryonic strategic capabilities can be seen as a set of different capabilities (or as a competence) that was articulated. For instance the embryonic strategic capability in managing large investment projects was a result of technological capabilities in process engineering, knowledge about suppliers, skills to specify the equipment, capabilities in furnaces designing and building and layout designing; and knowledge about glass composition. Therefore VGC had to integrate that knowledge to be able to use it as the capability to manage investment projects. The success of that integration seems to be related to the fact that this activity had a fairly practical focus and drew on knowledge that had been created and integrated previously in the routine undertaking of investment projects. This success did not require explicit knowledge management oriented to strengthening the knowledge creation process in this area. On the other hand, in those embryonic strategic capabilities that did require the continual integration of knowledge across organizational units for knowledge creation and renewal, and needed to be supported by R&D activities, VGC had more difficulties in build-

ing up competence. Such was the case of those capabilities concerned with electronic control systems and glass composition. The incipient knowledge management until 1990 limited that achievement. In the 1990s due to the instability of the organizational support to build strategic capabilities, associated with the instability of the technology strategy, those competencies were even farther from being built.

4. VGC rose to the third largest glass container maker in the world level without ever solving many problems. Knowledge accumulation continued at different speeds and in different directions between different plants, and also between Dirtec, Fama and plants. Even before being able to integrate knowledge across organizational units inside the country, VGC had to share and integrate knowledge across organizational units located in different countries. The differences between VGC and AGCC created a new dimension that made the differences in the learning strategies, speed of the learning process and depth of knowledge across organizational units even more complex.

5. From 1994 some attempts were made to develop more explicit knowledge management in two dimensions: sharing knowledge at the organizational level, and integrating knowledge across organizational units. These attempts sought to use, adapt, integrate and change existing knowledge and also contributed to creating new knowledge in certain areas. However the instability of the dual technology strategy in the 1990s made success difficult. Even though new ways of doing things were being encouraged, they were not diffused within Dirtec or VGC.

8.6   1909–96: A LONG AND DEVIOUS WAY OF BUILDING EMBRYONIC STRATEGIC CAPABILITIES BUT NOT STRATEGIC CAPABILITIES

Right up to the early 1970s VGC built the minimum essential knowledge base to survive in the market. From building basic production capacities it was able to gradually undertake innovation activities, learning to move from operating to building the minimum essential knowledge base (vertical movements up the y-axis in Figure 2.2 of Chapter 2), as can be seen in the developing countries literature in the descriptions of several firms. In the 1970s the accumulation process took on a different dimension. The firm started a Transition Process towards building strategic capabilities. As a result of both the experience and knowledge accumulated and the more formal R&D activities undertaken some embryonic strategic capabilities emerged. The process required the firm to combine, build and nurture different knowledge bases to undertake more complex innovation activities and to learn to move from simple knowledge bases to more complex ones (horizontal movements along the x-axis in Figure 2.2). The type of learning problems were similar to those described in the strategic management literature.

The Transition Process at VGC has two poles: a minimum essential knowledge base and fully developed strategic capabilities. However from the minimum essential knowledge base VGC could have moved in another direction. For instance it could have decided to continue to be a fast follower or to retain its embryonic strategic capabilities, and not try to build strategic capabilities. The description has shown that at various times VGC tried to build innovative technological capabilities of a different nature from those required to be a fast follower. For instance the firm pursued a 'technologically independent' strategy and built a number of embryonic strategic capabilities, Vitro-Tec sought to develop only strategic projects, and Ditac promoted the identification of areas of strength at the group level to develop core capabilities. All thus indicates that at times the firm was steering towards the pole concerned with building strategic capabilities.

VGC experienced difficulties in managing the knowledge to facilitate the process of building strategic capabilities. Twenty-five years after starting the Transition Process VGC continued to develop embryonic strategic capabilities, it built no strategic capabilities. Therefore the Transition Process was truncated.

The strategic management literature reviewed in Chapter 2 points out that the building of strategic capabilities is based on the ability to create new knowledge and integrate it with the already existing knowledge base to develop strategic assets. The management of knowledge facilitates the process of creation and renewal of knowledge and plays an important role in the process of building up strategic capabilities. A number of aspects of knowledge management are considered relevant in supporting the competitive advantages of firms, such as the conversion of individual into organizational learning, the coordination of learning and the knowledge integration, as described in Section 3.2 and 3.3.

The description presented so far in Part II of this book suggests that some features of knowledge management in VGC contributed to explaining the difficulties in building strategic capabilities. Four features of the knowledge management are particularly important: (i) the existence of a limited conversion of individual into organizational learning; (ii) the differences in the learning strategies across organizational units and the limited coordination of learning between them; (iii) the limited knowledge integration; and (iv) the instability of the knowledge creation process.

In addition certain other factors seem to have influenced those key features of the knowledge management. The firm pursued two technology strategies in parallel. It sought to be 'technologically independent' and to build strategic capabilities. At the same time it pursued a fast follower strategy. Both strategies were supported by decisions taken by the top management and received organizational support. However the organizational support for these strategies was unstable, which affected the aims and efforts to manage knowledge. Therefore the instability of the dual technology strategy was a factor that affected the knowledge management features. Another factor was related to the lack of consideration and management of the knowledge as a system. Even at times when the firm was making more consistent efforts to manage the knowledge to build strategic capabilities, it encountered difficulties in getting results. Several isolated mechanisms and organizational arrangements were established which were never articulated. Part III analyzes the problems in knowledge management underlying the truncated Transition Process.

PART THREE

Knowledge Management Problems Underlying
the Truncated Transition Process

Introductory Note

The previous three chapters have indicated that in the 1970s, after a long period of building the minimum essential knowledge base, Vitro-Glass Containers started a Transition Process towards building strategic capabilities. Twenty- five years later the Transition Process had not been completed. The firm built embryonic strategic capabilities but was not able to build strategic capabilities as a basis for distinguishing the firm competitively. The purpose of Part III is to discuss the main reasons for the failure to build strategic capabilities and complete the Transition Process.

As a technological capability, a strategic capability has two components: (i) a stock of technological knowledge, and (ii) an organized system for managing the stock of knowledge. The process of knowledge creation is related to the evolution of the stock of technological knowledge on which a strategic capability is based. The management of knowledge refers to the organizational dimension of the building of strategic capabilities. The management of knowledge affects the knowledge creation process and the use of the knowledge. By analyzing firms that have already built strategic capabilities, the strategic management literature has emphasized the role of knowledge management. As revealed in Part II, VGC experienced difficulties in managing the knowledge and, at the same time, still lacked knowledge in some areas. Therefore the evolution and interaction of both components of a strategic capability are crucial to explaining the failure to complete the Transition Process. For this reason, even though Part III analyzes the organizational dimension of building strategic capabilities, the analysis relates this dimension to the knowledge creation process. Therefore under the heading of knowledge management, the interrelation between both components of the strategic capabilities are analyzed here.

Central to building strategic capabilities are the conversion of individual into organizational learning, the coordination of the learning strategies, the integration of knowledge and the knowledge creation process. These are critical processes to the long-term capability building and have affected the limited success in completing the Transition Process. This book examines the main characteristics of these processes in VGC and discusses to what extent they explain the failure to build strategic capabilities in order to distinguish the firm competitively and complete the Transition Process.

This book also discusses several factors influencing these aspects of the firm's knowledge management and analyses to what extent they contributed to the difficulty to build strategic capabilities. Two main factors are given special attention, the failure to consider and manage the firm's knowledge as a system and the instability of the firm's dual technology strategy.

Part III contains an analysis of the problems due to the knowledge management that acted against completion of the Transition Process. It follows a theory-building structure that aims to interpret the story, to link some issues with the theoretical debate in the literature, and to present a number of reasons for the failure to build strategic capabilities and complete the Transition Process. Hence Part III is organized by issue. Chapter 9 analyzes four key features of the knowledge management that explain why the Transition Process was truncated. Chapter 10 analyzes two factors that influenced these key features of the firm's knowledge management.

9 Features of Knowledge Management Contributing to the Truncated Transition Process

9.1 INTRODUCTION

The strategic management literature reviewed in Chapter 3 considers that several knowledge management processes are relevant to support the competitive advantages of firms. The conversion of individual into organizational learning, the coordination of learning, knowledge integration and knowledge creation are considered central processes contributing to the building of strategic capabilities.

This chapter focuses on these four knowledge management processes and argues that the weaknesses in these processes were a major contributor to the truncated Transition Process described in Part II. In particular the limited nature of the conversion of individual into organizational learning, the limited coordination of learning strategies, the limited integration of knowledge across organizational boundaries, and the instability of the knowledge creation process are key features of knowledge management that contribute to explaining the failure to build strategic capabilities and the truncation of the Transition Process.

Section 9.2 summarizes in a structured way several symptoms or characteristics of the truncated Transition Process. Sections 9.3 to 9.6 describe each of the four features of knowledge management and explore their role in the truncated Transition Process. Section 9.7 presents some conclusions.

9.2 THE TRUNCATED TRANSITION PROCESS

As described in Part II, from the 1970s Vitro-Glasss Containers began a Transition Process to build strategic capabilities. Certainly the accumulation was quicker in some technical-functions, knowledge fields and technical areas than in others and these emerged as embryonic strategic capabilities. Whilst the firm created and accumulated knowledge and built a number of embryonic strategic capabilities, it has experienced great difficulty in building up strategic capabilities. Therefore in the 1990s the Transition Process has not been completed.

The truncation of the Transition Process displays certain symptoms. For instance as a result of an uneven knowledge accumulation process, in some areas there are embryonic strategic capabilities while in others there are none at all. The depth of knowledge is also uneven between the embryonic strategic capabilities, and within a particular embryonic strategic capability between organizational units. This type of unevenness can be regarded as a symptom of the truncated Transition Process. In addition the failure of the embryonic strategic capabilities which were accumulated to reach the stage of strategic capabilities is another symptom. The purpose of this section is to summarize in a structured way these two symptoms.

9.2.1 Unevenness in the Depth of Knowledge

The existence of unevenness in the depth of knowledge is a fact of organizational life and not just a characteristic of the Transition Process. However the type, level and evolution of the unevenness is a symptom of an incomplete Transition Process. The unevenness illustrates that the firm did not build strategic capabilities. As a result of this the Transition Process was truncated. Three types of unevenness are analyzed below: by technical-function, by knowledge field and between organizational units.

Unevenness by technical-function

The description of the process of building up of technological capabilities, presented in Chapters 6 to 8, reveals that VGC was able to undertake different types of activities by technical-function over time, moving from operating to innovating. Following the framework presented by Bell and Pavitt (1995), based on Lall (1992), an assessment of the level of technological capabilities reached by technical-function in each period was presented in Sections 6.5, 7.5 and 8.5. This assessment was based on the type of activities undertaken, which revealed different depths of knowledge and abilities to do things over time. Based on that assessment, Table 9.1 summarizes the depth of knowledge by technical-function at the end of each period of time.

The table illustrates that the firm was building up its technological capabilities, and was moving from basic to intermediate innovative technological capabilities and even to advanced in several technical-functions.

Over time certain technical-functions were developed more quickly than others. For instance intermediate innovative technological capabilities were achieved before 1970 in investment activities, production activities centered on the process, the supply of capital goods and the linkages with other firms.

As described in Chapter 6, the first three areas were of special concern from the earliest days as they were involved in adapting the technology to the firm- and country-specificity, assuring the continuity of the production process and supporting the expansion of the firm. Efforts in these directions fostered the accumulation of knowledge from the outset. The process of knowledge specialization from the 1970s allowed this accumulation to continue reaching advanced innovative technological capabilities in some of them, whereas the activities undertaken in other technical-functions, such as the production activities centered on the product, the linkages with clients and the linkages with the Science and Technology System were of a most elemental nature and changed at a much slower pace. In each period the type of activities undertaken in these latter technical-functions denoted a lesser depth of knowledge.

Table 9.1   Depth of knowledge by technical-function, 1909–90s

Technical-functions	After accumulating the minimum essential knowledge base: 1909–70	During the Transition Process: 1970–90s	
		At the end of the 1980s	In the 1990s
Investment project management	Intermediate	Intermediate/ Advanced	Advanced
Production-product centered	Basic	Intermediate	Intermediate
Production-process centered	Intermediate	Advanced	Advanced/ Intermediate
Capital goods	Intermediate	Advanced	Advanced/ Intermediate
Linkage with suppliers	Basic	Intermediate	Intermediate/ Advanced
Linkage with other firms	Intermediate	Intermediate	Intermediate/ Advanced
Linkage with clients	Basic	Basic	Intermediate
Linkage with the Science & Technology System	Basic	Basic	Basic

Source:
Own analysis of information from interviews.

Within each period the accumulation was uneven, combining activities of differing nature and complexity. For instance basic innovative technological capabilities in some technical-functions coexisted with intermediate or advanced in other technical-functions. These differences reveal that there was a wide range of depths of knowledge held by technical-function over these periods of time. As a result of the uneven paths referred to above, the depth of knowledge by technical-function in the 1990s has been different.

Unevenness by knowledge field

At the level of knowledge fields, the evidence suggests that the depth of knowledge also varied. It is difficult to measure and compare depths of knowledge of different natures. For instance patents can be a good measure of knowledge related to the electronic control systems but not of knowledge related to applied mechanical engineering or glass composition. These fields have less propensity to patent because of the ease with which they can be copied by competitors. In another even more operative technical area, such as Job Changes, patents do not enter the equation. Hence an assessment of the knowledge depth was made using the results of development projects and some innovation related activities described in Chapters 7 and 8, which include a variety of indicators of performance. Table 9.2 below resumes some results of development projects and activities carried out by VGC and assesses the depth of knowledge in the main knowledge fields used by the firm.

Table 9.2 illustrates the uneven depth of knowledge by fields in the organization from shallow knowledge in applied mechanical engineering to deep in glass composition and to very deep in electronic control systems. VGC was close to the frontier of technological knowledge in electronic control systems and glass composition in the 1980s. The depth of knowledge was assessed as very deep in electronic control systems because of VGC having been granted a patent close to the first patent in the world and having the capability to apply this knowledge to other equipment, as highlighted in Section 7.4.1.2.

The depth of knowledge in glass composition was assessed as just deep because VGC achieved independence in this field and used its own formula, but it did not nurture this knowledge base. In contrast in applied mechanical engineering the knowledge base is hardly the minimum essential to survive in the market. Even though the firm has practical knowledge, a more formal base of knowledge is required to solve some of the practical problems. As described in Section 9.2.2, electronic control systems and glass composition are embryonic strategic capabilities with different depths of knowledge, while applied mechanical engineering does not look like an embryonic strategic capability.

Table 9.2 Depth of knowledge by field, 1970–90s

Knowledge fields	Some evidence of the knowledge depth	Assessment
Glass composition	• The use of an own glass formula from the 1980s • The certification of the ISO-9001 in several plants, which reveals the use of good quality glass	Deep
Electronic control systems	• A patent of the electronic control system in 1978, eight years after the first such patent in the world • Other patents resulting from applying the knowledge in electronics to other equipment • The use of Vitro's electronic control system since 1990	Very deep
Applied mechanical engineering	• Several adaptations and improvements were carried out to the IS machine • Difficulties are still encountered over mastery of the principles of the machine's mechanisms and coupling them with different equipment technology, which is an important knowledge in the industry	Shallow

Source:
Own analysis of information from interviews.

The uneven depth of knowledge between fields affected the evolution of the set of embryonic strategic capabilities. For instance the electronic control system was designed to control the glass forming process, so it requires knowledge about glass composition and mechanical engineering. The knowledge in applied mechanical engineering is necessary to understand the mechanical sequence of the machine's mechanisms. Therefore a balance between the base of knowledge in electronic control system and mechanical engineering is necessary to improve the operation of the electronic control system. The unevenness between the depth of knowledge in electronic control systems and mechanical engineering has affected the knowledge creation process in electronic control systems and weakened this embryonic strategic capability.

Unevenness between organizational units

Unevenness was also found between organizational units related to the same knowledge field. Several authors from the SML asserted that to be able to apply and increase the knowledge, firms were required to share some common knowledge between their organizational units.[1] In the case of VGC, even though both common and complementary knowledge between Vitro-Tec, Dirtec and the plants was required to assure the implementation, feedback and upgrading of the equipment, plants did not possess the basic knowledge required for that activity in all fields. Based on the results of the development projects described in Chapters 7 and 8, Table 9.3 presents an assessment of the extent to which plants had the required basic knowledge. This will demonstrate that even though the advantages of the knowledge specialization in terms of the acceleration of the knowledge creation process were present, the unevenness between the organizational units is a symptom of the truncated Transition Process.

At the level of the organizational units, Table 9.3 illustrates that there was an asymmetrical depth of knowledge by the organizational units related to each knowledge field. Vitro-Tec and Dirtec – in different periods – were in charge of the strategic R&D activities and played a different role in the knowledge creation process to that played by the plants. However the plants lacked the basic knowledge required to accurately undertake and implement projects and contribute to the upgrading of the knowledge in electronic control systems and applied mechanical engineering. For example plants needed some basic knowledge in electronics to allow them to understand the functioning of the electronic control system, deal with its operation and obtain good performance, and be able both to integrate their knowledge with Vitro-Tec and Dirtec and to suggest improvements. However only a few plants possessed this basic knowledge and even the more knowledgeable plants lacked a real understanding of the functioning.[2] For this reason the assessment of the plants's depth of knowledge was shallow. Similarly because plants were more knowledgeable about machine operation than applied mechanical engineering, they had difficulty in identifying the source of problems in the line, as the case of the plunger mechanisms revealed (see Boxes 9.4 and 10.1). Therefore the assessment in applied mechanical engineering was also shallow. In the case of glass composition no problems of lack of knowledge were identified during the field work. This, alongside the production of good quality glass containers in all plants, suggests that the plants's depth of knowledge was deep.[3]

---

[1] See for instance Iansiti and Clark (1994), Leonard-Barton (1995a), Nonaka and Takeuchi (1995) and Pisano (1997).

[2] Interview with Dirtec's technical staff and AGCC's technical staff.

[3] A different argument could be that in this case the plants's knowledge is less important to nurture the knowledge base in glass composition than in the other knowledge fields.

Table 9.3 Depth of knowledge in each field by organizational unit, 1970–90s

Knowledge fields	Type of knowledge by organizational units		Assessment of plants's knowledge
	Vitro-Tec/Dirtec	Plants	
Glass composition	• R&D (research, development and minor improvements)	• Use of the glass formula to produce glass containers and carry out quality control • No problems of lack of knowledge were identified	Deep
Electronic control systems	• R&D (research, development and minor improvements)	• Operation and maintenance of the electronic control system • The demand from the plants for changes were the result of their unfamiliarity with electronics and lack of understanding of the functioning of the electronic control system • Uneven knowledge by plants, while Monterrey, Querétaro and Toluca plants have a basic knowledge, others including AGCC's plants were unable to solve some operational problems	Shallow
Applied mechanical engineering	• R&D (only some developments and basically minor improvements)	• Operation, maintenance and continuous improvements of the equipment • Plants are familiar with the equipment and ask for changes • Plants lack mechanical engineering knowledge and so they have difficulties to identify the problems generated by some improvements to the overall functioning of the IS machine	Shallow

Source:
Own analysis of information from interviews.

The imbalance of knowledge between the organizational units in electronic control systems and applied mechanical engineering affected the performance of the equipment, the effectiveness of the feedback to the units in charge of the R&D activities and therefore the knowledge creation process in those fields. Overall the type, level and evolution of the unevenness illustrates the lack of any strategic capabilities and the truncated Transition Process.

9.2.2 Embryonic Strategic Capabilities that did not Become Strategic Capabilities

Even though VGC created and accumulated knowledge and built a number of embryonic strategic capabilities, it experienced great difficulty in developing strategic capabilities. This is a symptom of the truncated Transition Process. The set of embryonic strategic capabilities built are similar in the sense that they are not used to distinguish the firm competitively. However there are differences in the depth of knowledge accumulated, the type of knowledge that supported their development and their evolution. These characteristics of the embryonic strategic capabilities and the failure to build any embryonic strategic capability in an area of great practical experience are summarized below.

Investment project management and Job Changes

The knowledge accumulated in different technical-functions and knowledge fields was the base to develop abilities to carry out certain technical activities, such as investment project management and Job Changes. For instance the ability to manage large investment projects was the result of capabilities in process engineering, awareness about suppliers, abilities to specify equipment, abilities to design and build furnaces, abilities to design layouts and knowledgeability about glass composition, as highlighted in Section 8.5. VGC had to integrate all these knowledge bases to be able to build and use a capability for investment projects management. Therefore the abilities developed in this area can be seen as a set of articulated capabilities, or as a competence in the sense of Prahalad and Hamel (1990). Whilst that capability/competence required inputs from different knowledge bases, including any R&D activities involved, the interviews revealed that there was no evidence of consistent and persistent efforts to coordinate the learning strategies pursued by the organizational units specialized in those knowledge bases, to share and codify related knowledge or to integrate knowledge between the units. The investment project management was one of the directions of the knowledge accumulation since the early days and along the Transition Process. However the investment activities have had quite a practical focus and VGC used knowledge from other areas that was integrated through the routine undertaking of investment projects. In that sense the knowledge creation process was oriented to making effective use of the existing knowledge rather than to creating new knowledge in this area. This has weakened the potential of this embryonic strategic capability to become a strategic capability.

VGC accumulated rich experience in large investment projects management because it had the opportunity to create new plants in Mexico and Central America, and to enlarge others by adding more furnaces and lines. It learned from these experiences and built expertise, as described in Sections 6.2.2, 7.4.2 and 8.3.2. Firms from advanced industrial countries generally have limited experience in such activities due to the maturity of their markets and the consolidation of the industry. The last new plant in the US was created by Owens-Illinois in 1981, while VGC established Toluca in 1986 and Mexicali in 1992 and, in addition, was undertaking re-building up to the present time. Therefore investment project management can be seen as a firm-specific capability or as an embryonic strategic capability cultivated up to the present through practical experience. However the aim was not in building a strategic capability in this area to distinguish the firm competitively, or at least the knowledge was not managed to get a strategic advantage. In the 1990s VGC has been licensing its own technology in investment project management and know-how in glass container manufacture to Latin American firms, which seems to be a direct result of that embryonic strategic capability. This new activity is pushing the embryonic strategic capability in investment project management forward in the direction of building a strategic capability.

The Job Changes activity is another case of an embryonic strategic capability based on very practical experience. VGC has been able to cost-effectively fill small orders from customers. The US producers have focused on large production runs to meet the needs of their major customers, whereas VGC has experience in small runs for its many small customers. In addition VGC's plants have a lot of experience in working with different colors, also associated with smaller orders. Therefore Job Changes have emerged as an embryonic strategic capability due to the short length of the production runs and as a result of a particular effort concentrated to utilizing existing knowledge to improve this activity, particularly in the 1990s. In fact this was one of the directions of the knowledge accumulation that has received increasing support during the 1990s and has been nurtured by some developments undertaken by Dirtec in these years. As highlighted in Section 8.2.3, one of the six projects of technological upgrading was oriented to improve this activity, and half of the improvements listed in Table 8.1 directly affected this activity. However the knowledge creation process has not been nurtured by applied research activities because of the contraction of these activities in the 1990s and the practical focus of the Job Changes. That was a set back for the future strengthening of this activity.

The fact that Job Changes is an area of best practice in relation to AGCC, as highlighted in Section 8.3.1, suggests that VGC has a relative expertise in this technical area. However this embryonic strategic capability was not managed to become a strategic capability, actually it was not recognized as an embryonic strategic capability until it was compared with AGCC in the middle of the 1990s.

The embryonic strategic capabilities that emerged in investment projects and Job Changes could have been strengthened by more applied research, and the coordination of the learning strategies and the integration of knowledge between organizational units. However the features of the knowledge management, analyzed later in this chapter, also contribute to explaining the failure to build strategic capabilities from these embryonic stages.

Electronic control systems and glass composition

The creation of knowledge in electronic control systems and glass composition was based on more formal R&D activities oriented to utilizing the existing knowledge and also creating new knowledge. A wealth of knowledge was accumulated in these fields from the 1970s and they became embryonic strategic capabilities, as described in Section 7.4.1.2 and Box 7.2. However the evolution of the R&D activities was unsettled and so was the knowledge creation process in these areas, as analyzed in more detail in Section 9.6. The R&D focus of these activities demanded that knowledge be integrated between Vitro-Tec, Dirtec and the plants.

However the focus on individual learning, the differences in the learning strategies and its limited coordination, and the limited knowledge integration, analyzed in more detail in Sections 9.3, 9.4 and 9.5, along with differences in the depth of the knowledge possessed by these units and the uneven depth of knowledge by fields, seem to have been major stumbling blocks to integrating knowledge between the organizational units. For these reasons VGC was less able to build up in these areas the type of competence that existed in the more practical areas.

Moreover the process of knowledge creation and the building up of strategic capabilities in areas such as electronic control systems and glass composition was even more vulnerable to changes in technology strategy than the more practical based embryonic strategic capabilities. In Section 10.2.3 it will be argued that the failure to perceive the learning dimension of the R&D activities, associated with the lack of perceiving knowledge as a system, conducted to link closely the R&D activities with the 'technologically independent' strategy. Section 10.3.4. will discuss that the instability of the dual technology strategy affected the support of the R&D activities and weakened particularly those embryonic strategic capabilities more related to these activities.

The failure to build a strategic capability in coupling equipment

Coupling equipment technology is an important capability in the glass container industry today. VGC has great experience in undertaking this activity. However it hardly built any embryonic strategic capability in this area. There were different perceptions about the role of the adaptation activity and uneven efforts were undertaking in this activity, which goes to explain the failure to build a strategic capability in coupling equipment technology.

The adaptation activity of VGC dates back to as early as 1909, when the first Owens machines were installed, and has continued to be important. The earliest experiences were basically associated with the need to make the foreign technology fit the firm - and country-specific conditions. Later this activity was nurtured by the continuous upgrading of equipment in the attempt to keep abreast of the technological frontier and by in-house developments. Hence the carrying out of adaptations has become a routine activity. Table 9.4 is a *résumé* of the main motives for adaptation being undertaken from the outset.

The intensity and characteristics of the adaptation activity undertaken by VGC from the earliest days contribute to explaining the peculiarities of its equipment technology. Nowadays VGC has idiosyncratic equipment that combines different technologies. This equipment technology is referred to as Vitro/Owens-Illinois, Vitro/Emhart or Vitro/Maul in Chapters 6, 7 and 8. Such peculiarity has necessitated that adaptation activities be continued.

Table 9.4   Main motives to undertake adaptation activities

- The use of raw materials with a different composition

- The different climatic conditions in Mexico that determined the need to adapt the furnaces, the height and ventilation system of the buildings, the layout, etc.

- The operation of different equipment technologies in the same plant, particularly since the 1940s, such as new foreign equipment technology, in-house developments and also earlier equipment technology that was maintained to the end of its useful life

- The introduction of machine mechanisms from different small suppliers in the already adapted IS machines

---

Source:
Own analysis of information from interviews.

Adaptations to equipment have ranged from very simple changes made in the production line to extensive mechanical engineering design undertaken by the technology function.[4] For instance all the plants adapt the electronic control systems by simply disconnecting the sensors, particularly the pass-gob sensor.[5, 6] In the case of the Emhart's electronic feeder mechanism installed at the Querétaro plant in 1996, it was necessary to carry out design engineering for it to be coupled with the Owens-Illinois's gob feeder already in operation. This work of adaptation was carried out jointly between Emhart Glass and the Advanced Machinery Department of Dirtec.[7] Therefore in many cases the adaptation activity has required a deeper understanding of both the equipment acquired and the nature of its coupling with the existing equipment, and filling in of the remaining gaps by independent efforts. Therefore in spite of the fact that it is not an activity oriented to creating new knowledge, it has required in-house innovative efforts.

Despite the obvious need for these adaptations, summarized in Table 9.4, and the effort required to undertake this activity, there have been differing views about the role and usefulness of this activity in the firm. A positive role is associated with two arguments that underlined the interviews. Firstly, because VGC has used idiosyncratic equipment it has not been able to just buy off-the-shelf. Therefore the adaptation activity has been needed in order to achieve the required performance from the equipment technology acquired. Secondly, the intensity of the adaptation and the in-house development activities allowed the building of an idiosyncratic equipment technology that is mainly Vitro/Owens-Illinois. The capability for combining equipment could be the basis for a strategic capability, particularly in line with the new trend in the industry to combine different technologies to obtain better performance from the equipment. However the ability to convert this strength into a strategic capability depends on how it is managed. Up to the present it has been a source of weakness due to the difficulties encountered in controlling the coupling of different technologies and the lack of steady organizational support to overcome them, as Box 9.1 below illustrates.

The negative role of the adaptation activity is associated with two further arguments that emerged from the interviews. Firstly, in some cases the adaptations were made by plant personnel with insufficient understanding of the functioning of the equipment. Instead of asking Dirtec for technical assistance or training, the plants carried out continuous improvement projects to increase the equipment performance. In these cases the adaptation was not

---

[4]　Interview with a Manager of the Advanced Machinery area from Dirtec's Advanced Engineering Department.
[5]　As described in Section 7.4.1.2, the pass-gob sensor is an electronic trigger that allows a reduction of the optic in the bottle.
[6]　Interview with the Electronic Maintenance Leader of the Monterrey plant.
[7]　Interview with a Manager of the Advanced Machinery area from Dirtec's Advanced Engineering Department and the Director of Dirtec.

really a requirement for increasing the equipment performance but in fact revealed that the plants did not have the know-how to operate the equipment and needed more training.[8] The disconnection of the pass-gob sensor is an example of this argument. Secondly, continuous adaptation and upgrading of the equipment generated the need to create and accumulate knowledge in applied mechanical engineering to support the capability for coupling different technologies.[9] Therefore if adaptation is undertaken the creation of that knowledge is a requirement, must be a target and demands specific efforts and investments. If this knowledge is not accumulated, as indeed happened, the adaptation activity is likely to generate problems rather than offer advantages. In addition, whilst the adaptation is part of the R&D activities, this second argument was strengthened by the diffused perception that the adaptation activity does not require very much research. However due to the intensity of both the adaptation activity and the upgrading of the equipment, coupling technologies required deeper knowledge about the equipment than that required for the simple activity of adapting and demanded applied research in mechanical engineering to overcome imbalances, intolerance and other unfitness.

The coexistence of both approaches about the role and usefulness of the adaptation activity contribute to explaining the weaknesses in the coupling of different equipment technologies. Box 9.1 below illustrates this issue.

The continuous adaptation and upgrading of the equipment required knowledge of mechanical engineering that far exceeded the depth of knowledge already built in this field. There has been no systematic knowledge accumulation and no understanding of the need to support this activity with applied research in mechanical engineering. Even during Vitro-Tec's time, knowledge in mechanical engineering to support the coupling of equipment technologies was not a clear direction of the knowledge accumulation process. Whilst the adaptation activity continued to be very important, the emphasis in applied research was on creating new knowledge rather than on strengthening the knowledge to support the adaptation activity and the coupling of different equipment technologies. The strategic bias of Vitro-Tec contributed to this focus. While the adaptation activities were supported in some sense by the mechanical engineering knowledge that had been built up for other purposes, there was neither the aim to coordinate the learning strategies and integrate the knowledge across organizational units, nor the understanding of the usefulness of the R&D activities for that matter. The decentralization of Vitro-Tec, the

---

[8] Interview with a Manager of the Advanced Machinery area from Dirtec's Advanced Engineering Department.
[9] Interviews with technical staff of Dirtec's Transfer of Technology and Advanced Engineering Departments.

change in the focus of Fama and the reduction in R&D activities in the 1990s further weakened the knowledge in mechanical engineering. The difficulties to create knowledge in coupling different equipment technologies were made worse by the different views about the role of the adaptation activity. Even though the coupling of equipment technologies could be considered as an embryonic strategic capability based on practical experience, it was difficult to convert this embryonic strategic capability into a strategic capability. Actually it is hard to say that this is an embryonic strategic capability, certainly it is more incipient than others.

To sum up, the unevenness by technical-function, by knowledge field and between organizational units; the actual stage of development of the embryonic strategic capabilities and the failure to build strategic capabilities are symptoms of a truncated Transition Process. The following sections describe four features of the knowledge management and explore their role on the truncated Transition Process.

9.3   LIMITED CONVERSION OF INDIVIDUAL INTO ORGANIZATIONAL LEARNING

A central process in building strategic capabilities is the conversion of individual into organizational learning. Learning is a process that happens primarily at the individual level, and organizational learning is not the simple sum of all the individual learning, as described in Section 3.2.1. The process of conversion of individual into organizational learning is neither simple nor automatic. It requires specific conditions and efforts. Two key activities for the organizational learning process are the sharing of knowledge and the codification of knowledge, which in turn facilitates the sharing.

The description presented in Chapters 7, 8 and 9 revealed that throughout its history VGC has had a continuous concern to learn. Many mechanisms were used and different organizational arrangements were established to support this activity. Their importance and focus have changed over the years according to the level and directions of the knowledge accumulation process. Up to 1970 learning occurred essentially at the individual level. From the 1970s, as the firm started the Transition Process, VGC became more aware of the need to implement specific actions to support the process of organizational learning to facilitate the building of strategic capabilities. From 1970 to 1993 there were learning mechanisms and organizational arrangements aiming at that target, but they were still incipient and not articulated. From 1994 a more consistent effort was made to promote the conversion of individual into organizational learning and new organizational arrangements were set up. However the firm found it difficult to change its way of doing things and improve the process of organizational learning.

---

*Box 9.1   Coupling equipment from different technology sources: a
failure to build a strategic capability*

Coupling equipment from different suppliers was a practice rooted in the 1920s,
when VGC introduced Lynch technology while the Owens technology was still in
operation. This practice grew as the result of adaptation activity, continuous search
for the latest equipment, introduction of improvements based on in-house
developments and the existence of idiosyncratic equipment.

The capability for combining equipment acquired from different suppliers has
become very important in the industry in the last 10 years. The standard equipment
technologies for the IS machines (Emhart Glass or Owens-Illinois) being combined
with machine mechanisms produced by small specialized suppliers allows the
standard equipment to reach a higher level of efficiency.[10] The small specialized
suppliers sell such mechanisms to be coupled to standard equipment technologies.
In the 1990s VGC introduced some of these new mechanisms and coupled them
with its equipment, as did AGCC.

The activity of coupling equipment in VGC is more than fixing mechanisms
provided by different suppliers. VGC cannot ask for a Quantum plunger mechanism
to fix in its Vitro/Owens-Illinois or its Vitro/Maul/Owens-Illinois machines. It has
to be able to design the coupling by itself because none of the other suppliers
understands or produces for the idiosyncratic equipment VGC has.[11] AGCC also
couples mechanisms from different suppliers. However AGCC has used basically
standard equipment, so the coupling of the mechanisms to its equipment has been
a very practical and trouble free activity.[12] It can ask for a Quantum plunger
mechanism to fix in its Emhart Glass, Owens-Illinois or Maul machines. Therefore
the complexity of the activity in VGC is higher than in AGCC. VGC has to
understand the mechanical principles of its idiosyncratic equipment and of the
mechanisms acquired from other suppliers to be able to couple them. So it is necessary
for it to undertake R&D activities to support the coupling.

Nevertheless the wide practical experience, the efforts to undertake R&D
activities and increase the knowledge creation process in applied mechanical
engineering have been less intense. Equipment technology was changing even while
Dirtec's technical staff were still analyzing earlier equipment technology. They did
not dedicate enough time to understanding the mechanisms and there was no
documentation of the differences and relationships between mechanisms. They were
forced to couple the new equipment technology they had obtained without any in-
depth knowledge about it.[13] The case of coupling a plunger mechanism with the
molding equipment, described in Boxes 9.4 and 10.1, dramatically illustrates this
weakness. The result was that it was necessary to make increased efforts to achieve
good performance and to overcome the defects generated by a bad coupling, and
the need for even more adaptations.

---

[10] Interview with the Manager of Fama's Production Engineering Department and the Director
of Dirtec.
[11] Interviews with Dirtec's technical staff from the Transfer of Technology and Advanced
Engineering Departments.
[12] Interviews with the Leaders of the Maintenance and Process Engineering Departments of
the AGCC's Elmira plant.
[13] Interview with Dirtec's technical staff.

The main purpose of this section is to identify the extent to which individual learning was transformed into organizational learning, by analyzing how much knowledge was shared at a collective level and the extent to which potentially codifiable tacit knowledge was actually codified. Section 9.3.1 analyses the weaknesses in sharing and codifying knowledge from 1970 to 1993. Section 9.3.2 describes a set of new organizational arrangements established since 1994 to increase the conversion of individual into organizational learning and analyses the extent to which they actually work.

9.3.1 Weaknesses in Sharing and Codifying Knowledge: 1970–93

During the time VGC was building up the minimum essential knowledge base, the firm was not very complex and the organizational boundaries were not very rigid. Even though the learning mechanisms were basically oriented to support individual learning, it was quite easy to share a few areas of knowledge at the organizational level. As the businesses and the knowledge base grew, knowledge became more specialized by technical-function, knowledge field and technical area in different organizational units and the organization became larger and more complex. In this context it was necessary to set up specific organizational arrangements to enable learning, including several that were specially designed to facilitate the sharing and codifying of knowledge. Such procedures were particularly necessary when the firm started the Transition Process from building the minimum essential knowledge base to building strategic capabilities to distinguish the firm competitively.

Table 9.5 contains the main learning mechanisms the firm used from very early on and the organizational arrangements for learning that were basically implemented since the firm began the Transition Process. Some of these were directly oriented to sharing knowledge, such as the periodical technical audit of plants by Dirtec; others were directed to codifying knowledge and thus facilitating knowledge sharing, such as the publication of the proceedings of the technical meetings to analyze experiences. The last column of the table shows some characteristics of their functioning.

At first sight the evidence presented in Table 9.5 suggests that the learning mechanisms and organizational arrangements for learning used by VGC were no different from those widely described in the literature. However a more detailed analysis of their functioning reveals that their effectiveness in terms of the learning at organizational level was low. The scope of the sharing and codifying of knowledge was limited. This issue is analyzed below.

Table 9.5 Learning mechanisms and organizational arrangements, 1970–93

Learning mechanisms	Organizational arrangements	Characteristics of the functioning
From internal sources		
R&D activities	• 80% of the time of Vitro-Tec's personnel and 20% of Dirtec's personnel was assigned to major improvements • Patents have to be applied for • Teamwork for project development	• 10-15% of the actual time of Dirtec's technical staff was dedicated to major improvements, even when Vitro-Tec was decentralized to the divisions • Even though patents were applied for, there was an incomplete documentation of the projects, in fact no log-books were filled in • Few experiences of teamwork.
Technical meetings to analyze experiences	• Annual activity organized by Dirtec • The proceedings were published	• The proceedings of the meetings to analyze experiences were not circulated • No feedback mechanisms were established from Dirtec and Fama to the plants
Monitoring plants's experiences	• Periodical technical audit by Dirtec	• No feedback mechanisms were established from Dirtec to the plants • Little documentation and sharing of the experiences between plants
Training	• Elaboration of manuals, videos, etc. • A technical library was set up in each plant	• Difficulties in upgrading the manuals
Bulletins	• Bulletins were published by Vitro-Tec	• Some efforts to diffuse information
From external sources		
Licensing agreements and purchase of equipment	• Participation in conferences • Technical assistance and consultations • Analysis of the patents	• Focus on upgrading the equipment more than on learning about new practices • Little effort in combining external and internal practices
Hiring personnel		• Difficulties to combine the new knowledge possessed by the hired technicians with present practices
Visits to competitors' facilities	• Personnel from different level undertake this activity	• Focus on identifying the upgrading of the equipment • Little effort in learning on new practices • Partial sharing of the individual learning

Source:
Own analysis of information from interviews.

9.3.1.1 Insufficient sharing of knowledge

A more detailed analysis of the functioning of some mechanisms and organizational arrangement allows identification of the scope of tacit knowledge sharing. For instance visits to competitors' facilities had been an important source of knowledge and a mechanism for learning from external sources, over the years. After the 1950s frequent visits were undertaken by personnel from the shop floor, Dirtec and also from the corporate offices. Once VGC signed the Technical Agreement with Owens-Illinois in 1974 it regularly sent a large number of personnel to visit the Owens-Illinois's facilities. Even during periods of more tight control of expenditure, such as the beginning of the 1980s and the 1990s, this activity continued to be supported. However in spite of the financial effort given to learning through this mechanism, between 1970 and 1993 no organizational arrangements were in place to allow the knowledge acquired by the personnel to be shared. Therefore it continued to be individual learning.

The main characteristics of the visits to competitors' facilities as a learning mechanism are described below. First, from very early on the main target was to identify the scope for upgrading of the equipment. This information was diffused within the firm and many of the upgrades were incorporated.[14] In addition small operational changes were identified and sometimes introduced. Second, although personnel acquired additional information about their competitors, such as type of equipment used, their strengths and weaknesses, etc., this information was not shared in the same way. The interviews revealed a clear fragmentation of the information about competitors. While some topics were clearly understood by certain personnel, others had doubts. Third, most of the visits were very short and VGC encouraged the observation of technology in operation rather than the development of experience in competitors' facilities. This latter is a much more powerful way of acquiring tacit knowledge, as Nonaka and Takeuchi (1995:63–4) illustrated in the case of the Matsushita Electric Industrial Co. Fourth, a few longer visits allowed time to identify changes in the work organization, layout design, managerial practices and ways of doing things. For instance some interviewees remarked that they actually learned more from the management of knowledge than from the equipment. In particular from Toyo Glass some learned about the promotion and appraisal system to stimulate the creation of knowledge,[15] whilst others learned different ways of doing things from Owens-Illinois.[16] However this learning was neither

---

[14] Interview with a firm's employee engaged in 1930, who was Upkeep from 1950 to 1980, and with several of Dirtec's technical staff.
[15] Interview with a technical employee who spent one month at Toyo Glass.
[16] Interview with an employee who spent one year at Owens-Illinois's facilities.

shared nor incorporated in VGC's facilities and behaviors. Unlike the case of Chaparral Steel, described by Leonard-Barton (1992b:35), the personnel were not empowered to apply what they had learned to the firm. To sum up, the functioning of this learning mechanism meant that only in the case of equipment upgrading can it be said that the organization learned at all. In other issues, such as work organization, managerial practices and ways of doing things, this was an important learning mechanism but only at the individual level.

In the case of the knowledge acquired by hiring foreign personnel, it seems that VGC did hire technicians but made no consistent organizational effort to share in their knowledge and incorporate it with the existing knowledge and established ways of doing things. In the first decades of operation, due to the key managerial roles played by the hired technicians and the still shallow knowledge base of VGC, foreign hired technicians were likely to effect changes in the way things were being done, as shown in the case of Chaparral Steel (Leonard-Barton, 1995a:17). They were empowered to apply their knowledge to the firm, therefore the tacit knowledge held by those hired personnel was also reasonably shared. After the 1970s, the conditions conducive to sharing the knowledge held by new hired personnel changed. VGC had already built up internal knowledge that had to be taken into account and integrated with external knowledge. In addition the managerial role of new hired technicians was weaker and so they were not empowered as hired people had been in the former period. VGC had built up a more complete and specialized organizational structure and only hired technicians for specific knowledge areas. These factors made the sharing of external knowledge more difficult. Hired experts participated in certain developments with VGC personnel, however they could not change essentially the existing ways of doing things. Therefore this mechanism was more efficient at increasing the number of personnel with knowledge in the firm than in contributing to learning at the organizational level.

In the case of the meetings to analyze experiences, they have been used as a learning mechanism since the 1950s to varying degrees. However no explicit organizational arrangements were established to facilitate feedback from Dirtec and Fama to the plants. VGC invested in this learning activity, but took no steps to increase the efficiency of the mechanism. The material presented at the technical meetings is contained in the conference proceedings and resides in technical staff offices. The quality of the material has increased over time, revealing the accumulation of knowledge.[17] It seems that this mechanism has allowed the sharing of tacit knowledge and generated a certain amount of codified knowledge. However the extent to which it has been shared within VGC as a whole or whether it was only shared between the participants in the seminars is not clear. It is also unclear how much it was drawn upon to support

---

[17]   Interview with the Director of Dirtec in the 1970s and 1980s.

new development projects. Indeed no reference to these conferences proceedings was made during the description of such projects. So it appears that it has been even less fruitful as a way of increasing the existing knowledge base.

All this evidence suggests that there was an effort to nurture the learning processes at the individual level and to increase the sharing of knowledge. However the functioning of the organizational arrangements to share the knowledge was incomplete. Learning has remained basically at the level it was acquired – individual, team, plant or division – and it has been difficult to share tacit knowledge or to convert individual learning into learning at the organizational level. Therefore deliberately or not the effort to increase individual learning has been more consistent than the effort to share what has been learned.

9.3.1.2   The neglect to codify the codifiable tacit knowledge

Knowledge codification is a key activity in the conversion of individual into organizational learning because it facilitates the diffusion of information within the firm and supports the process of knowledge sharing. The efforts to codify knowledge carried out by VGC were even less intense than the efforts to share knowledge. It would be true to say that knowledge codification was neglected by the firm. A few organizational arrangements were designed to codify knowledge, such as publishing the proceedings of the meetings to analyze experiences, publishing bulletins, etc. However, as shown in Table 9.5, their functioning was also incomplete.

The case of insufficient documentation of innovation projects reveals the neglect of knowledge codification. The documentation of innovation activities started in the 1970s when these activities were more formally undertaken. During the time of Vitro-Tec the most important means of documenting improvements and developments were patents, some project records and bulletins. However there was no systematic activity. For instance the patents were not accompanied by filling in completed log-books to document the whole innovation project, as mentioned in Table 9.5. The case of the legal battle with Owens-Illinois related to the patent of the electronic control system dramatically illustrates the problems arising from neglecting the codification of knowledge (see Box 9.2).

Even in the case of standard operating procedures there was a neglect of codification of codifiable tacit knowledge – that knowledge that could and should be codified. As the firm was building up its minimum essential knowledge base there was no systematic documentation of the standard operating procedures. In the case of the operation of the equipment, VGC started recording a type of job history in the 1950s, as highlighted in Section 8.4.2. This was a very elementary documentation of the characteristics of the bottles run. However these records were neither used to plan the same type of production run nor written into operating procedures. The Upkeeps had tacit knowledge and they relied on it more than on written documents. Therefore that knowledge remained tacit and individual. During the 1970s and 1980s, even though VGC had started the Transition Process, documentation of the standard operating procedures was still not properly undertaken. It was in the 1990s, in the context of acquiring the international quality control norm ISO-9001, that this documentation was actually accomplished.

Box 9.2   How they lost a legal battle with Owens-Illinois [18]

Vitro-Tec was granted a patent for an electronic control system in 1978 (see Section 7.4.1.2). Its electronic control system included a pass-gob sensor as one of its main features. Some years later Owens-Illinois was granted a patent which included that sensor. Owens-Illinois issued an affidavit to support its claim and presented its log-book of the project. Vitro-Tec did not have records of the whole history of the project development, it had not completed a log-book. In fact there was not the routine to fill in log-books. Vitro-Tec was not able to show the process of invention and the date the sensor was developed, therefore it could not prove it was the first to invent the pass-gob sensor.

In spite of neglecting the documentation of knowledge, some codified knowledge has resulted from activities explicitly intended for other purposes, such as the training program (Catve) and the AST award.

Even though Catve was not explicitly intended to codify knowledge, it was very important in contributing to this activity. Different forms of codified knowledge were elaborated for each course module, such as a program, guides, working notebooks, videos and manuals, as described in Table 9.5 and in Section 7.4.3.1. Catve documented the technical activities in manuals. There is a manual for each area of technical knowledge, which includes approximately 90 per cent of the basic technical knowledge according to the company.[19] These manuals and other documents were developed on the basis of tacit knowledge possessed by VGC's employees and codified knowledge – designs and manuals from VGC, Owens-Illinois, Emhart Glass, etc. Therefore Catve was effective in converting tacit knowledge into codified knowledge, and also in elaborating that codified knowledge into other forms of codified

---

[18] Interviews with the Leader of the electronic system project and the Leader of Ditac's Patent Department.

[19] Interview with the present and former Leader of Catve and the Leader of the Monterrey plant's Training Center.

knowledge, following the modes of knowledge conversion proposed by Nonaka and Takeuchi (1995). This last form of knowledge conversion denotes a concern for translating foreign codified knowledge into more comprehensive codified knowledge, which could be more easily understood by the company's employees. In addition a technical library was created in the Human Resources area of each plant to provide a location for the course modules. Personnel had easy access to this part of the organizational memory of VGC. However the extent to which this technical library was used was not made clear during the interviews.

The 'AST award' implemented by the Vitro-Group was designed specifically to reward a better performance. It was also directed to identifying the best practices in the firm. To be able to participate plants have to change some ways of doing things and have to document their activities. Therefore the 'AST award' increased the documentation activity within VGC.[20]

Even though Catve and the 'AST award' stimulated the conversion from tacit into codified knowledge, it was for a different reason. It seems that the generation of an important amount of codified knowledge was not considered to be an important by-product. Therefore there were no efforts made to update that codified knowledge.

The evidence presented so far has revealed that the codification of knowledge was neglected from the early days. The existence of codified knowledge was not perceived as a requirement to enrich the performance of different activities. As in the case of the sharing of knowledge, the functioning of a few organizational arrangements oriented to strengthening the codification of knowledge was incomplete. Therefore knowledge remained essentially tacit and codifiable tacit knowledge remained non-codified.

This neglect of knowledge codification also affected the sharing of tacit knowledge. Tacit knowledge is difficult to transmit, so to be shared it has to be firstly converted in some form of codified knowledge. The sharing of tacit knowledge, therefore, became a more difficult task that contributed to the limited conversion of individual into organizational learning observed during 1970–93.

9.3.2 Difficulties in Increasing the Conversion of Individual into Organizational Learning: From 1994 On

The company began to recognize the limited conversion of individual into organizational learning and by 1994 had put in place several new and very specific organizational arrangements explicitly designed to try to overcome the problems and increase the sharing and codification of knowledge. This

---

[20] Interview with the Director of Dirtec.

book analyzes them in considerable detail in terms of 'how they actually worked'. The main characteristics are described below.

The methodology used was first to identify the new organizational arrangements through interviews with Dirtec's managers, and second to evaluate how those organizational arrangements actually worked through interviews with a broad range of lower level personnel directly involved in development projects. The evidence obtained from lower level Dirtec personnel and plant employees revealed significant differences between some of the newly established organizational arrangements and the actual ways of doing things. Table 9.6 presents the new organizational arrangements designed to share and codify knowledge by 1994 and the actual practices, or the way that the work got done.

Some of the organizational arrangements were explicitly designed to share knowledge, for instance the cross-division teamwork for project development, and the procedures to communicate to Dirtec failures experienced and changes in the equipment carried out by the plants. Others were designed to increase the knowledge codification and also to contribute to the knowledge sharing, such as filling in log-books and publishing bulletins.

However, as illustrated in Table 9.6, there was a difference between 'how things should be done' according to the official organizational arrangements and 'how things were actually being done'. The new prescribed practices were not fully working as revealed by the failures to complete log-books, the irregularity in publishing the bulletins, or the omission of plants to communicate failures experienced and changes to the equipment carried out by themselves. In these cases, as in others, the old practices persisted and coexisted with the new ones. For instance by 1994 a new organizational arrangement was established to allow the knowledge acquired from visiting competitors' facilities to be shared: Dirtec's technical staff who visited competitors' facilities were required to write a report. The written reports were kept by the Technology Management Department. This mechanism was explicitly designed to codify what was learned as a way to facilitate the sharing of knowledge. However interviews revealed that most of Dirtec's technical staff did not routinely read the reports to look for information. Actually it was found that only two of the 70 technical staff routinely read the reports.[21] In addition many plant personnel also visited competitors' facilities but they did not have the experience or the skills to write a report. In relation to the log-books, even though Dirtec's technical staff knew they ought to document the projects because this was included as part of their job description, they did not have the time to do so. This time restriction became particularly intense in the 1990s due to the focus on the day-to-day running of the business and on increasing the operational efficiency. The codification of the knowledge was seen as the last and least

---

[21] Interview with Dirtec's technical staff.

Table 9.6 New organizational arrangements and the actual practices, 1994–7

Learning mechanisms	New organizational arrangements	How they actually worked
From internal sources		
R&D activities	• Log-books have to be completed • Cross-division teamwork for project development	• Log-books are not regularly filled in • The award system rewards individual plants and discourages cross-plant and cross-divisional teamwork
Teamwork at the plant level	• A prize was established to reward projects of continuous improvement • Experimentation is allowed for continuous improvement	• Overstocking of projects and difficulties in selecting the best ideas to be standardized or for being further developed by Dirtec
Monitoring plants's experiences	• Procedures to communicate to Dirtec failures experienced and changes in the equipment carried out by the plants • Manuals of the operating procedures which were required to be filled in	• Plants did not communicate unless they could not solve the problem • The award to continuous improvement teams encourage plants to keep and develop their ideas instead of communicating them to Dirtec • The manuals of the operating procedures were filled in to get the ISO 9001 certification, they do not include innovation related activities
Bulletins	• Four bulletins were published by Dirtec	• They are not printed regularly
From external sources		
Purchase of equipment	• Collaborative technological developments	• Little organizational support to promote projects of collaboration
Visits to competitors' facilities	• Written reports on the results	• Two out of 70 staff usually read the reports
Acquiring firms	• Infrastructure of communication between subsidiaries • Exchange of visits • Technical assistance and Consultations	• Recognition of some areas of Vitro's expertise as a by-product • Slow process of interaction

Source:
Own analysis of information from interviews.

important stage of project development which resulted in a continuous lag of codifying the development and results of the projects.

Regardless of the setting up of new organizational arrangements to share and codify the knowledge and to increase the conversion of individual into organizational learning, this conversion remained limited. Analysis of the differences between the established organizational arrangements (how things should be done) and how they actually worked illustrates the difficulties of incorporating new practices and radically changing the way of doing things. It reveals the rigidities of firm's behavior and the difficulty of changing this behavior described by organizational theorists and the innovation theory.[22] The old practices of a little sharing and codifying of knowledge still persisted and coexisted with the new ones, resulting in a limited conversion of individual into organizational learning.

The methodology used to evaluate how the learning mechanisms and organizational arrangements actually worked allows identification of the differences between the formality and the reality in the firm. Formality is how things should be done according to the new organizational arrangements and the new practices, while the reality is how things actually were. When managers were asked to identify the importance of the learning mechanisms by completing a questionnaire and assessing their importance with a number, they answered according to the formality. The reality revealed the persistence of old practices. The questionnaires were completed during the first week of field work in the firm. However the assessment of the learning mechanisms obtained from the managers during this first week should be modified according to the evaluation of the actual practices based on the interviews carried out over a month with a range of lower level personnel. Table 9.7 presents a manager's assessment based on the questionnaire and an assessment of the direction of the change based on the interviews.[23] The direction of the arrows reveals the direction of the change in the manager's assessment based on the reality. The number of arrows reveals the intensity of the change. For instance R&D was considered a very important mechanism and was evaluated with the maximum score of a (5) by the manager. However, as already mentioned, some of the new organizational arrangements established to support these activities and increase the sharing and codifying knowledge were not functioning, for instance log-books were not periodically filled in and the award system rewarded individual plants and discouraged cross-plant and cross-division teamwork. Therefore R&D was more efficient as a mechanism for individual learning

---

[22] See for instance Cohen and Sproull (1996), Levitt and March (1988), Nelson and Winter (1982) and Dodgson (1993).

[23] There were few differences between the assessments of different managers of Dirtec. The analysis is based on the assessment of the highest-level manager.

than as a way to learn at the organizational level. For this reason the manager's assessment of R&D as a very important learning mechanism should be significantly reduced, hence the assessment based on the reality presents two arrows down in the table.

Table 9.7 Comparative assessment of the learning mechanisms based on the manager's viewpoint and 'how things actually worked'

Learning mechanisms	Manager's assessment based on the formality (1st week)	Assessment based on the reality (a month)
R&D	5	↓↓
Meetings to analyze experiences	4	↓↓
Training	4	↑
Bulletins	4	↓↓
Licensing agreements	5	↓
Hiring personnel	4	↓
Visits to competitors' facilities	5	↓↓
Acquiring firms	4	↑↑

Note:
1= not important, 5 = very important
Source:
Questionnaire to a manager and own analysis of information from interviews.

The difference between formality and reality was also referred to by Argyris and Schön (1978, quoted by Dodgson, 1993:389), who argued that there is a gap between actors's rationalized statements of what they do and what actually occurs in the firm. Those differences observed in the firm denote that the new organizational arrangements did not work properly and that old and new practices coexisted. The coexistence of different practices was also associated with the existence of a dual technology strategy that characterizes the condition of being a firm in a Transition Process, as analyzed in Section 10.3.

The existence of differences between formality and reality suggests some issues related to the research design in firms of this type. While a short visit to the firm revealed the type of learning mechanisms formally used and the established organizational arrangements, a very detailed analysis was required to obtain an understanding of how they actually worked (see Box 9.3).

Box 9.3   Organizational arrangements and actual practices:
Implications for the research design

In the first week of my field work I obtained an assessment of the importance of the learning mechanisms by managers of different Dirtec Departments. That assessment was mainly based on: (i) the type of learning mechanisms used, (ii) the established organizational arrangements, and (iii) how things have to be done. However the interviews with a broad range of lower level personnel, directly involved in development projects, gave a different picture of how they actually worked. This result suggests that when interviewed, managers answered according to the established organizational arrangements and 'how things should be done', including the organizational arrangements recently set up or in process of implementation. This is the picture that I received in the first week in the firm. But the actual behavior was predominantly based on the old way of doing things, which were clearly revealed by the stories of project development told by different team members.

The difference between formality and reality suggests that it is not easy to understand what is really going on inside the firm. There is a mix of old and new practices which makes the evaluation of the firm's behavior difficult. This evidence has a methodological impact in terms of reliance on the information obtained from this firm, for instance: (i) To what extent do interviews with managers or high level technical staff allow us to identify how things are actually being done?, (ii) How long does a visit to a company have to be in order to understand what is really going on? and (iii) How much narrower does the focus have to be if you have only a short time available?

Even though this situation is a characteristic of VGC, it is likely to be prevalent in other firms in a Transition Process. Moreover, the evidence obtained in AGCC – a firm with a slow follower technology strategy – revealed that this situation is not unusual. Actually there is a world-wide diffusion of information about the best practices, the Japanese way of doing things, new theories of organizational learning, etc. Firms receive this information and try to implement at least some practical recommendations, without combining them with their actual practices, resulting in the prevalence of old practices and in a mix of learning practices. This feature suggests that the description of VGC presented here may be a more general problem.

To sum up, one of the research questions was to identify the extent to which individual learning was transformed into organizational learning. The first step was simply trying to identify the extent to which this happened. The answer was that it did not happen very much. Both the sharing and codifying of knowledge were weak, therefore the conversion of individual into organizational learning was limited. This is associated with the emphasis that VGC put on supporting individual learning and with its difficulties in changing the old way of doing things. Even though new organizational arrangements to learn were established in the 1990s to increase the sharing and codifying knowledge, they have not been very successful in changing the way of doing things. This has affected the creation of knowledge and the building of strategic capabilities and so has contributed to the limited success in completing the Transition Process. Some factors that influenced the limited conversion are analyzed in Chapter 10.

9.4 DIFFERENT LEARNING STRATEGIES AND LIMITED COORDINATION OF LEARNING

Organizations have different learning processes on-going. The organizational units pursue different learning strategies so, as Dodgson (1993:388) asserted, they apply different levels and direction of resources to learning and they learn at different rates. As a result the knowledge accumulated by areas is different and, in some sense, it has to be different because an organization has different requirements of knowledge. However, as referred to in Section 3.3, organizations have to coordinate their learning processes in some way to be able to integrate the knowledge across organizational boundaries and build strategic capabilities.

A feature of the knowledge management system at VGC is that there were considerable differences across the organization in learning strategies and there were few attempts to coordinate those different approaches to learning. The purpose of this section is to analyze this feature.

The differences in the learning strategies by organizational units were not dramatic during the time that VGC was building up its minimum essential knowledge base. On the one side, the knowledge possessed by different organizational units within VGC and within the Vitro-Group was shallow and roughly the same. On the other, the Vitro-Group was not a large and complex organization nor did it have rigid organizational boundaries. The learning strategies pursued by the organizational units were similar, or it could even be said that there was one global learning strategy. However as the Vitro-Group expanded its business and increased its base of knowledge it became a larger and more complex organization, as did VGC, and significant differences in the learning strategies pursued by the organizational units arose. In particular once VGC started the Transition Process more complex innovation activities were undertaken by certain organizational units, as described in Section 7.4, which required coordination of learning activities across departments, units, business-functions and divisions.

The main differences of the learning strategies across Vitro-Tec, Dirtec, Fama and VGC's plants during the Transition Process are presented below. The analysis focuses on two issues: (i) the different aims of their learning strategies according to the organization of the technology function and the attempts to coordinate these strategies; and (ii) the obstacles to success due to the role played by the divisions.

1. Different aims of the learning strategies within Vitro-Tec, Dirtec, Fama and VGC's plants

The process of building the minimum essential knowledge base was accompanied by a process of knowledge specialization. For instance, Fama emerged in the 1940s as a result of the knowledge already accumulated in design engineering, and then specialized in design engineering and machine manufacturing, as highlighted in Section 6.2.3. As a result of the technological capabilities already accumulated, a formal organization of the technology function was set up in 1977 at the Vitro-Group level. This established a division of labor between Vitro-Tec, Dirtec, Fama and the plants, with different aims, as described in Section 7.3. Vitro-Tec was in charge of the R&D activities and was predominantly oriented to strategic projects (80 per cent of its technical staff's time), Dirtec was primarily oriented to short-term projects using traditional approaches and sources of knowledge (80 per cent of its technical staff's time), Fama was in charge of the machine related knowledge and the plants kept operations running and focused on continuous improvements.

Even though the aims of the learning strategies of these units were different, each played a specific role in the organization of the technology function. Therefore there was an attempt to coordinate the learning strategies between organizational units. However these coordinated learning strategies were modified by the divisions, so significant differences emerged and the coordination was actually limited, as analyzed below.

2. Pressures to change the learning strategies by the divisions and limited coordination

The organizational units related to the innovation activities in glass containers were located in different divisions. Dirtec and the plants were located at VGC while Vitro-Tec and Fama were in other divisions, as Table 9.8 summarizes.

Divisions at the Vitro-Group had some degree of autonomy to make technology related decisions. Some divisions were more keen to pursue a 'technologically independent'[24] strategy and sought to build strategic capabilities based on R&D activities, such as Vitro-Basic Industries. Others, who followed more closely a fast follower technology strategy, sought to build other types of technological capabilities, such as VGC. The different perceptions of the divisions and their technology strategies changed the aims of the actual learning strategies pursued by the organizational units and affected the intensity of the effort to follow those related to the organization of the technology function. The impact of the divisions on the behavior of each organizational units is analyzed below.

Table 9.8   Divisions where the organizational units were located, 1970–90s

Organizational unit	Location: 1970-90	Location: 1990s
Dirtec	VGC	VGC
Vitro-Tec	Vitro-Basic Industries	—
Fama	Vitro-Basic Industries	Vitro-Packaging
Plants	VGC	VGC

VGC, Dirtec and plants

In spite of the role assigned to Dirtec according to the organization of the technology function and the aims of its learning strategy, there were some biases associated with the technology strategy more supported by VGC. The Divisional President of VGC from the early 1970s until 1986, and later the CEO of the Vitro-Group, took the view that the division had to be a fast follower of Owens-Illinois. Hence Dirtec had to be oriented to supporting that technology strategy. Dirtec had to focus on projects basically oriented to assuring effective transfer of the Owens-Illinois technology, supporting the reduction of costs, solving the day-to-day problems and increasing operational efficiency. Dirtec was closer to the plants and less interested in development activities than was expected. Most of the projects had a shorter horizon than had been envisaged by the organization of the technology function,[25] as highlighted in Section

---

[24] As referred to in footnote 2 of Chapter 6, a number of managers used the phrase 'technologically independent' which meant trying to innovate and develop technology in certain areas, leading them to the international technological frontier, while continuing to purchase equipment and technology in other areas.

[25] Interview with the two Directors of Vitro-Tec.

7.3. Plants were only concentrated in the operation and continuous improvement projects. In the 1990s, due to the new organization of the technology function, Dirtec formally assumed the more formal R&D activities previously assigned to Vitro-Tec. However Dirtec did not significantly change the aims of the learning strategy established by its division and so the strategic projects in glass containers were reduced.

Even though Dirtec was under a certain amount of pressure to undertake strategic projects, the pressures from VGC to be oriented to the short-term were more powerful than those from the technology function.

Vitro-Basic Industries, Fama and Vitro-Tec

Fama was in charge of the design and manufacture of the equipment and from the outset carried out activities geared towards improvements. Very early on it also produced a major incremental innovation – the paste mold machine to make glassware products – which was patented, as described in Box 6.2. From the 1970s the Unit of Technological Research was more focused on development activities in relation to what was expected according to the organization of the technology function. Fama was located at the Vitro-Basic Industries Division. This division – which produced the machinery, equipment and raw materials – along with other divisions and certain other Vitro-Group's top managers had the ambition to convert VGC and the Vitro-Group into a 'technologically independent' company. The technology strategy favored by Vitro-Basic Industries helps to explain why Fama showed a more long-term innovation focus than Dirtec and the plants. Vitro-Tec had the same bias as Fama but in this case towards more research than had been expected. It was only interested in strategic projects. It acted as a R&D laboratory quite isolated from the production side.

Therefore Vitro-Tec, Dirtec, Fama and the plants followed different learning strategies. These strategies were also different in relation to the organization of the technology function. The intensity of their efforts to learn were different and so they learned at different speeds. The coordination of the learning strategies was limited. The bias of the units generated by the technology strategies of the divisions affected the interaction between them, generated misunderstandings and limited the integration and creation of knowledge. As a result Dirtec and the plants were slower in their learning about certain technical-functions and in some knowledge fields than Vitro-Tec and Fama, but were faster in other areas, resulting in their achieving a different and unrelated depth of knowledge. There was also an uneven depth of knowledge between Dirtec and the plants, which was discussed in Section 9.2.1.

Fama's learning strategy was closer to Vitro-Tec than to Dirtec and the plants. This meant there were differences in the learning strategies between

Fama and its main clients – the plants. In the 1990s as the plants were required to produce dramatic rises in efficiency and product quality there was more interaction and coordination of activities.[26] Fama was more oriented to plant requirements and plants were more demanding.

The following examples illustrate the difference in the aims of learning between the organizational units. The expectations in relation to the Technical Agreement signed with Owens-Illinois in 1974 were different between organizational units. This agreement was regarded by some units and technical staff as a source of knowledge to nurture the process of knowledge creation, and a means to maintain a continuous benchmarking to improve in-house developments. However for others it was just the main source of ready-made technology. Another example is related to the way of approaching the reduction in energy consumption, which was one of the guidelines in the 1980s. VGC approached this issue from the point of view of reducing waste and asked for solutions. This meant that the issue was addressed as an engineering problem. However Vitro-Tec was not interested in carrying out R&D merely to speed up the incorporation of the latest improvements made by Owens-Illinois or to undertake minor improvements. On the contrary Vitro-Tec wanted to develop strategic projects. Vitro-Tec, therefore, took the strategic approach by looking for different sources of energy or changes in the use of energy.[27] These differences generated a disconnection between VGC's needs and Vitro-Tec's ambitions and caused misunderstandings between them.

To sum up, the learning strategies were highly diversified across the firm. The organization of the technology function revealed an attempt to coordinate the learning strategies between units. However the organizational units did not strictly follow the learning strategy established in the organization of the technology function. Their aims were more influenced by the divisions they belonged to. This resulted in significant differences between the learning strategies of units and a limited coordination of learning which in turn affected the creation of knowledge and the effective building of strategic capabilities, contributing to the failure to complete the Transition Process.

9.5   LIMITED KNOWLEDGE INTEGRATION

Knowledge integration was found to be an important basis for building strategic capabilities by the strategic management literature reviewed in Section 3.3. The knowledge specialization process determines that each organizational unit accumulates different knowledge bases or different specialisms within the same

---

[26] Interview with the Manager of Fama's Process Engineering Department.
[27] Interview with the Director of Vitro-Tec during 1977–87.

knowledge base, so it is necessary to integrate knowledge across units to strengthen the knowledge creation process and be able to build strategic capabilities. The main purpose of this section is to analyze the scope of the knowledge integration process and the existence of links between organizational units.

VGC has followed a long process of knowledge specialization and the organizational units are rather specialized. However there is limited integration of knowledge between VGC and other divisions of the Vitro-Group, between plants, between different business-functions, between organizational units within the technology function and even between Dirtec's departments. The process of knowledge specialization has been quicker than the process of building bridges between the specialized organizational units.

For instance Dirtec had problems in coordinating the activities of improvement and development if they involved areas of knowledge assigned to different departments. Due to its knowledge specialization, the Advanced Machinery Department's responsibility finished when a new development – a kit or a new equipment – was installed in a plant. After that the Process Engineering or Technology Transfer Departments took over responsibility. Thus there was a break in the information flow, with little sharing of information and integration of knowledge between departments.[28] This problem was exacerbated when it was necessary to coordinate across business-functions, such as between technology and production or technology and marketing. The case of coupling new plunger mechanisms with molding equipment from different technology sources, described in Box 9.4 below illustrates this issue.

What this case revealed was that knowledge, technical-functions and responsibilities inside Dirtec and within VGC were rigidly distributed across organizational units. The activity of coupling different technologies required the coordination of activities and the integration of knowledge across organizational units, but no-one in the organization had been assigned this function. The cross-function and cross-discipline teamwork undertaken since 1994 to integrate knowledge was the only way to solve the problem. However due to the limited practice of integrating knowledge, the lack of bridges between the organizational units and a highly isolated way of doing things it took four years to actually coordinate the activities and find the solution to the problems, which had surfaced in the Guadalajara plant in 1992, but in fact had been hidden since 1988.

Another example of the limited knowledge integration is related to the different specialization in mechanical engineering between VGC and Fama. VGC specialized in the operation of the machines and in undertaking continuous improvements, and Fama was responsible for their design and manufacture. Instead of integrating the knowledge related to this field to improve significantly the design, each organizational unit had been specialized and there had been

---

[28] Interview with Dirtec's technical staff from several departments.

little interaction between them.[29] Even though they had to interact in order to discuss the machine specifications, install the machines, solve certain operational problems and undertake small improvements, the interaction and knowledge integration oriented to carry out substantial improvements of the equipment was infrequent. This limited the creation of knowledge in mechanical engineering, a rather weak knowledge base in spite of being a vertically integrated company as analyzed in Section 9.2.2. Actually the knowledge boundaries of the firm in equipment are narrower than the production boundaries, as argued in Section 10.3.3.

Even Vitro-Tec, which was more concerned with supporting the knowledge creation process, undertook uneven efforts to integrate knowledge across organizational boundaries. On the one side, it established some cross-function and cross-discipline teams for this purpose, such as in the case of the development of the electronic control system described in Section 7.4.1.2. On the other side, Vitro-Tec was focused on R&D activities and put little emphasis on the links with the production side. It did not yield much in terms of business; actually very few developments were taken into the market. Sometimes the problem was that VGC and other divisions had not undertaken any previous market research for the development projects. On other occasions, this problem was related to Vitro-Tec's focus on strategic R&D activities and its lack of commitment and organizational arrangements to link these activities to the market. The weak links between R&D and production required specific efforts to build bridges, but this issue was not adequately tackled. This was not a distinctive problem of VGC, as referred to in Section 3.3, other large innovative firms also experienced difficulties in linking the activities of R&D and production.[30]

Since 1994 the firm has recognized its limited knowledge integration and has made some attempts to overcome this. At the Dirtec level the team for coupling the plunger mechanism with the molding equipment is an example. At the group level, in 1996 Ditac led an exercise across the divisions looking for the areas of strength and of potential synergy within the Vitro-Group to support the knowledge creation process. Some areas were identified as embryonic strategic capabilities and commitments to support processes of knowledge integration were established. In the case of glass composition, a cross-division team was established and meets every month, as highlighted in Section 8.4.1. The cross-function and cross-discipline teams have been the main integrative mechanisms used occasionally in the past and reinforced recently. However neither overlapping problem solving, redundancy of knowledge, integrators or other integrative mechanisms listed in Table 3.2 – that were used by several firms to facilitate the knowledge integration – nor other firm-

[29] Interview with technical staff of Dirtec and Fama.
[30] See for instance Rothwell (1977) and Cooper (1988).

specific mechanisms for the same purpose were referred to in the interviews about development projects.

Box 9.4   Weak knowledge integration: Coupling plunger mechanisms with molding equipment

The introduction of new plunger mechanisms from Toyo Glass in 1988 and Owens-Illinois in 1990, without any change in the Maul's molding equipment, resulted in bad performance due to a deficient coupling of different technologies. From 1988 plants were experiencing problems without identifying their origin. They were applying different types of short-term solutions to the problems but not consulting Dirtec. In 1992 the Guadalajara plant was experiencing a very low 'pack to melt' ratio of 60 to 70 per cent. Many containers had defects, such as blur and choked neck, which the plant had not been able to solve. Dirtec was called in and a team was put in charge of looking for the origin of the problem and for a solution to it. The problem was found to be a failure in coupling the plunger mechanisms with the molding equipment. The Dirtec team realized that one of the obstacles to early identification of the origin of the problems was that there were different perceptions of those problems.
1. The Operation Manager (plant) presented the problems in terms of the final result and he asserted that they could not form the finish of the containers, therefore the glass forming process must be at fault.
2. The Molding Leader (plant) considered that the forming process was right because they were using the standard measures indicated by Central Design (Marketing-function).
3. The IS Machines Leader (plant) indicated that the installed machines followed the specifications of the manufacturer given by Dirtec (Technology-function).[31]
However those areas were using a different technology base to support their perceptions. Central Design was using Maul-Fama technology for molding and a container design adapted to Owens-Illinois. The IS machines area, particularly for the plunger mechanism, was using basically Owens-Illinois technology or Toyo/Owens-Illinois. Even though each area independently was right, jointly they were wrong. For a finish of 2.625″, the plunger's constant is of 2.312″ according to Maul's molding, while there were 3 or 4 Owens-Illinois's plunger constants, depending on the plunger diameter, determining several different guide-plunger-finish packages.[32] Central Design's wrong assumption that all plants had the same molding and guide-plunger-finish package meant that each plant had to make adjustments to get a reasonable operational efficiency.

One of the main difficulties in identifying and solving problems of coupling different technologies was that they were located in the intersection of different knowledge specialisms. To solve this type of problem it was necessary to coordinate the activities undertaken by all the units involved and integrate knowledge across business functions. From 1994 Dirtec set up multidisciplinary teams including members from Central Design, plants, and from its Process Engineering and Transfer of Technology Departments, that then had the ability to discover the origin of many of the problems.[33] Another dimension of the project related to the continuous upgrading of equipment and the limited time to learn and codify knowledge is analyzed in Box 10.1.

---

[31] Dirtec, internal document.
[32] Dirtec, internal document.

These experiences, although positive, were isolated cases of knowledge integration. They confronted a long tradition of working separately, the existence of barriers to coordinate the activities across organizational boundaries and little support from top and middle-level management for processes of knowledge integration. The inability to recognize the need and potential of the coordination of activities and integration of knowledge was not unique to VGC. As Mitchell (1986) points out referring to large innovative firms, even though the linkages and synergy may be understood by the technical areas, it is unlikely to be recognized across all management levels.

Following Tidd, Bessant and Pavitt (1997:65), the effort to develop specialized knowledge in VGC was higher than the effort to exploit this knowledge through integrating it across organizational boundaries. This depends on specific actions of knowledge management to strengthen the bridges – which were limited – to facilitate the integration of the knowledge.

To sum up, VGC did not build the capability to integrate internal knowledge, which was found by several authors to be a crucial aspect of building strategic capabilities, or even a strategic capability *per se*.[34] Indeed the knowledge integration process was limited and the efforts to increase this process were still incipient. This has weakened the knowledge creation process and the building of strategic capabilities in the areas where embryonic strategic capabilities have emerged, and in doing so has contributed to explaining the truncated Transition Process.

9.6   INSTABILITY IN THE KNOWLEDGE CREATION PROCESS

The building up of strategic capabilities is a gradual process that takes time. It requires the existence of a clear purpose, a corporate-wide understanding that it is a long-term goal and organizational support. Knowledge creation is a critical process involved in building strategic capabilities that also requires time, stability and persistent organizational support. The main purpose of this section is to analyze the stability of the knowledge creation process in the main areas of accumulation.

The description of the process of knowledge accumulation since the firm started the Transition Process, presented in Sections 7.4, 8.3 and 8.4.1, revealed five main areas of knowledge accumulation that can be considered as embryonic strategic capabilities: glass composition, electronic control systems, the management of Job Change, process engineering and investment project

---

[33]   Interview with the manager of Dirtec's Process Engineering Department.

[34]   See for instance Clark and Fujimoto (1991), Henderson (1994) and Iansiti and Clark (1994).

management.[35] The description also showed that the directions of knowledge accumulation and the intensity of the effort to create knowledge in each area changed over time. The five main areas of knowledge accumulation and the three main changes in the direction of this process during the Transition Process are presented in Table 9.9. The number of arrows represents the intensity of the organizational effort to create knowledge in each area by period. This assessment was based on the description presented in the sections referred to above.

Table 9.9 Changes in the direction of the knowledge accumulation

Areas of knowledge accumulation	1970–90	1990–3	1994–6
Electronic control systems	↑↑↑↑	↑	↑↑
Glass composition	↑↑↑↑	↑	↑↑
Job changes	↑	↑↑↑	↑↑↑↑
Process engineering	↑↑	↑↑↑	↑↑↑
Investment projects management	↑↑	↑↑	↑↑↑

Source:
Own analysis of information from interviews.

This table illustrates the changes in the direction of knowledge accumulation. In each period the main directions were different. From 1970 to 1990 the main areas of knowledge accumulation were electronic control and glass composition. As highlighted in Section 7.4, the organization of the technology function, the strengthening of the R&D activities, and a number of learning mechanisms and organizational arrangements to learn were set up in that period, all contributed to strengthening the knowledge creation process and to building embryonic strategic capabilities in those areas. For this reason the assessment of these two areas has four arrows in this period. On the other hand, the accumulation in the other areas was based more on the practical experience of Dirtec and plants, therefore the assessment of the intensity of effort to create knowledge was considered lower.

---

[35] There are two other emerging areas of accumulation in the middle of the 1990s that still were not at the stage of embryonic strategic capabilities by 1996. They were related to the Samurai and the 'Enhanced Value Finisher' projects. Both projects have a strong customer orientation.

At the beginning of the 1990s there was a change in the direction of accumulation towards the more practical areas of Job Changes, process engineering and investment project management. These areas were more consistent with the new emphasis of the technology strategy in this period towards increasing operational efficiency in the short-term. The main technological upgrading projects of Dirtec supported these embryonic strategic capabilities. However there was a general contraction of the applied research activities and the development activities were driven by minor improvements. For this reason the assessment of these areas increased but has only two or three arrows. Accumulation in the areas of glass composition and electronic control systems practically stopped, keeping only minor improvements to avoid obsolescence, as described in Section 8.3.2. Hence the assessment is reflected in only one arrow.

From 1994 the most practical areas remain the main directions of knowledge accumulation. Actually knowledge accumulation in the areas of Job Changes and investment project management was further strengthened, therefore the assessment presents more arrows than in the beginning of the 1990s. Process engineering remains with the same assessment due to the fact that there were weaknesses in this area, particularly in coupling equipment technologies as analyzed in Boxes 9.1 and 9.4. The old directions of knowledge accumulation were reconsidered as relevant areas and new efforts started to be undertaken through the identification of areas of strengths and potential synergy, as described in Section 8.4.1. Hence the assessment presents more arrows than in the former period however, due to the incipient character of the efforts, it contains only two arrows.

Table 9.9 also illustrates that the evolution of the organizational effort to support the knowledge creation process by area was uneven. In the cases of Job Changes, process engineering and investment projects management there was a steady increase of the effort over the three periods. However in the cases of electronic control and glass composition the intensity of the effort over the three periods was basically unstable. An intense organizational effort to support the knowledge creation process was undertaken from 1970 to 1990, during 1990–3 the knowledge creation process was practically stopped and from 1994 there was an incipient increase of effort.

The main changes and the most unstable evolution occurred in the knowledge fields that required more formal R&D activities – electronic control and glass composition.

This instability was associated with changes in the organization of the technology function and the effective support of the R&D activities. The story of the development of an electronic control system for the IS machines, described in Box 9.5 below, illustrates the instability of the knowledge creation process in this specific field.

Box 9.5   The vicissitudes of the accumulation in electronic control knowledge

The electronic control project described in Section 7.4.1.2 is an example of the Vitro-Group's creating knowledge in a new field – electronics. The project followed a devious process of implementation with changing organizational support.

1. The project started as a hidden project at Fama in the early 1970s with little organizational support.
2. The project received organizational support in the late 1970s. During the 1980s it was transferred to Vitro-Tec and a team was formally constituted, knowledge existing in different organizational units was integrated (e.g. from Vitro-Tec, Fama, Dirtec and the plants), different knowledge fields were integrated (e.g. electronics and mechanical engineering) and different projects were joined (e.g. the electronic control and the 90 degree push-out mechanism projects). As a result a family of products was developed (e.g. Vitro II-A, Vitro III-A, an electronic push-out mechanism and an electronic gob distributor), some patents were granted and the knowledge accumulated was applied to other areas (e.g. furnace controls, feeder controls, and decoration and annealed furnace controls).
3. By 1990, when Vitro-Tec was decentralized to the divisions and the R&D activities were weakened, the project was stopped. It was supposed to progress towards the Vitro IV model – a self-controlled electronic control – which could not be accomplished. In the 1990s only minor improvements were undertaken to the Vitro III-A model to avoid obsolescence of the control system and to introduce some plant requirements (e.g. adding an automatic rejecter of hot bottles, and new programs to freeze the finish, to freeze the preform and to freeze the bottles).[36]
4. Since 1995 at the level of VGC, and since 1996 at the Vitro-Group level, electronic control knowledge was recognized as an embryonic strategic capability. The need to increase the organizational support of R&D activities in this field was again considered.

As this example illustrates, the development of the project was not a straightforward process. It was not approached as a strategic project over the whole period closely following the path of the R&D activities. The organizational support was unstable as was the knowledge creation process in electronics.

The more practical areas – Job Changes, process engineering and investment projects management – were less affected by those factors. Their increased importance over the three periods of time reveals their independence of the changes in the organization of the technology function and of strategic R&D

---

[36] Interview with the project leader and the Manager of Dirtec's Electronic Technology Department.

activities. This is also the result of the new focus of VGC in the 1990s towards increasing operational efficiency and reducing costs.

The shifts in the direction of the knowledge accumulation from the 1970s and the non-existence of a gradual process of knowledge creation in the areas more closely related to the more formal R&D activities affected the process of building strategic capabilities in glass composition and the electronic control systems. That process requires a long term purpose and a steady support. However being a firm in a Transition Process – a very fragile stage – VGC has been exposed to pressures to accumulate knowledge in different directions, which has affected its knowledge creation process in these two areas. In fact the process has been essentially unstable. This instability also affected accumulation in the more practically based embryonic strategic capabilities, because the knowledge creation process in these areas could be strengthened as a by-product of the accumulation in glass composition and electronic control systems. The instability of the dual technology strategy is a key factor in explaining the instability of the knowledge creation process, as analyzed in detail in Section 10.3.4.

9.7   CONCLUSIONS

Strategic capabilities are based on the ability to create new knowledge and integrate it with the already existing knowledge base. The management of knowledge plays a crucial role in building up strategic capabilities. Several processes, such as the conversion of individual into organizational learning, the coordination of the learning processes, and the integration of knowledge, are considered relevant, as referred to in Sections 3.2 and 3.3. All of these contribute to strengthen the knowledge creation process, which is the basis for building up strategic capabilities.

The evidence presented in this chapter has revealed some features of the knowledge management at VGC that are not in line with the type of behavior expected according to the SML. Even though they are on-going processes in the firm, their scope is still limited. The conversion of individual into organizational learning is limited, there are different learning strategies and a limited coordination of learning, the knowledge integration across organizational boundaries is limited and the knowledge creation process has been unstable. Even though these features of the knowledge management contributed to building embryonic strategic capabilities in electronic control systems, glass composition, process engineering, investment projects management and Job Changes, they have undoubtedly affected the building of strategic capabilities over these embryonic strategic capabilities. Therefore they contribute to explaining the failure to complete the Transition Process.

1. The limited conversion of individual into organizational learning is based on the weaknesses of the process of sharing and codifying the knowledge. The weaknesses in sharing knowledge are associated with the stress VGC put on supporting individual learning. The neglect to codify knowledge over the years contributes to explaining why codifiable tacit knowledge remains non-codified. The weak knowledge codification has furthered the limited sharing. Even though new organizational arrangements were established in the 1990s to facilitate the sharing and codifying of knowledge, they have not been very successful in changing the way of doing things in the firm. The differences observed between formality and reality in firm's behavior denoted that the new organizational arrangements did not work properly and that old and new practices coexist. As a result knowledge basically remained at the level of when it was acquired – individual, team or plant level – and the organizational learning was limited.

2. Knowledge specialization comes alongside the knowledge accumulation process. As the knowledge was being specialized, the learning path followed by each knowledge field, technical area and technical-function was closely related to the direction and speed of the learning processes of the organizational units in charge of it. The differences in the learning strategies between the organizational units increased from the 1970s when VGC started the Transition Process. The evidence revealed that Vitro-Tec, Dirtec, Fama and the plants followed different learning strategies and learned at different speeds. Some units were enthusiastic to pursue a fast follower strategy, while others followed more closely a 'technologically independent' strategy. Hence they created and accumulated knowledge of a different nature and depth. Even though the organization of the technology function revealed an attempt to coordinate the learning strategies between units, actually such coordination was limited and the learning strategies of the units were basically driven by the divisions they belonged to. That weakened the efforts to build strategic capabilities. The existence of distinct learning strategies followed by different organizational units within the firm is an issue barely analyzed by the SML. In particular the problems arising from those differences and the way of dealing with them is not approached by the firm-level research, even though it is an important fact that affects the knowledge creation activities and the building of strategic capabilities. In that sense the evidence provided by the VGC's case contributes to setting some of its characteristics.

3. The evidence has revealed that VGC experienced difficulties in integrating the knowledge internally across organizational boundaries, such as business-function, plant and department; it also found it difficult to

integrate knowledge with other divisions of the Vitro-Group to look for potential synergy. The bridges between units to facilitate the knowledge integration are indeed very weak, which affects the knowledge creation process and the building of strategic capabilities. Knowledge specialization with little concern for creating strong bridges to integrate the knowledge generated results in a fragmentation of the knowledge existing within the firm. Even though VGC extended its production boundaries and acquired different plants and a machine manufacturing firm, it seems that its knowledge boundaries were less extended than its vertical production boundaries.

The limited integration of knowledge across organizational boundaries, along with the difficulty in sharing what was learned from external sources of knowledge, reveals that VGC has neither built the capability for internal integration nor for external integration referred to in certain SML.[37]

4. The embryonic strategic capabilities were based on five main areas of knowledge accumulation. The evidence shows that there have been continuous shifts in the direction of the accumulation and in the intensity of the effort to create knowledge in each area. This has resulted in a highly unstable knowledge creation process in each area, which has affected the accumulation in specific directions and reduced the potentiality to build strategic capabilities. The instability was higher in glass composition and electronic control systems, two embryonic strategic capabilities closely related to the more formal R&D activities. This instability also affected the accumulation in the more practically based embryonic strategic capabilities, which were nurtured as a by-product of that process.

5. Unevenness in the depth of knowledge accumulated by technical-function and by knowledge field is a characteristic of VGC. Moreover the stock of common knowledge that each organizational unit is required to have to be able to integrate knowledge between different units is also uneven, even in the main areas of knowledge accumulation. All this unevenness is a symptom of the non-existence of strategic capabilities and the truncated Transition Process. The four features of the knowledge management contributed to that result.

VGC built embryonic strategic capabilities as a result of learning to move from operating to innovating (vertical movements up the y-axis in Figure 2.2) as described by the DCL, and by combining different knowledge bases looking

---

[37] See for instance Clark and Fujimoto (1991), Henderson (1994), and Iansiti and Clark (1994).

for building more complex ones (horizontal movements along the x-axis) as referred to by the SML. However this later movement has been incipient and incomplete. The process of knowledge specialization in VGC overcame the pace of the changes in the management to promote organizational learning, coordinate the learning processes and integrate the knowledge across organizational units. The characteristics of the management and the way of doing things have continued to be based on individuals instead of on a coordinated way of working. Even though there were some attempts to change this behavior, VGC found it difficult to change its way of doing things. The features of the knowledge management were significant in weakening the knowledge accumulation, resulting in building only embryonic strategic capabilities and failing to convert them into strategic capabilities. The inability to perceive knowledge as a system and the instability of the dual technology strategy influenced the knowledge management and furthered the difficulties encountered to build strategic capabilities to distinguish the firm competitively, as analyzed in Chapter 10.

10 Factors Influencing the Knowledge Management Features

10.1 INTRODUCTION

Ever since VGC began the Transition Process to building strategic capabilities in the 1970s, the technology strategy pursued has been characterized by duality and instability. The duality was associated with the fact that the firm pursued two technology strategies in parallel. It sought to be 'technologically independent'[1] and build strategic capabilities. At the same time it pursued a fast follower strategy. Both strategies were supported by decisions taken by the top management and received organizational support. The instability was related to the fact that the organizational support for each strategy was unstable over the whole period. The Transition Process has two poles and VGC took decisions directed towards these different poles, which reinforced one strategy in relation to the other. This instability affected the aims and efforts to manage knowledge over time, therefore this is a factor that influenced the features of the knowledge management.

The features of the knowledge management were also influenced by the lack of consideration and management of knowledge as a system. In particular when VGC undertook more efforts to manage knowledge to build strategic capabilities, it lacked a systemic view to articulate mechanisms, organizational arrangements and processes. Several mechanisms, organizational arrangements and practices were established and a number of processes were encouraged without being articulated. The lack of interrelatedness happened at the level of the organizational units, which worked quite independently of each other.

The inability to perceive and manage knowledge as a system and the instability of the dual technology strategy were factors that influenced the knowledge management. The purpose of this chapter is to analyze the extent to which those

---

[1] As referred to in footnote 2 of Chapter 6, this phrase meant trying to innovate and develop technology in certain areas, leading them to the international technological frontier, while continuing to purchase equipment and technology in other areas.

factors affected the knowledge management features and then furthered the difficulties to build strategic capabilities and accomplish the Transition Process.

Section 10.2 discusses the extent to which, and how, the non-perception of knowledge as a system affected the conversion of individual into organizational learning, the coordination of learning strategies, the integration of knowledge across organizational boundaries and the knowledge creation process. Section 10.3 discusses the effects of the instability of the dual technology strategy. Finally Section 10.4 presents some conclusions.

10.2 THE NON-PERCEPTION OF KNOWLEDGE AS A SYSTEM

As described in Section 2.3, a strategic capability is increasingly seen as an interdependent knowledge system. As Leonard-Barton (1992a and 1995a) has pointed out, this system includes different dimensions such as employee knowledge and skills, technical systems, managerial systems and values and norms in the organization. Each of these dimensions is a subsystem that has to be internally consistent. Along the same lines as described in Section 3.2, a learning organization has to carry out a number of learning activities. Each activity has to be deliberately managed as a system, which includes a mind-set, a set of mechanisms and a pattern of behavior according to Garvin (1993). Therefore a systemic approach to knowledge is at the base of building strategic capabilities.

The meaning of a knowledge system and its interrelatedness between different practices and mechanisms is revealed by the effect of the same practice in two different knowledge systems. One characteristic of a learning organization described by Leonard-Barton (1995a:10) is that everybody participates in the problem solving and does not wait for the specialist, as practiced by personnel at Chaparral Steel. However in the context of a different knowledge system, such as VGC, that behavior does not help because it generates lack of standardization and unfitness in the production line. As highlighted in the case of coupling the plunger mechanism with the molding equipment in Box 10.1 below, sometimes a plant's own solution increased the problems and made it more difficult to overcome them. Therefore individual mechanisms introduced in other contexts do not necessarily work because knowledge is a system. As Teece and Pisano (1994:550) mentioned, 'few routines are 'stand-alone'; coherence may require that a change in one set of routines ... requires changes in some other'. Therefore the whole set of learning mechanisms, organizational arrangements and routines have to be considered as a system that has to be articulated.

Drawing on this approach, the characteristics of the management of knowledge were analyzed to identify the extent to which VGC had such a systemic view. VGC made several attempts to manage knowledge to build strategic capabilities. It took several decisions, implemented organizational arrangements and encouraged learning mechanisms oriented to strengthen the conversion of individual into organizational learning, the coordination of learning strategies, the integration of knowledge and the knowledge creation process. However each decision, activity and process was viewed on its own, without taking into account the interrelationships between them. For instance VGC continually changed its equipment when looking to introduce the latest technology, without changing skills, knowledge and ways of doing things at the pace that generated imbalances. In that sense it is argued that VGC did not manage knowledge as a system.

This section discusses the extent to which not perceiving knowledge as a system has influenced the features of knowledge management analyzed in Chapter 9, and furthered the difficulties in building strategic capabilities. Detailed arguments of how this factor affected each of the key features are analyzed below.

10.2.1 Effect on the Conversion of Individual into Organizational Learning

Knowledge not being considered as a system has influenced the conversion of individual into organizational learning and contributed to explaining why this conversion is limited. Two arguments will be analyzed: (i) the lack of internal coherence of the efforts for sharing knowledge; and (ii) the failure to consider all the dimensions of the equipment upgrading, particularly the learning dimension.

Lack of internal coherence of the knowledge sharing efforts

As analyzed in Section 9.3, the firm has used several learning mechanisms and has set up a number of organizational arrangements explicitly designed to assist learning, which individually have contributed to the sharing and codifying of knowledge. However it has been less aware of the differences between the individual and organizational dimensions of the learning processes, and of the positive or negative impact of the organizational arrangements not designed for learning over the sharing of knowledge.

The learning mechanisms and organizational arrangements for learning listed in Tables 9.5 and 9.6 were explicitly designed for learning and were managed deliberately. Each was oriented to a specific goal, however their significance in the process of conversion of individual into organizational learning is not straightforward. Some of them have positively influenced the sharing of knowledge, either at the plant or at the firm level, and only a few have had a broad impact on sharing knowledge. However there were other organizational arrangements not explicitly designed for learning which have had either a positive or a negative impact on the sharing of knowledge and therefore on the conversion of individual into organizational learning. Some cases identified during the interviews are listed in Table 10.1 below and their impact on the sharing of knowledge is marked. An arrow up represents a positive effect and an arrow down represents a negative impact on sharing knowledge. The assessment is based on the description of the process of building up technological capabilities presented in Chapters 6, 7 and 8 and draws on the analysis presented in Section 9.3.

The results presented in this table reveal the different effects of the learning mechanisms and organizational arrangements on the sharing of knowledge. There is some coherence within the learning mechanisms and organizational arrangements that were explicitly designed for learning. They were directed to sharing the existing knowledge at the plant or at the firm level, and each one has generated a positive result as the up arrows illustrate.[2] For instance the meetings to analyze experiences were undertaken by personnel from different units, including Dirtec and all the plants, allowing knowledge sharing at both levels as illustrated by the up arrows. The teams for continuous improvements were organized at the plant level and the results had little diffusion across the firm. So this mechanism only facilitated the sharing at the plant level. The log-books were oriented to increase the knowledge codification to support the sharing at the firm level, as the arrow up indicates. Only the 'Award for the continuous improvement projects' had contradictory impacts at the firm level, as illustrated in Table 10.2 and analyzed below. However, although all of them individually contributed to knowledge sharing, there was no clear articulation between all the mechanisms and organizational arrangements explicitly designed to improve learning to ensure the spread of the knowledge within the firm. It is not clear that they stimulated and facilitated the sharing of knowledge across different knowledge bases, organizational units and activities of the firm. Additionally this result requires consideration of the interrelationships between the different elements, which were not taken into account. Actually the stress was put on individual learning as analyzed in Section 9.3.

However a major problem is associated with certain organizational arrangements designed for other purposes, which have had either a positive or a negative impact on the sharing of knowledge. The case of the diary report of the 'pack to melt' ratio illustrates this issue. Each day plants have to report to the Director of Operations the efficiency reached the previous day. Each job change, color change, breakdown of the machine or any other interruption in

---

2   Here I am not considering the extent to which the organizational arrangements actually work. This issue was analyzed in Section 9.3.

the line affects the daily performance. This report requirement has pressured plants to be focused on how to assure the best performance in a short time, and how to solve problems that appear each day.[3] To do this they must share knowledge at the plant level to solve problems, which explains the arrow up. For instance if there is a machine breakdown, the priority is for them to be able to start up the line or the machine section by themselves. If the solution, whatever it is, does not generate further problems Dirtec is not informed about the changes made to the machine, so knowledge is not shared at the firm level which explains the arrow down. Only if problems do arise Dirtec is called in. Additionally the plants are more interested in supporting continuous improvement projects undertaken by themselves, which have a rapid impact on the operational efficiency level, rather than in participating in long-term development projects headed by Dirtec.[4] This also explains the arrow down of the diary report of the 'pack to melt' ratio at the firm level. Therefore the diary report of the 'pack to melt' ratio is an organizational arrangement not designed for learning which has empowered the indicators of efficiency over other plants's behavior associated with learning. Even though it contributes to the sharing of knowledge at plant level, it negatively affects the sharing of knowledge within the plants.

Table 10.1 suggests that there are interrelations between different dimensions of the firm's activities, which affect the sharing of knowledge. Therefore it is necessary to approach knowledge as a system to capture the nature and scope of all the learning mechanisms and organizational arrangements that either purposely or not affect the processes of sharing the knowledge.

The case of the awards illustrates the lack of a systemic approach to analyzing all the dimensions that affect the sharing of knowledge.[5] Even though there had been some sporadic awards to stimulate innovation activity, it was only at the end of the 1980s when a more organized set of awards came into being. Certain new prizes were established and were directed to different aims. The 'Technological Development Annual Award' was established in 1991 'to stimulate the creative and innovative efforts of the personnel'.[6] The 'Adrián Sada Treviño (AST) award' was created in 1989 and came into operation in 1991. This is an integral quality award which covers a broader range of issues than the international quality control norm ISO-9001.[7] Vitro-Group established an annual competition and a prize. In order to compete plants were required to complete a very broad and qualitative questionnaire. Plants had to present

---

[3] Interviews with Dirtec's technical staff and plant personnel.
[4] Interviews with Dirtec's technical staff.
[5] The award system can be considered as one managerial system in the framework proposed by Leonard-Barton (1995a). It is part of the incentive system.
[6] Vitro S.A. (1991:60).
[7] Interview with the General Manager of the AGCC's Elmira plant.

their performance and describe the mechanisms developed to achieving it. The 'AST award' has offered considerable potential for the provision of stimuli to increase operational efficiency, codify the knowledge and diffuse the company's values. It has contributed to the identification of the best organizational practices within VGC. Finally the 'Award for the continuous improvement projects' has been directed to stimulating the activity of the teams. It has also been an incentive to document the many small improvements identified by plants. Even though the three awards cover different aspects of the innovation related activities, their effect on sharing knowledge is contradictory. Some awards have had both positive and negative impacts on the effectiveness of other organizational arrangements to learn in relation to sharing and codifying knowledge, as described in Table 10.2.

Table 10.1   Contradictory impact of learning mechanisms and organizational arrangements on the sharing of knowledge

Learning mechanisms and organizational arrangements	Designed for learning	Designed for other purposes	Impact on knowledge sharing	
			Plant level	Firm level
Meetings to analyze experiences	✓		↑	↑
Monitoring the plants's experiences	✓			↑
Bulletins	✓			↑
Log-books	✓			↑
Teamwork for project development	✓			↑
Teams for continuos improvement	✓		↑	
Training, particularly Catve	✓		↑	↑
Continuous improvement's award	✓		↑	↓↑
Technological development's award	✓			↑
AST award		✓	↑	↑↓
Rotation of personnel		✓		↑
Engage relatives		✓		↑
Diary report of the 'pack to melt'		✓	↑	↓
Policies to increase standardization		✓		↑
Organizational changes		✓	↑	↓

Source:
Own analysis of information from interviews.

For instance while the 'Technological Development Annual Award' rewards teamwork for project development as the arrow up illustrates, the 'AST award' and the 'Award for the continuous improvement projects' discourage cross-plant or cross-division teamwork for project development as the arrows down indicate. Therefore even though teamwork for project development has a positive effect on sharing knowledge at the firm level as can be seen in Table 10.1, its final effect is weakened by the influence of those awards.

Table 10.2   Contradictory impact of the awards on certain organizational arrangements

	Award for continuous improvements	AST award	Technological Development Award
Meetings to analyze experiences	↓	↓	↑
Monitoring the plants experiences	↓	↓	
Teamwork for project development	↓	↓	↑
Teams for continuous improvement	↑	↑	
Documentation	↑	↑	↑

Source:
Own analysis of information from interviews.

In relation to the effect of the 'AST award', whilst workshops for transferring the best practices related to the management model were carried out at the Vitro-Group level as a result of the 'AST award', the sharing of knowledge was less encouraged. The 'AST award' has been more efficient in stimulating the increase of the operational efficiency than in identifying and diffusing the best organizational practices related to innovation activities within the Vitro-Group and within VGC. This award promotes competition rather than interaction between plants, so it negatively affects some mechanisms and organizational arrangements more oriented to sharing the knowledge, such as meetings to analyze experiences or monitoring plants experiences as the arrows down show. In fact it has weakened any positive effects of them on the sharing of knowledge indicated in Table 10.1. The 'Award for the continuous improvement projects', in stimulating plants to carry out projects by themselves, operates in the same direction.

In general the awards have encouraged individual work rather than work by groups, and interaction inside one plant instead of knowledge sharing and synergy within VGC, and even less within the whole Vitro-Group. There is no other powerful organizational arrangement that compensates for the negative impact of these awards on the sharing of knowledge. It seems that the awards do not conform to a system directed to a broad objective, instead they appear to be a set of awards that rewards different activities.

The evidence presented so far suggests that knowledge was not perceived as a system. There has been no coordination of the organizational arrangements that explicitly or implicitly affect the sharing of knowledge. Moreover there are some organizational arrangements which have affected the sharing of knowledge in different directions. Particularly important are those that being designed for other purposes have had either positive or negative impacts on the organizational arrangements that were explicitly designed for learning and should have had a positive effect on the sharing of knowledge. Some of these have been very powerful in the 1990s due to their relationship with the technology strategy focused on increasing the operational efficiency. Although it is difficult to avoid contradictory effects, the whole set of organizational arrangements could be managed in a more coherent way to increase the limited conversion of individual into organizational learning.

The failure to consider all the dimensions of the equipment upgrading

The failure to manage the frequency of changes in the equipment, by not taking into account the learning dimension associated with those changes, is other evidence of knowledge not being considered as a system.

A common view of the firm has been to identify technology with equipment and follow a sort of 'hardware' technology strategy. Such a view considers that technological accumulation involved continuous introduction of new machines and complementary equipment. Because VGC has been concerned with the state-of-the-art, it sought out the best equipment technology, acquired the machines and the complementary equipment and continuously upgraded them to keep pace with the technological frontier. However introducing the latest equipment neither masters the equipment technology nor changes the way of doing things to get better performance from the equipment. This requires specific learning efforts. In addition each new machine or complementary piece of equipment needed to be understood and adapted to the equipment technologies still in operation, which also requires learning efforts. These are the learning dimensions of technological upgrading that demanded an understanding of the technology as knowledge, management of the knowledge and consideration of the interrelations between the different dimensions of the knowledge system.

VGC has managed to keep pace with the technological frontier by upgrading equipment. However personnel have not had time to understand and dominate one technology before they were forced to deal with a new equipment technology.[8] The firm has not taken into account that each equipment upgrading or technology change has required learning activities associated with the understanding of new codified knowledge, upgrading the former codified knowledge and also acquiring new tacit knowledge. Therefore the firm has not managed the frequency of the changes in a structured way.

The case of the introduction of the NNPB process of double cavity illustrates this issue. Since 1988 there have been many upgrades of the IS machines for the introduction of the NNPB technology. These upgradings have necessitated intensive work to understand and adapt different equipment technologies, and also to update the codified knowledge existent in the firm. The problems confronting the team involved are described in Box 10.1 below.

Box 10.1 reveals the frequency of upgrading, some of the problems generated, the need for learning associated with each upgrading and the lack of understanding by VGC's management of that dimension. Each upgrading of equipment was basically managed as an isolated incident without evaluating the other activities required to support it. Due to the frequency of the changes, the firm did not have time to properly understand the changes and learn from them, particularly because of lacking a deliberate purpose and organizational support to do it.

The way of managing the frequency of changes in the equipment without taking into account the learning dimension associated with those changes affected the conversion of individual into organizational learning. Learning remained at the individual level and codifiable tacit knowledge was not codified. The inability to consider knowledge as a system is at the basis of that way of upgrading. It furthered the limited conversion of individual into organizational learning analyzed in Section 9.3. VGC also failed to understand the learning dimension of the R&D activities, as analyzed in Section 10.2.3.

The learning dimension of the upgrading was only given consideration in the 1990s with the introduction of the NNPB triple cavity technology of Owens-Illinois. The introduction of this technology received more organizational support than any other and specific learning efforts were undertaken to prepare for its introduction. As described in Section 8.2.2, managers from Dirtec and the plants implemented certain actions to internalize external tacit knowledge to accelerate the assimilation, such as sending personnel to receive training and acquire experience in operation, maintenance and job changes. This change in the firm's behavior related to the NNPB triple cavity technology is still very restricted. The extent to which this change will become general behavior is still too early to be assessed.

---

[8]   Interviews with Dirtec's technical staff.

---

*Box 10.1   Continuous equipment upgrading and lag in learning and
            knowledge codification*

By 1988 VGC was using Maul's molding, and Owens-Illinois's and Maul/Fama's plunger
mechanism. It was interested in adapting its IS machines for the introduction of the
NNPB double cavity technology to produce lightweight containers. It bought a Toyo
Glass's NNPB machine, five sets of Toyo Glass's plunger mechanisms for the NNPB process
to fix in its already installed machines, and the detailed engineering of the NNPB technology
to be able to manufacture the machines. Toyo Glass had 'improved' Owens-Illinois
technology. Dirtec and Fama worked on the adaptation of the Toyo Glass's plunger
mechanisms and NNPB technology to the Maul's molding. This work of adaptation changed
some characteristics of the equipment, which became Toyo Glass/Vitro; required an
understanding of imbalances generated; and demanded an update of Toyo's designs.[9] By
1990, when Dirtec's technical staff was still working to solve the problems generated by
the introduction of Toyo's NNPB technology, VGC decided to use Owens-Illinois as the
main source of technology. New Owens-Illinois's plunger mechanisms were introduced
into some already installed machines. The molding equipment remained basically Maul,
and they slowly started to change it to an Owens-Illinois base. New mechanisms had to be
understood, new problems of coupling were generated and new acquired designs had to
be adjusted to couple different equipment technologies.[10]

   These changes to the equipment technology were accomplished in a shorter time than
were the understanding of them and finding solutions to the problems generated by them.
The work of coupling was usually carried out as a simple adaptation with no time to learn
about the new equipment. Plants were informed by memorandum about the measures that
had to be taken when using each new plunger mechanism. However there were many different
mechanisms, which generated different types of imbalances and required different changes.
Plants had many defects in the containers and were applying different type of solutions to
the problems, including modifications to their equipment, which were neither reported
to Dirtec nor incorporated in the designs.[11] Therefore new imbalances were being generated.
In 1992 when the Guadalajara plant was not able to solve the defects Dirtec was called in.
As described in Box 9.4, the origin of the defects was found to be a failure to couple
different technology basis. The diagnosis revealed that 58 per cent of the machines installed
in all the plants were affected by this problem.[12]

   By 1996, even though they had progressed, the adaptation of all the machines and
processes was still not finished. They controlled the coupling in the Blow-Blow process
and had accomplished 80 per cent of its installation. They had the solution for the Press-
Blow process and had completed 20 per cent of its installation. They did not start the NNPB
process. Once a general solution was found the project did not receive further funding from
VGC and the technical staff were re-assigned to other projects. The designs had not been
updated, the documentation of the project was still incomplete and the understanding of
the solutions to all the problems had not been reached.[13] However these dimensions of the
upgrading were not taken into account by top management. As a result the limited
understanding remained as individual learning of the team members. Dirtec had to support
the continuation of this project with resources from the Samurai project.[14]

---

[9]   Interview with the project leader.
[10] Ibid.
[11] Ibid.
[12] Dirtec, internal document.
[13] Interview with the project leader.
[14] Interview with the Director of Dirtec.

To sum up, the lack of internal coherence between all the learning mechanisms and organizational arrangements that affect the learning processes, and the failure to consider the learning dimension of the equipment upgrading suggest that VGC has not managed knowledge as a system. Even though the firm has made some efforts to intensify the processes of sharing and codifying the knowledge, strengthen the learning processes and be technologically updated, not considering the interrelationships between different organizational arrangements, learning mechanisms and the existing tacit and codified knowledge has affected the scope of the sharing of knowledge, the knowledge codification and so the scope of conversion of individual into organizational learning.

10.2.2 Effect on the Coordination of Learning and Integration of Knowledge

The non-perception and management of knowledge as a system has influenced the coordination of learning and integration of knowledge and goes to explaining why the extent of these processes has been limited.

The organization of the technology function set at the end of the 1970s reflected an attempt to look at the technology function as a system and to coordinate the learning processes. Each unit played a different role covering different aspects of the innovation activities. The different learning strategies were supposed to be articulated. As described in Section 9.4, the coordination was limited. The divisions pursued different technology strategies or put emphasis on different targets, which affected the learning strategies of their organizational units.

Divisions were interested in their businesses without perceiving the interrelation between their activities and the activities of other divisions, particularly in technology-related activities. However even though the divisions were defined as product-divisions, there are several interrelations associated with: (i) the vertical integration; and (ii) the technology-related diversification followed by the Vitro-Group. As the exercise carried out by Ditac (Direction of Technology of the Vitro-Group from 1990) in 1996 revealed, there are a number of common knowledge bases between several divisions, such as melting (furnace design and maintenance), glass composition, glass forming, decorating and electronic control of the processes, as described in Section 8.4.1. This exercise was the base for re-examining the Vitro-Group as a knowledge system, as Vitro-Tec and the organization of the technology function did during the 1980s. The success of this new effort depends again on the extent to which the divisions perceive themselves as being part of such a system.

So far, knowledge has not been managed consistently as a system. The learning strategies within the Vitro-Group have differed and the coordination of learning has been limited. As a result divisions have continued to work rather independently.

Knowledge not being perceived as a system is the basis of the limited concern to build strong bridges between different organizational units to facilitate the integration of knowledge. Some attempts to integrate knowledge were analyzed in Section 9.5. Cross-function and cross-discipline teamwork was the main integrative mechanism that began to be used, besides informal communication networks. This was one of the integrative mechanisms listed in Table 3.2 that was found to be powerful in facilitating the integration of knowledge across organizational boundaries in a number of firms. Cross-function and cross-discipline teamwork were useful ways of dealing with the problems associated with the introduction of the new plunger mechanism in VGC, described in Boxes 9.4 and 10.1, and revealed the potential of such mechanisms. Although there were also other experiences of teamwork, they had very little impact on the way things were done. There was no tradition of cross-boundary teamwork within units and within the organization as a whole, and the successful experiences were insufficient to radically change how learning was organized within the firm. Although a 'Technological Development Annual Award' was established to reward teamwork in project development, teamwork was not perceived as part of a set of interrelated mechanisms pushing in the same direction to generate processes of knowledge integration. It was oriented to solving specific problems and sometimes the results were rewarded. As in the case of the learning mechanisms and organizational arrangements for learning, the integrative mechanisms worked in isolation. The potential for teamwork to facilitate knowledge integration between different organizational units, functions and disciplines was unevenly recognized because interrelations of the knowledge system were not recognized. Another factor that affected the potentiality of teamwork was the instability of the technology strategy, as analyzed in Section 10.3.1.

In general VGC has failed to build strong bridges between the organizational units undertaking a project and either the end users or those units likely to be involved in further stages of the project. They also failed to forge consistent links with units that could contribute to increasing knowledge in a specific area. Instead of integrating knowledge, the links between the uneven organizational units resulted in a transfer of technology from one to the other, as the case of the links between Fama and VGC illustrates. The direction of the transfer of technology between Fama and VGC has changed over time depending on the depth of the knowledge achieved by each unit, the learning strategies and the location of the design capabilities inside the Vitro-Group. The transfer was from VGC to Fama until the 1960s, then up to 1990 it went from Fama to VGC, and in the present decade it has again been from VGC to Fama.

To sum up, the failure to perceive and manage knowledge as a system is one of the reasons for the limited coordination of learning and the limited knowledge integration.

10.2.3 Effect on the Stability of the Knowledge Creation Process

The evolution of the knowledge creation process has been affected by the perception of R&D activities only as generators of innovations. For this reason R&D activities were only related to the technology strategy of being 'technologically independent'. The learning dimension of the R&D activities was not recognized, which weakened the support for these activities and therefore of the knowledge creation process. This perception of the R&D activities is again a result of the failure to consider knowledge as a system.

As referred to in Section 3.2, Cohen and Levinthal (1989:569) pointed out that whilst firms can generate innovations from R&D activities, they also learn through such activities and enhance their ability to identify, assimilate and exploit the existing knowledge. Along the same lines Tidd, Bessant and Pavitt (1997:184) pointed out that the learning accumulated through long-term R&D projects may be useful to developing innovations in the future. This learning dimension of R&D activities is more difficult to identify and assess and was neglected by both firms and the literature until the late 1980s.

In the case of VGC, learning that resulted from R&D activities seems to have been more important than the generation of major innovations. Fama and Vitro-Tec developed certain innovations and were granted a number of patents. Those innovations were mainly improvements and adaptations to the designs of world technology leaders and only a few were more significant innovations.[15] The patents granted, referred to in Section 7.4.1.1, were not licensed so VGC did not obtain any direct economic benefits from these innovations. Thus R&D activities as generators of world-level innovations or as generators of economic benefits were not very successful. However VGC introduced these in-house improvements and made adaptations to the equipment installed in its own plants and contributed to improving the performance of the equipment. Unfortunately it is difficult to measure the economic impact of these activities and to identify how much any increase in the performance of one production line is associated with a specific improvement in one piece of equipment.[16] The electronic control system was certainly a significant innovation and was introduced in all the plants after 1990. Its economic benefit was more easily measurable because it was a complete piece of equipment. However it took a

---

[15] Interview with technical staff from Ditac's Patents Department and Dirtec's Advanced Engineering Department.
[16] Interview with the Manager of Dirtec's Process Engineering Department.

long time for the economic results to be appropriated because although the project was initiated in the early 1970s, manufacture and diffusion within the plants started only in 1990, as described in Section 7.4.1.2 and discussed in Box 9.5 and Section 10.3.4. The long duration of the project reduced the appreciation of its economic benefit.

In addition the R&D activities carried out by VGC were important in terms of allowing it to speedily incorporate the new developments introduced on the market by the world technology leaders. VGC has continuously upgraded equipment to keep pace with the technological frontier. This process was accompanied by an intense activity of adapting the upgrading to meet the firm- and country-specific conditions and coupling with the equipment already installed. The adaptation and coupling of equipment was facilitated by the technological capabilities already accumulated. The R&D activities surely contributed to creating the knowledge base required and accelerated the learning processes. However this output of the R&D activities, which is not easily measured, was not recognized by top management as being of economic benefit.

The economic benefits of the R&D were also underestimated because the technology function did not build on the ability to predict and measure the cost of the developments, precisely plan the time period and estimate the profits of the projects.[17] Even the conventional project appraisal techniques, that can only be of use for some short-term projects,[18] were not fully utilized. In addition the costs of the developments were underestimated. For instance there was no budget for building prototypes, so that cost had to be included, and so hidden, in repair costs.[19] All these factors reduced the confidence of top management in the usefulness of the R&D activities as part of the knowledge system of the company.

In addition, as had been discovered in other companies, the perception of the benefits of the R&D activities differed between technology managers and the top management. The technology managers were aware of the difficulties of getting a full estimation of the economic benefits of the R&D activities. They realized that there were some dimensions of the R&D activities that could not be measured, particularly the learning accumulated.[20] This judgment reveals, though they did consider that R&D activities had a dual role. However top management evaluated R&D activities by the number and impact of patents and by the economic benefits of these activities.[21] Therefore the role of R&D activities was seen to be generators of major innovations and thus related to the technology strategy of being 'technologically independent'.

---

[17] Interview with the Director of Ditac.
[18] See for instance Mitchell and Hamilton (1988) and Tidd, Bessant and Pavitt (1997: chapter 6).
[19] Interview with a design engineer from Dirtec's Advanced Machinery Department.
[20] Interview with the Directors of Ditac and Dirtec.
[21] Interview with the Divisional President of VGC.

R&D could be also related to the fast follower strategy. Even pursuing a fast follower strategy, maintaining a defensive strategy of R&D or an imitative strategy, conducting R&D to effectively adapt the innovations to quickly catch up and being an active learning firm are key activities.[22] As Nelson and Winter (1982:124) noted, imitator firms, although not generating breakthrough inventions, can be considered to be innovators because most of the problems are really solved independently. However VGC followed a short-term version of this technology strategy, as highlighted in Section 8.1 and discussed in Section 10.3, so the R&D activities were not significant for supporting it. In addition VGC did not view minor changes as innovations. For instance the embryonic strategic capabilities based on more practical knowledge were not formally supported by R&D or recognized as being supported.

Thus although the learning resulting from R&D activities seems to be more important than the innovations and patents granted, the effect of not considering knowledge as a system contributes to explaining why this positive effect of the R&D activities was not perceived by top management. That view, in conjunction with the difficulty of presenting the R&D activities as a valuable investment, meant that R&D activities were very vulnerable to changes in support from top management and to the business and technology strategies. The resulting fragility of R&D activities adversely affected the knowledge creation process in all the embryonic strategic capabilities, and particularly influenced the instability of the knowledge creation process in these embryonic strategic capabilities based on R&D. Even in the case of the more practically based embryonic strategic capabilities, VGC lost the potential of the greater contribution that the R&D activities could have made in another context. Therefore it deepened the difficulties to build strategic capabilities, which required purposeful and sustained support.

In an attempt to overcome these weaknesses from 1996 the technology managers began to make efforts to measure the 'value of technology'. Several projects were evaluated and an approximation of the economic benefits were made. These assessments were directed towards supporting the new projects proposed to top management and obtaining from them greater technological commitment.[23]

The failure to understand the learning dimension of the R&D activities also contributes to explaining the difficulties of integrating the knowledge across organizational units, as well as the inability to systematically learn from competitors and integrate external knowledge and the failures in codification of the innovation related activities. These activities assumed less importance if the learning role of the R&D activities was not taken into account.

---

[22] Footnote 1 of Chapter 6 describes the main technology strategies.
[23] Interview with the Directors of Ditac and Dirtec.

10.3 THE INSTABILITY OF THE DUAL TECHNOLOGY STRATEGY

Since VGC started the Transition Process two technology strategies have coexisted in parallel: one directed towards being a fast follower of Owens-Illinois and the other directed to strengthening in-house developments in order to be 'technologically independent' in certain areas.[24] The former course involved converting all the plants to the original Owens-Illinois technology, avoiding any in-house developments. It was conceived as a short-term version of the fast follower strategy without any R&D activities, even those oriented to quick assimilation of technology. The second strategy was based on the idea that VGC and the Vitro-Group had already created a body of knowledge, had built some embryonic strategic capabilities and therefore should continue undertaking R&D activities in those particular areas.

Whilst both strategies coexisted in parallel, they were neither consistent nor articulated. Top management was taking simultaneous decisions related to each of these strategies, sometimes in relation to the same areas. Therefore there was never any clear decision about the direction of the knowledge accumulation in the long-term. Additionally – and even more importantly – the support for each technology strategy was not stable and at some stages one was more supported than the other, and vice versa.

The technology strategy of being 'technologically independent' has its roots in the 1940s when Fama was created. Initially the strategy had a broad focus without defining areas of specialization, and coexisted with a sort of followership strategy to introduce the new equipment launched on the international market by the technology leaders. This technology strategy has survived until today with a clearer definition of the areas where VGC wants to have technological leadership. However there have been two key ruptures in the evolution of this technology strategy. The first was in 1974 when VGC decided to sign a Technical Agreement with Owens-Illinois. This was in the context of flourishing in-house technological capabilities, looking for

---

[24] During the stage of building up the minimum essential knowledge base to survive in the market firms basically pursue a technology strategy of slow followers. After this they can pursue a fast follower strategy and remain as a close second or look to building strategic capabilities by following a leadership technology strategy. Taking the Transition Process up to the point of being an active learning fast follower can be a rational place to be for a firm from a developing country, and also for many firms from the advanced economies that are not the most innovative ones. This fast follower strategy has to be supported by R&D activities more in the role of learning than in creating innovative outputs. However VGC has enunciated a strategy of technological leadership and at times has tried to build strategic capabilities, which means that the idea of the pole of the Transition Process was to build strategic capabilities and not to be only an active learning fast follower.

different sources of knowledge, developing in-house technology and starting a Transition Process towards building strategic capabilities. However VGC had begun to export to the US and was under pressure to solve certain technical problems. The technology strategy was supposed to be unique but with different goals being articulated. On the one hand the goal was to solve some of the technical problems with the Technical Agreement and catch up with Owens-Illinois, while on the other hand the aim was to maintain in-house developments for the long-term.[25] In fact this was the origin of a fast follower technology strategy, that coexisted with the 'technologically independent' strategy and put pressure on for a deviation of the development activities promoted by this strategy. This latter strategy of achieving technological leadership was again reinforced between the end of the 1970s until the end of the 1980s. The organization of the technology function and the creation of Vitro-Tec were the main events, as described in Section 7.3.

By 1990 VGC was faced with three main pressures: (i) risky changes in the economic and technological context; (ii) pressures associated with the acquisition of AGCC and the need to update its facilities; and (iii) changes in the power inside the Vitro-Group which favored the promoters of a fast follower technology strategy. Under these conditions there was a second rupture and the technology strategy of being a fast follower of Owens-Illinois was strongly supported. An important effort was put on assimilating Owens-Illinois technology and increasing the operational efficiency and product quality. Two main facts supported that strategy, as described in Section 8.2. One was the introduction of the new Owens-Illinois's NNPB triple cavity technology with the explicit prohibition of adapting it with any in-house improvements, and the other was the decentralization of Vitro-Tec towards divisions and the discouragement of the development and improvement activities.

From 1994, but with more support from 1996, the technology strategy of becoming 'technologically independent' was again revived. However this time an attempt was made to identify the areas where technological leadership was most desirable, as described in Section 8.4.1.

An example of the coexistence of the two technology strategies can be found in Vitro-Group's mission statement for 1993 and the technology strategy stressed at that time. The fast follower technology strategy had been strengthened since 1990 but Vitro-Group's mission statement stated that they wanted to be the lowest cost producer and to have 'technological self-reliance'.[26] Whilst in order to achieve this in-house development needed to be maintained and strengthened, the conversion of the equipment to the Owens-Illinois technology required a reduction of in-house developments.

---

[25] Interviews with the two Directors of Vitro-Tec and the Director of Fama in the 1980s.
[26] Vitro SA (1993b:20).

Something that underlined the instability of the dual technology strategy was that top management did not realize that each swing in the technology strategy required a huge investment. This was particularly important when the magnitude of the installed capacities and the mix of equipment technologies made any decision to change the technology base economically difficult. Thus, management made decisions, such as to convert the equipment towards 100 per cent Owens-Illinois technology, but did not invest enough money to support the decision. The result was that the duality of the technology strategy and the mix of equipment technologies had to continue. In addition the decision to be a fast follower of Owens-Illinois did not change the technology culture and the dynamic of adaptation and development deeply rooted in VGC's behavior. Moreover VGC had a tradition of technology being important and the Board of Directors had continually approved decisions which accorded with that view.

The following example illustrates how the equipment was dealt with as a result of the dual technology strategy. In the case of the NNPB technology of triple cavity VGC pursued a fast follower technology strategy. Non-improvement was incorporated and also the electronic control system was an Owens-Illinois's Com-soc instead of the Vitro III electronic control system. In the 1990s the emphasis on this strategy was such that the decision to use Owens-Illinois technology was understood by the employees as relating to all the equipment and not only to the NNPB triple cavity technology. Everybody said 'we have to use 100 per cent Owens-Illinois technology',[27] therefore the message received by them was 'you must not adapt or improve'. However in spite of the subtle messages and actions the strategy oriented to developing the technology and the embedded routines of adapting and improving the equipment persisted. Plants, Dirtec and Fama had learned through experience that they had to adapt and improve the equipment to achieve better operation, and in the 1990s the level of operational efficiency was a crucial indicator. The comparison between the differences in the specification of two IS machines ordered by the Guatemala plant from Fama in 1992 and 1996, presented in Table 10.3, illustrates the persistence of that behavior.

The Guatemala plant placed two orders for the same basic machine – a type E 41/4inch IS machine, double cavity with eight sections. The machine supplied by Fama in 1996 incorporated 37 changes in relation to the machine acquired in 1992, most of them based on in-house improvements on the original designs. The source of the changes and some examples of them are presented in Table 10.3.

This table illustrates how in the 1990s they continued undertaking improvements to the original Owens-Illinois designs in spite of the predominance of the fast follower strategy. Only three of the 37 changes

---

[27]   Interviews with Dirtec's and Fama's technical staff and Monterrey plant's personnel.

incorporated in the new machine originated from the upgrading by Owens-Illinois of the original design provided to VGC. In contrast most of the changes were proposed and undertaken by Dirtec. They consisted of upgrading the Vitro/Owens-Illinois equipment, improvements to the Owens-Illinois's designs and improvements to Vitro's own equipment. In addition other changes, basically related to the operation of the equipment, were specified by plants and designed by Dirtec.

Table 10.3 Adaptation and improvements of an IS machine in the 1990s

Source of improvements	Number of changes	Examples of changes in the machine's specifications
Owens-Illinois	3	• Upgrading of the finish equipment • Upgrading of the invert mechanism
Dirtec	24	• Change in the gob distributor from mechanical to electrical • New locations of components and pipes of the external piping to operate the plunger • Fine adjustment in the take-out mechanism • Change in the manipulation of information of the Vitro II-A electronic control
Plants	10	• Change in the layout of the fuel oil piping of the invert mechanism • Elimination of pipes and air valves of the guards and brackets of the eight sections IS machine
Total	37	

Source:
Adapted from Fama's internal document, 1996.

The improvement activity that continued to be undertaken in the 1990s was based on the traditional strategy of adapting and developing technology. This was a characteristic strongly embedded in firm behavior which received some organizational support in this period. In addition AGCC became a new source of changes to the equipment. Therefore in spite of the message from top management to use 100 per cent Owens-Illinois technology, VGC continued to be led by two different technology strategies.

The duality of the technology strategy brought different learning strategies, set different priorities and aims, gave different messages and promoted different directions in knowledge accumulation. It put pressure on the personnel of Dirtec, Fama and the plants and reduced the effectiveness of each strategy. Personnel had to combine projects and practices related to both strategies, which reduced the focus on getting the best result from only one of them. The instability of the dual technology strategy has provoked discontinuity in on-going projects, continually changed the intensity of the effort to accumulate in each direction, and affected the potential to build up strategic capabilities and accomplish the Transition Process. The result of the instability of the dual technology strategy also affected top management's perception of the knowledge accumulated by different divisions of the Vitro-Group, which reinforced the lack of purpose to build strategic capabilities. More detailed arguments of how the instability of the dual technology strategy affected each of the features of the knowledge management are discussed below.

10.3.1 Effect on the Conversion of Individual into Organizational Learning

The instability of the dual technology strategy is a factor that has negatively influenced the conversion of individual into organizational learning. Each strategy supported different practices. On one side, the strategy of being 'technologically independent' supported a major concern to share and codify knowledge to support the knowledge creation process. On the other, the short-term version of the fast follower strategy was less concerned with sharing and codifying knowledge, or was interested in sharing and codifying other types of knowledge. The dual technology strategy nurtured the coexistence of a mix of practices. The instability of the technology strategy made it more difficult to change the way of doing things.

The instability of the technology strategy generated problems about settling the practices to share and codify knowledge during 1970–93. That instability weakened the efforts to learn at organizational level, which depended on the settling down of the practices to share and codify knowledge that had been established by 1994. The easiest way to deal with the instability was to continue the old way of doing things.

The changing interpretation of teamwork and the incomplete codification illustrate the effects of the instability of the dual technology strategy on the conversion of individual into organizational learning.

Changing meanings of teamwork

Teamwork took on a different meaning at VGC and in general at Vitro-Group over the years. This was due to the continuous changes in the support to each technology strategy, which in turn established different priorities and promoted different practices. The changes in the nature and spread of the teamwork demonstrate the effect of the instability of the technology strategy on the settling down of some practices.

Teamwork as organized by Vitro-Tec in the 1980s was closer to the meaning used in the SML. It was designed to share knowledge and increase the knowledge base in the context of the technology strategy of being 'technologically independent'. Technical staff worked in cross-function, cross-knowledge field and cross-division teams for product and process developments. Dirtec's, Fama's and plant's personnel were part of these teams. The plants supported the tests and were a source of ideas and tacit knowledge to improve the prototypes and first models. Teamwork for project development was associated with the support to carry out R&D activities and contributed to sharing knowledge at the firm level. It also facilitated the integration of knowledge across organizational boundaries to make effective use of existing knowledge and to create new knowledge. However this practice had been practically abandoned by 1990 due to the strengthening of the technology strategy of being a fast follower, the focus on efficiency, the decentralization of Vitro-Tec towards the divisions and the discouraging of R&D activities.

The idea of teamwork with a different meaning was revived by the top management in 1993. Teamwork was then seen as just working in teams.[28] The activity was explicitly oriented towards cost reduction and increased operational efficiency, which were the main aims of the technology strategy predominant at that time. The firm looked to identify the best practices and reduce duplication of activities to allow an efficient down-sizing and re-engineering process, and teamwork was oriented to that aim.[29] In this context teams were set up to work on continuous improvement to increase operational efficiency. To achieve this, knowledge had to be shared primarily at the plant level, to which these teams contributed. However, as analyzed in 10.2.1, the contribution to knowledge sharing was contradictory. The teams were made up of personnel from one particular plant with the aim of solving a specific problem and knowledge was shared basically at that level.

The renaissance by 1996-7 of the strategy to develop technology reinstated teamwork for product and process development to share and create knowledge. For instance the project set up by Ditac in 1996 to identify the areas of strength within the Vitro-Group opened the discussion about the need to organize teamwork at the Vitro-Group level in some knowledge fields to exploit synergy across divisions.[30] However this was an isolated attempt that was far from

---

[28] Vitro S.A. (1993b and 1994).
[29] Ibid.
[30] Interview with the Director of Ditac.

Learning and Knowledge Management in the Firm

successful in diffusing this practice within the firm. The meaning of teamwork mentioned above remained predominant in the 1990s.

These examples illustrate the changes in the meaning and practices of teamwork at VGC that were associated with the different emphasis in the technology strategies. Such changes generated a confusion about the nature of the practice within the firm and the aim of this activity. Even though everybody in the firm accepted this concept, there were difficulties in establishing a practice of teamwork that facilitated the sharing of knowledge and the conversion of individual into organizational learning. The successful experiences mentioned before were sporadic and had little impact on the firm's behavior.

Incomplete codification

The instability of the technology strategy affected the efforts to codify knowledge. For instance personnel were moved to different activities according to the changing emphasis of the technology strategy before accomplishing the codification of projects. As analyzed in Section 9.3, the codification activity was seen as the last and a minor stage of the project development, therefore personnel were switched to other activities or projects before they could complete documentation of the project they had been working on. This instability made it more difficult for personnel to internalize the new organizational arrangements oriented to strengthening the knowledge codification and to change their practices. This also helps to explain why although technical staff had log-books they were not filled in, as analyzed in Section 9.3.2.

The instability of the technology strategy also affected the 'organizational memory' of the firm. This 'organizational memory' is the store of knowledge of the firm and according to Huber (1996) is a key element for organizational learning. For instance the change in the location of the technology function and the discouraging of R&D activities since 1989 resulted in a discontinuity in the documentation of technology related activities. When in 1994 Dirtec implemented new organizational arrangements to increase the codification of knowledge, it found that there was a break in the organizational records. For instance it was not possible to compare the positioning exercises of the RMS carried out at the beginning of the 1980s (see Box 7.2) with the present positioning.[31] Such exercises were undertaken at the time that Dirtec was developing its own glass formula under the 'technologically independent' strategy. However they were discontinued in the late 1980s and personnel were assigned to other activities. When glass composition was reconsidered as an embryonic strategic capability and new positioning exercises began to be

---

[31] Interview with the leader of the Glass Laboratory.

supported by the renaissance of that particular technology strategy, there was an incomplete history of the evolution of this knowledge field by the main players in the international market. Therefore the instability of the technology strategy negatively influenced the limited knowledge codification.

To sum up, the instability of the technology strategy weakened the efforts to share and codify knowledge and learn at the organizational level. It increased the usual difficulties encountered in changing the way of doing things, so it has negatively influenced the settling down of those practices oriented to increasing the sharing and codifying of knowledge.

10.3.2 Effect on the Learning Strategies and the Coordination of Learning

The many changes in the technology strategy influenced the operation of the technology function, the relative importance of each organizational unit in the knowledge accumulation process, the aims of each unit to build specific abilities and the support to implement development projects. Thus the instability affected the learning strategies, furthering the difficulties to coordinate them across organizational boundaries.

In this period there were also many organizational changes directed to integrating related businesses and streamlining operations. The Vitro-Group looked for different structures to manage its glass containers operations and to ensure operational streamlining. In 1991 the glass containers operations of Mexico, the US and Central America were formally integrated into one new division named Vitro Glass Containers of North America. In 1994 the Mexican and Central American subsidiaries and the US subsidiaries separated into two structures, and in 1995 all the glass container operations were once more integrated.[32] The organizational location of the activities that provided the raw materials and capital goods also underwent many changes. All these organizational changes added to the instability of the day-to-day activities and long term projects, influenced the operation of the technology function and affected the learning strategies of the units.

The instability experienced by Fama – the organizational unit in charge of the technical-function of supplying the capital goods – dramatically illustrates those issues. There were many organizational changes that modified Fama's location in the organizational structure of the Vitro-Group, and many shifts in its market-target and in the degree of novelty of the machines that Fama had to supply. These changes were related to the instability of the dual technology strategy of VGC and affected the aims of the learning strategies, the speed of the learning processes and the depth of knowledge in this technical-function. The following Table 10.4 is a *résumé* of the most relevant changes.

---

[32] Vitro S.A. (1991, 1992, 1993a, 1994, 1995 and 1996a).

Table 10.4   Instability and shifts of Fama's learning strategy

	Changes that faced Fama	Effects on the learning strategy
Changes in the market-target	**1940s** • Satisfy VGC's and Vitro-Glassware's demand for molds and equipment to produce glass products	
	1950s-70s • Supply VGC and Vitro-Glassware • Undertake improvements and develop some in-house equipment technology	• Effort to build innovative technological capabilities, including R&D activities
	1974 • VGC decided to sign a Technical Agreement with Owens-Illinois • Fama had to manufacture and adapt the equipment to VGC specific conditions	• Effort to reproduce the Owens-Illinois's machines designs, which reduced the stress on R&D
	1980s • Supply VGC and also export all over the world	• Effort to penetrate the international market • Accumulation of knowledge from foreign clients
	1990s • Satisfy VGC's demand in Mexico and Central America and AGCC's demand • VGC decided to introduce the Owens-Illinois's NNPB process and Fama had to focus on the manufacture of that new equipment • Fama had to start the manufacture of the electronic control systems	• The knowledge accumulated from foreign clients was abandoned • Effort to reproduce the Owens-Illinois's NNPB process, so the R&D activities were stopped
Organiza-tional changes	• 1974–89: located at Vitro-Basic Industries • 1989: Fama became a division • 1991: located at Vitro-Capital Good, a new division • 1994: located at Vitro-Packaging, a new division, the engineering personnel were transferred to Dirtec • 1996: located at Vitro-Chemical, Fibers and Packaging, a new division	• Instability, which required continuous alignment to different divisional technology strategies and set different aims
Changes in Fama's size	• 1981: 2600 employees • 1982: 1500 employees • 1990–3: 36% reduction of personnel • 1994–5: 7% reduction of personnel	• Loss of skilled personnel, disintegration of teams, unlearning

Source:
Own analysis of information in Vitro's Annual Reports and several interviews with Dirtec's and Fama's technical staff.

Until the 1970s Fama was oriented to supplying VGC with machines, undertaking improvements to foreign designs and also developing some in-house equipment technology. In the 1970s VGC realized it had low productivity and Fama was experiencing some mechanical problems with the 6 inch IS machine. It was likely that Fama could have solved the problems,[33] but VGC decided to sign a Technical Agreement with Owens-Illinois, as described in Section 7.2.1. VGC argued that it produced and sold bottles and not machines and it needed to increase its productivity level.[34] It was basically a short-term decision. Fama had to reproduce the Owens-Illinois's designs, adapt them to the firm- and country-specific conditions and manufacture the machines. R&D activities were reduced because all the effort was concentrated into working on the Owens-Illinois's designs.[35]

However in the 1980s VGC's demand for machines reduced because of the Mexican crisis of 1982. Fama then had to redirect its efforts towards the international market to compensate for the contraction of the internal market. In 1987 Fama exported 40 per cent of its production. It had the opportunity to acquire knowledge from other glass container makers who were its clients. It was not allowed to incorporate this knowledge in the machines produced for the international market due to secrecy agreements. However Fama began to accumulate a stock of technological knowledge different from that of VGC.[36] VGC was able to take advantage of this newly acquired knowledge, but did not recognize its potential. At the same time that Fama was accumulating technological knowledge, VGC changed its technology strategy. The fast follower technology strategy came to fruition by 1990 and VGC decided to convert its equipment to 100 per cent Owens-Illinois technology. Fama once again had to concentrate all its efforts into reproducing the Owens-Illinois technology and its R&D activities were once again brought to a halt, as described in Sections 8.2.1 and 8.2.4. Each of these changes affected Fama's learning strategy in different directions and modified the technological links between Fama and VGC.

In addition from 1974 to 1996 Fama was located in five different divisions. These organizational changes affected not only its organizational location but meant that Fama had to align itself to different divisional strategies and aims, which necessitated continuous adaptation to changing conditions. These organizational changes were related to the search for operational streamlining at Vitro-Group level, and also to the changes of the technology strategy of VGC and the redefinition of the vertical integration strategy. Finally the

---

[33] Interview with a manager of Advanced Machinery of Dirtec's Advanced Engineering Department, the ex-Directors of Vitro-Tec and the Director of Fama.
[34] Ibid.
[35] Ibid.
[36] Interview with the Director of Fama in the 1980s.

continuing reduction in Fama personnel from 2 600 in 1981 to less than 1 000 in 1996 disintegrated teams, reduced the number of skilled workers and meant that knowledge was lost.

The instability of the dual technology strategy and all the changes that it generated greatly affected the learning strategy followed by Fama and, in fact, changed the aims and affected the speed of its learning processes. It can also be said that in this technical-function there was a process of 'unlearning'. As the case of Fama reveals, the instability of the technology strategy enlarged the differences in the learning strategies of the organizational units and influenced the ease to coordinate learning within the firm.

Behind this instability there were some power conflicts going on between the divisions that also affected the coordination of learning between Fama, Vitro-Tec, Dirtec and the plants. VGC occupied a stronger position in the Vitro-Group than did Vitro-Basic Industries or the other divisions that subsequently provided the vertical integration. Some decisions in relation to the role of Fama and Vitro-Tec seem to have been associated with retention of power and not improving operational efficiency or the existing equipment technology. An example of this is related to the decentralization of the technology function to the divisions and the elimination of Vitro-Tec, which seems to have been related to reducing the power of Vitro-Basic Industries. Unlearning in R&D activities was an unfortunate result of this decision. Another example is related to some of the changes in VGC's technology strategy that reduced the dependence of VGC on Fama, also located at Vitro-Basic Industries, even when VGC could have taken advantage of the on-going learning processes at Fama.

10.3.3 Effect on the Knowledge Integration

Different technology strategies require different strategies of R&D and demand distinct types of knowledge. The Leadership strategy is characterized by maintenance of a state-of-the-art R&D capability and building strategic capabilities. The Fast Followers strategy is characterized by maintenance of a defensive strategy of R&D or an imitative strategy, conducting R&D to effectively adapt the innovations to quickly catch up, constantly monitoring the markets and being an active learning. The Slow Follower strategy is characterized by the introduction of innovations when they are diffused and not conducting R&D. The aims and scope of the knowledge integration differ according to those technology strategies. The extent to which knowledge is actually integrated across the internal boundaries of the firm influences the extension of the knowledge boundaries over the production boundaries of the firm.

The instability of the dual technology strategy pursued by VGC influenced the efforts to carry out R&D and continually changed the aims of the knowledge integration, weakening that process. In doing so it affected the knowledge boundaries of the firm.

The glass container industry is a mature industry. The equipment innovations are crucial for the path of technical change in the industry and mechanical engineering is a key knowledge base. However there are two types of firms: (i) vertically integrated firms which also produce the equipment, such as Owens-Illinois, Heye Glas and VGC; and (ii) only glass container makers, such as AGCC, Saint Gobain and Bormioli. These two types of firms have different types of production boundaries, the former are integrated backward to producing the equipment, the latter are not. In addition there are specialized suppliers of equipment, such as Emhart Glass. The technology strategy chosen by the glass container makers is related to its production boundaries – level of vertical integration – and it strongly influences the knowledge base in mechanical engineering.

The technology leaders in the glass containers industry are Owens-Illinois and Emhart Glass. Heye Glas has leadership only in certain very specific equipment technology. Owens-Illinois has pursued a technological leadership strategy, by maintaining a state-of-the-art R&D capability and building the basis for strategic capabilities in equipment technology to compete. Its R&D activities have nurtured the knowledge base in mechanical engineering. Owens-Illinois has actively integrated its knowledge in glass container and equipment manufacture across organizational boundaries, to extend its knowledge boundaries over its production boundaries and built the basis for strategic capabilities to distinguish the firm competitively. Heye Glas on a smaller scale has followed a similar path.

Other glass container makers pursue either a slow or a fast follower technology strategy. They have to create a knowledge base in mechanical engineering according to their production boundaries and chosen technology strategy. If they are vertically integrated, they have to build innovative technological capabilities in supplying capital goods and so create a depth knowledge base in mechanical engineering. If they are only glass container makers, they still need in-house knowledge in mechanical engineering to interact with their equipment suppliers and to control their manufacturing process. However the depth of the knowledge base seems to be more related to the technology strategy than to the production boundaries. For instance Saint Gobain and Bormioli, being only glass container makers, have adopted a fast follower strategy. They have constantly monitored the markets and conducted R&D in equipment to effectively adapt the innovations in order to catch up quickly and also to improve the equipment they buy.[37] They have extended

---

[37] Interviews with the Director of Dirtec and a manager of Advanced Machinery of Dirtec's Advanced Engineering Department.

their knowledge base in mechanical engineering over their vertical production boundaries, which do not include equipment manufacture.

AGCC, in contrast, has pursued a slow follower strategy. R&D activities, and particularly with regard to applied research in mechanical engineering, have been very weak. AGCC has relied on commercial suppliers and acquired equipment basically off-the-shelf. It has had to be able to find equipment to accurately match its requirements, so it has developed the capacity to describe very accurately the specifications of the equipment. Whilst commercial suppliers try to sell, AGCC has learned how to buy according to its own requirements. Instead of requiring design capabilities, it has had to learn about and understand its processes to support its decisions about what to buy and from whom; to develop a capacity to describe the requirements of the equipment; and to develop the ability to fix the equipment acquired from different suppliers in its production lines. In addition AGCC has had to learn to be a demanding client in order to be able to operate the equipment at a reasonable level of efficiency.[38] In terms of mechanical engineering, the slow follower strategy did not demand a deeper knowledge base than that required to buy, operate and provide maintenance for the equipment.

VGC pursued two technology strategies, one of a fast follower and the other to achieve leadership in certain areas. Both strategies set different aims for the R&D activities; demanded different types of knowledge and different scope for the integration of knowledge; and required a different depth of knowledge in mechanical engineering. The instability of this dual technology strategy weakened the efforts undertaken in both directions. As a result the extension of the knowledge boundaries in relation to the production boundaries does not fit with either technology strategy. The knowledge in mechanical engineering is shallow, as analyzed in Section 9.2.

VGC is a vertically integrated company, has carried out R&D activities and has had a Technical Agreement with Owens-Illinois for more than 20 years. Although VGC does produce some equipment, the Technical Agreement has reduced the pressures for VGC to increase its mechanical design capabilities. It could consult its technology source whenever necessary. Also it has not been necessary for it to develop the skills to describe its requirements or to buy equipment because of its having one main supplier.[39] The Technical Agreement has supported the fast follower strategy, but it has reduced the pressure to carry out R&D to effectively and quickly adapt the innovations launched by Owens-Illinois. Therefore it has not been necessary to extend the

---

[38] Interviews with the Manager of the Engineering Department of AGCC's Technical Center and managers of Dirtec's Advanced Engineering Department.
[39] Interviews with the Director of Dirtec and a manager of Advanced Machinery of Dirtec's Advanced Engineering Department.

knowledge boundaries in mechanical engineering as far as the production boundaries. In fact the Technical Agreement has supported the short-term version of the fast follower technology strategy pursued by VGC. Because of its unrelatedness to more formal R&D activities, this technology strategy has not demanded knowledge integration processes to nurture the creation of new knowledge.

As a result of the 'technologically independent' strategy and by having Fama and Vitro-Tec, VGC did build certain mechanical design capabilities and carried out a number of in-house developments. This has extended the knowledge base in mechanical engineering over what is required by a glass container maker, and has required that the knowledge be integrated across organizational boundaries to contribute to the knowledge creation process in this field.

However as a result of the instability of the dual technology strategy VGC has created a base of knowledge in mechanical engineering that is essential for the firm's operation and equipment upgrading, but is still shallow. One of the results of the duality and instability of the technology strategy is the idiosyncratic equipment installed. There is no supplier that can offer machine mechanisms that precisely fit with VGC's equipment.[40] Therefore VGC has had to rely on its in-house capabilities to adapt complementary equipment to its idiosyncratic existing equipment or to update it. This has pressured VGC to keep the R&D activities, integrate knowledge across organizational boundaries to do that, as Box 9.4 illustrated, and increase its knowledge base in mechanical engineering.

Unfortunately during the Transition Process VGC has been exposed to different pressures and has not made a clear decision about its technology strategy in the long-term. It has not set out clearly 'what to buy and what to develop' and it has not been consistently either a leader or a fast follower in any area. The instability has affected any efforts to integrate knowledge, changing the type of knowledge relevant to be integrated and the intensity of effort to undertake this activity, as illustrated by the changes in the support to the projects on-going analyzed in Section 10.3.4. This has resulted in a *sui generis* mix of equipment, which it has found difficult to understand accurately and dominate, and in a shallower knowledge base in mechanical engineering than would be expected from a firm that manufactures equipment and undertakes R&D activities. Although VGC manufactures equipment, its knowledge boundaries in mechanical engineering were not as extended as its production boundaries. This reduced the possibility of building up strategic capabilities in related areas, such as Box 9.1 illustrates in the case of coupling different equipment technologies.

---

[40] Interviews with several of Dirtec's technical staff.

10.3.4 Effect on the Stability of the Knowledge Creation Process

In Section 9.6 it was argued that the instability of the knowledge creation process in the main areas of accumulation is one of the features of the knowledge management at VGC. This feature is one of the reasons for not building strategic capabilities. The instability of the dual technology strategy is a key factor in explaining the instability of the knowledge creation process. The changes in the support to projects and the failure to recognize embryonic strategic capabilities illustrate the effect of the instability of the dual technology strategy over the knowledge creation process.

Changes in the support to on-going projects

The many changes in the support for each technology strategy during the Transition Process provoked dramatic alterations in the innovation related activities, changes in the relative importance of the organizational units involved, continuous start-up and halting of the projects, modifications in the main directions of the knowledge accumulation and instability in the knowledge creation process. There has been no gradual and consistent knowledge accumulation in the main directions, as illustrated in Table 9.9. Particularly unstable has been the accumulation in the areas that were clearly related to more formal R&D activities, as analyzed in Section 9.6. The technology function has worked like the 'swing of a pendulum' following the instability of the technology strategy. Hence areas that were emerging as embryonic strategic capabilities could not develop to become strategic capabilities. Table 10.5 below presents the many shifts of development projects in the main knowledge fields and of the R&D activities, first in one direction, then the other, then back again and so on.

Table 10.5 illustrates the devious process of knowledge creation in each field associated with the changes in the stress of the technology strategies. For instance in the cases of the electronic control systems and glass composition, the projects were supported by a 'technologically independent' strategy during the 1980s. However the weakening of this strategy at the beginning of the 1990s and the strengthening of the fast follower strategy meant that these projects almost came to a stop. The reconsideration of the former strategy and the identification of these as embryonic strategic capabilities resulted in a revival of those projects by 1996–7. However when the pendulum swung back to having an interest in these areas becoming strategic, there was found to be a gap in the information, in the benchmark exercises and in the accumulation of knowledge. Therefore increased efforts were required to update the knowledge and restart the knowledge creation process. A more detailed description of the vicissitudes of the electronic control project is presented in Box 9.5.

In this way the many changes in the projects and R&D activities, generated by the instability of the technology strategy, affected the knowledge creation process and reduced the knowledge accumulation in the main directions. The potentiality to convert the embryonic strategic capabilities in strategic capabilities as a result was limited. This evolution of the embryonic strategic capabilities reveals that in the long-term there was no clear and persistent purpose to build strategic capabilities. Whilst the potentiality to do so was there, it was not exploited.

As the SML widely stressed, building what they called core competencies is a long-term process that requires continuous improvement. The continuous changes in support for the R&D activities weakened particularly the effort to create knowledge, accumulate it in the same direction and so build up strategic capabilities.

Failure to recognize the embryonic strategic capabilities

One of the most dramatic results of the instability of the dual technology strategy was that the top management had no confidence in in-house technological capabilities. As a result of decisions being taken in different directions and the direction of the knowledge accumulation being changed, it took a long time for the top management to recognize the depth of knowledge already accumulated by VGC and the whole Vitro-Group in certain areas. The instability of each technology strategy and the inconsistency in following a unique technology strategy hid the potentiality of some embryonic strategic capabilities to become strategic capabilities, and contributed to explaining some 'mistakes' involved in important technology related decisions. Box 7.1 described the first steps involved in carrying out a collaborative technological development with Heye Glas. The failure to carry on that agreement, described in Box 10.2, illustrates the issue.

This case illustrates the effect of the dual technology strategy and its instability on the recognition of the potential of certain embryonic strategic capabilities to become strategic capabilities to distinguish the firm competitively. VGC could have been the leader in the NNPB technology with Heye Glas, but it lost the opportunity.

Another example is related to the failure to identify the knowledge in electronic control systems as an embryonic strategic capability. The electronic control system developed in the 1970s was oriented to the glass forming process, instead of being only an electronic timing drum like those produced by other companies and diffused in the industry. The original idea and knowledge base that allowed the development of a different type of control were the result of designing a control system for the glassware production (see Section 7.4.1.2). The knowledge was related to the specific conditions and businesses that the Vitro-Group had at that time and the directions of the searching activities that

Table 10.5 Continuous changes in the support to the knowledge creation process, 1970–90s

Projects, activities and knowledge fields	The swing of the pendulum	
	Greater support to the 'technologically independent' strategy	Greater support to the fast follower strategy
Centralized R&D activities	• 1978–89: strengthened by the creation of Vitro-Tec and the organization of the technology function • 1996–7: thinking about 'what to buy or to develop' and having some R&D activities centralized	• 1990: decentralization of Vitro-Tec and contraction of the R&D activities
Mechanical engineering	• 1940–70: Fama accumulated knowledge • 1970s: Fama established its UIT, so it was interested in development projects • 1980s: learning from foreign customers and accumulation of knowledge • 1989: Fama developed an in-house IS machine	• 1974: Technical Agreement with Owens-Illinois, so it had to carry out efforts to reproduce foreign designs • 1990: Fama had to manufacture the Owens-Illinois's NNPB IS machines and convert the installed IS machines to the Owens-Illinois technology base, the development activities were stopped

Table 10.5 (Continued)

Electronic control systems	• Early 1970s: creation of the prior knowledge base • 1977: set the project in Vitro-Tec • 1978: the first patent was granted • 1980s: the Vitro I, II, III models were developed and several patents were granted • 1990: Fama started the manufacture of the product • 1990: stop the project and so the creation and accumulation of knowledge, the Vitro IV model was not developed • 1996–7: thinking the electronic control as an embryonic strategic capability
Glass composition	• Early 1980s: set the project in Dirtec, R&D activities, benchmarking, developing of a new glass formula • Late 1980s and early 1990s: stop the project and so the process of creation and accumulation of knowledge • 1996–7: thinking the glass formulation as an embryonic strategic capability

the technology function carried out. Therefore it could have formed the basis for a firm-specific knowledge. However the project was not viewed or managed as a strategic project. The condition of being a firm in a Transition Process and the instability of the dual technology strategy largely contributed to this failure to build any strategic capability in electronic control systems.

Box 10.2 The failure to recognize the potential of the new NNPB technology

In the beginning of the 1980s Vitro-Tec set up a project to reduce the weight of the bottles. There was the opportunity to carry out this technological project in collaboration with Heye Glas. The team undertook benchmark exercises, identified the development from the science side, and met and interacted with Heye Glas as a potential technological partner. VGC was at the knowledge frontier with that potential partner. By 1982 Heye Glas offered to make a joint venture to develop the NNPB technology. However the joint venture for this technological development was not signed. Top management decided not to sign the agreement, the project was stopped and the efforts to create knowledge in this area were significantly reduced. VGC already had the Technical Agreement with Owens-Illinois, and top management was afraid of the reprisals from Owens-Illinois. Additionally the market did not still give signals of requiring a drastic reduction in the weight of the bottles.[41] Top management did not realize the potential of this project to be the base for building a strategic capability and having a technological leadership in this area, or it did not have the purpose to build that strategic capability.

The end of the story was that Heye Glas overtook Owens-Illinois in that technology. By 1986 Owens-Illinois announced Heye Glas to be the leader in the NNPB technology and signed an agreement with Heye Glas to develop this technology further. Owens-Illinois developed the triple cavity model and Heye Glas developed the double cavity model. By 1988–9 they separated, each one with its own model.[42] In 1990 VGC acquired the NNPB technology of triple cavity from Owens-Illinois.

Behind the failure to recognize the depth of knowledge in any area was the continuous comparison with the depth of knowledge, level of investment in R&D and number of patents of Owens-Illinois. The evaluation of the R&D activities by the number and impact of patents and by the economic benefits of

---

[41] Interview with the ex-Directors of Vitro-Tec.
[42] Ibid.

these activities, highlighted in Section 10.2.3, is illustrative of this issue. In addition a sort of internal benchmark with the Owens-Illinois based equipment was established in such a way that it reduced the reliability of in-house developments, mainly when they still were at an experimental stage. This fact was made clear by the plants's perception of the low performance of Vitro's electronic control system in relation to the Owens-Illinois's Com-soc, and by the disconnection of the pass-gob sensor – one of its main features – when it was installed at plants. In the case of the glass composition this was revealed by the difficulties encountered in introducing the new glass formula to substitute the formula in use provided by Owens-Illinois, as described in Box 7.2. These issues reveal some of the types of problems that a firm in a Transition Process encounters in trying to build up the knowledge base to build strategic capabilities.

The building of embryonic strategic capabilities described in Section 7.4 and 8.3 did not necessarily result from their having greater or more steady organizational support. Neither was there a clear and persistent discrimination in favor of enhancing the learning process during the Transition Process in these areas. Their emergence and evolution did not follow any clear strategic and long-term plan, as illustrated by the changes in the direction of the knowledge accumulation shown in Table 9.9 and the changes in the support to on-going projects shown in Table 10.5. Whilst it is not unusual that development projects emerge from hidden projects,[43] or as a result of solving problems, VGC failed to recognize their potential and, even when evidence of this potential was clear it did not provide persistent support. Therefore VGC had no clear and persistent purpose towards building strategic capabilities. The more practical areas, such as Job Changes, process engineering and investment project management, received more support over time. However top management failed to identify their potential and their need to be nurtured with R&D activities in order to build strategic capabilities. This failure and the lack of a clear and persistent purpose contribute to explain why the embryonic strategic capabilities did not progress to become strategic capabilities. Those are factors laying behind the instability of the technology strategy.

Similar failures can be detected in many other companies and are described in the SML as constraints to building strategic capabilities.[44] What is specific in the case of VGC is the variability of its approach. In some periods the firm seemed to understand the potential and be focused and in others not. This unstable approach did not favor the building of strategic capabilities.

Since 1994 attempts were made to strategically define 'what to buy and what to develop', based on the existing knowledge base. Electronic control

---

[43] See for instance Augsdorfer (1996).
[44] See for instance Mitchell and Hamilton (1988); Miyazaki (1993); Teece, Pisano and Shuen (1990).

Learning and Knowledge Management in the Firm

systems and glass composition were found to be two areas of embryonic strategic capabilities of VGC and also two of the five areas of potential synergy between the divisions of the Vitro-Group, as highlighted in Section 8.4.1. Hence they were considered strategic areas and efforts were made to strengthen them.[45] The reconsideration of the importance of these areas can be seen as a recognition of the failure of top management in the past to understand the potential of the knowledge accumulated in these areas. Successful building of strategic capabilities in these areas will depend on several issues including the purpose of top management, the effective support to do it and reduction in the instability of the knowledge creation process. These issues seem to have begun to be tackled.

10.4 CONCLUSIONS

This chapter has analyzed the effect of not perceiving knowledge as a system and the instability of the dual technology strategy on knowledge accumulation. The evidence suggests that these two factors have influenced the features of the knowledge management. Therefore they have increased the limited conversion of individual into organizational learning, the differences in learning strategies and the limited coordination, the limited knowledge integration and the instability of the knowledge creation process. This helps to explain the failure of embryonic strategic capabilities to become strategic capabilities and the truncated Transition Process.

1. The lack of internal coherence between all the learning mechanisms and organizational arrangements that affect the learning processes, the failure to perceive the links between the stocks of tacit and codified knowledge, the failure to consider the learning dimension of the innovation related activities and the lack of concern to build strong links between different organizational units reveals that VGC had no systemic view of learning as referred by Leonard-Barton (1992b), Garvin (1993) or Teece and Pisano (1994). This affected the conversion of individual into organizational learning, the coordination of learning, the knowledge integration and the knowledge creation process.

2. The failure to consider knowledge as a system has resulted in several learning mechanisms being used more as unrelated sources of knowledge than as learning. Learning processes require the interrelationship of mechanisms, organizational arrangements and practices. Moreover they require that specific efforts be carried out to

---

[45] Interview with the Directors of Dirtec and Ditac.

fit what is learned with existing ways of doing things and the existing knowledge base. Such efforts were rarely undertaken.

3. The evolution of the knowledge creation process has been affected by the perception of the R&D activities only as generators of innovations. Although the learning resulting from R&D activities seems to be more important than the innovations and patents granted, the effect of not considering knowledge as a system contributes to explaining why this positive effect of the R&D activities was not perceived by top management. That view, in conjunction with the difficulty of presenting R&D activities as a valuable investment, meant that R&D activities were very vulnerable to changes in support from top management and to the instability of the technology strategy.

4. The building up of strategic capabilities requires a long-term commitment and steady support. The successful building of technological capabilities experienced by firms from catching up countries was based on a consistent and persistent technology strategy over a considerable period of time. However the technology strategy of VGC was dual, unrelated and basically unstable. There was neither a clear and persistent purpose to build strategic capabilities nor to be a fast follower.

5. The duality of the technology strategy set different priorities, aims and practices; gave different messages; brought different learning strategies and promoted different directions of the knowledge accumulation. It put pressure on the work of Dirtec's, Fama's and the plants's personnel and reduced the effectiveness of each strategy.

6. The instability of the dual technology strategy provoked changes in the focus of knowledge management between creating new knowledge or utilizing and changing existing knowledge, in the relative importance of each organizational unit in the knowledge accumulation process and in the aims of each unit to build specific abilities. It generated continuous start-up and halting of on-going projects, and changed the intensity of the effort to accumulate in each direction, modifying the main directions of the knowledge accumulation. This instability is another reason why there was no consistent and persistent knowledge accumulation in the main directions, which limited the potentiality to convert the embryonic strategic capabilities in strategic capabilities and complete the Transition Process.

11 Conclusions

Technological capability building is an issue that has been widely discussed in the last 20 years by two different theoretical traditions based on firm-level empirical research. The first is the tradition of research on technological capability accumulation in industrial firms in developing countries (see for instance Dahlman and Westphal, 1982; Bell, 1984; Westphal, Kim and Dahlman, 1985, Katz, 1986 and 1987; Lall, 1987 and 1992; and Bell and Pavitt, 1995). This tradition has concentrated on the learning processes involved in building up the minimum essential base of knowledge to engage in innovative activity. The second tradition is the strategic management literature about building core capabilities or competencies in firms at the international frontier in advanced industrial countries (see for instance Prahalad and Hamel, 1990; Teece, Pisano and Shuen, 1990; Pavitt, 1991; and Leonard-Barton, 1995a). This literature has paid attention to the management of strategic knowledge assets in order to maintain, nurture and re-build strategic capabilities.

However firms like Vitro-Glass Containers that have already built the minimum essential knowledge base, developed a number of embryonic strategic capabilities but have not yet built strategic capabilities are not considered by those bodies of literature. Although at the top of the DCL's firms in terms of technological capabilities, they have not yet built any strategic capabilities. Therefore they have not arrived at the stage that the SML uses as a point of departure. Firms at that stage of accumulation do not fit in with the problems raised by either body of literature. On the one side, the DCL is centered on the technical dimensions of technological capability building and has paid inadequate attention to two issues: (i) the organizational and managerial aspects of this process; and (ii) the later stage of accumulation as firms approach the international technological frontier and seek to build the more complex and integrated knowledge bases needed to make strategic use of that knowledge. On the other side, the SML has given considerable attention to organizational issues, but with reference to knowledge management in moving from simple to complex knowledge bases in order to maintain, nurture and re-build the existing strategic capabilities. However this body of literature has virtually ignored how those strategic capabilities were initially accumulated.

The central aim of this book has been to examine the characteristics of the Transition Process from building the minimum essential knowledge to building strategic capabilities at the firm level. The central argument is that there is no simple linear progression from the early stage of accumulation of the minimum essential knowledge base to the management of knowledge as a strategic asset. Instead there is a complex Transition Process as firms build embryonic strategic capabilities on top of those minimum levels and then stretch beyond these to develop strategic capabilities. As they make this transition they have to build up deeper and broader stocks of knowledge and develop new types of knowledge management. Both the technological knowledge and the organizational dimensions are crucial to the completion of the Transition Process and building of strategic capabilities. This Transition Process is a barely explored issue between the two theoretical traditions mentioned above.

This book has addressed three research questions through a case-study of VGC at firm level.

1. What are the key issues of knowledge management in each stage of the technological capability building?
2. More specifically: What are the problems of the Transition Process? Why was the firm able to build innovative capabilities but not a set of strategic capabilities?
3. What are the factors that influenced the features of knowledge management during the Transition Process?

These research questions are reviewed in Sections 11.1 to 11.3. Finally Section 11.4 briefly outlines issues which were not broadly analyzed in this book and additional research questions that were not focused in this work but that deserve to become the subject of future research.

11.1 KEY ISSUES OF KNOWLEDGE MANAGEMENT IN DIFFERENT STAGES OF TECHNOLOGICAL CAPABILITY BUILDING

This book differentiated three stages of technological capability building. First, building the minimum essential knowledge base is the stage of accumulation where the firm enhances its technological capabilities in order to keep down costs, improve quality and upgrade the equipment to achieve parity with competitors. This stage is characterized by the accumulation of routine production capabilities, basic to intermediate innovative technological capabilities and simple knowledge bases. Second, the Transition Process was defined as a stage of accumulation from building the minimum essential knowledge base to building strategic capabilities to distinguish the firm competitively. This stage is characterized by the accumulation of intermediate to advanced innovative technological capabilities and embryonic strategic capabilities in a number of technical-functions, technical areas or knowledge fields based still on simple knowledge bases. Third, building strategic capabilities was defined as a stage of accumulation where the firm has advanced innovative technological capabilities in all the technical-functions and has already built a number of strategic capabilities that distinguish the firm competitively. These strategic capabilities are based on complex knowledge bases and the firm continually looks to maintaining, nurturing and renewing them.

The key issues of knowledge management are different in each stage. This book analyzed the first two stages of accumulation. The VGC case revealed that knowledge sharing and codification were key issues in managing knowledge in order to contribute to the knowledge accumulation process necessary to build the minimum essential knowledge base, as described in Chapter 6. At times, when the type of innovation activities undertaken required an extensive knowledge sharing, more effort was put on setting mechanisms to achieve this. In contrast, however, less effort was put on codifying the codifiable tacit knowledge and in making effective use of existing codified knowledge.

During the Transition Process VGC established a more formal organization of the technology function. Internal sources of knowledge became more important, particularly R&D activities, including applied research, product and process development activities, and minor improvement and adaptation activities. During the evolution of this Transition Process VGC was able to gradually undertake activities involving a higher degree of innovativeness, combining different knowledge bases and contributing to the building of more complex ones. It was able to build up embryonic strategic capabilities in electronic control systems, glass composition, process engineering, job changes and investment project management, as described in Chapters 7 and 8. The more formal organization of the technology function and the new innovation activities brought new learning problems, such as the need to integrate different knowledge fields and organizational units and coordinate the learning strategies pursued by different organizational units. Knowledge integration and coordination of learning strategies became key issues of knowledge management along with knowledge sharing and codification.

Certain learning problems occurred in each stage, two of which were particularly relevant: (i) the existence of an uneven depth of knowledge across the firm, and (ii) the identification of a set of organizational factors related to knowledge management that affected the accumulation of technological knowledge. Hence in both stages the technological and organizational dimensions were important to the progress of the accumulation process. The relevance of these organizational factors increases the need for explicit knowledge management. Therefore the focus of the DCL on technological learning and on the accumulation of technological knowledge rather than on the interaction between technological and organizational factors is narrow. Other learning problems, however, were different, in particular knowledge integration and the coordination of learning strategies became major issues in carrying out the Transition Process. Thus these would seem to be key issues in building primarily a strategic capability, an aspect which the SML does not deal with.

In relation to the framework presented by Bell and Pavitt (1995), based on Lall (1992), about the levels of technological capability building, this book provided evidence of the difficulties in classifying a firm by levels. VGC undertook activities of a different innovative nature by technical-function in each stage of accumulation. This case study revealed that it is easier to classify technical-functions than the firm itself. Mastery can be reached over certain technical-functions while in others the knowledge accumulated is much shallower. The VGC case also revealed that even within the same technical-function, the levels of achievement differ between organizational units.

11.2 KNOWLEDGE MANAGEMENT AND THE TRUNCATED TRANSITION PROCESS

The Transition Process that started in the 1970s has been truncated. VGC built embryonic strategic capabilities, as described in Chapters 7 and 8. However it was unable to progress further to create a coherent knowledge base from which to develop strategic capabilities to distinguish the firm competitively. In addition, as analyzed in Chapter 9, the firm suffered uneven depths of knowledge by technical-function, by knowledge field and between organizational units. Even though the existence of unevenness is a fact of organizational life, the level and evolution of the unevenness seem to be a consequence of the firm being in a Transition Process. The type of unevenness across the firm, the building of embryonic strategic capabilities and the failure of these to reach the stage of strategic capabilities are symptoms of the truncated Transition Process.

The research looked at the characteristics of the firm's behavior to identify problems encountered in trying to build strategic capabilities and thus complete the Transition Process. The SML considers that several knowledge management processes are relevant. This book examined four of these processes in detail: the conversion of individual into organizational learning, the coordination of learning, the knowledge integration and the knowledge creation.

Chapter 9 argued that the limited conversion of individual into organizational learning, the existence of different learning strategies and the limited coordination of learning, the limited integration of knowledge across organizational boundaries and the instability of the knowledge creation process are key features of VGC's knowledge management. These features constitute a weakness and are a major reason for the truncated Transition Process.

Limited conversion of individual learning into organizational learning

This feature of the VGC's knowledge management was based on the weaknesses in the process of sharing and codifying knowledge. These weaknesses are associated with the emphasis VGC put on supporting individual learning and its neglect to codify knowledge over the years. The weak knowledge codification exacerbated the limited sharing. Even though the firm established new organizational arrangements in the 1990s to facilitate the sharing and codifying of knowledge, they were not very successful in changing the way of doing things in the firm. Thus the conversion of individual learning into organizational learning was restrained.

The SML has analyzed successful conversions of individual learning into organizational learning (see for instance Senge, 1990; Cohen and Levinthal, 1990; Nonaka and Takeuchi, 1995; and Huber, 1996). However the specific problems that firms confront when they are actually undertaking that conversion were unexplored. The DCL has given very little attention to organizational learning. There has been a broad emphasis on individual learning to accumulate with no account taken of the individual and organizational levels. Kim (1995, 1997a and 1997b) is unique among those authors undertaking empirical work in dealing directly with problems related to organizational learning. However he adopts the same perspective by describing successful cases without dealing with the problems that must be overcome. In contrast this book has focused on the identification and understanding of the problems that need to be overcome rather than on describing successful projects in order to identify the best mechanisms and practices that contribute to success.

The VGC case is illustrative of three particular problems: (i) the lack of concern to codify the codifiable tacit knowledge, a problem which was related to several issues such as the lack of understanding of the importance of codifying, the lack of routines to actually do it, and a scant understanding of the potentially codifiable tacit knowledge; (ii) the difficulty in changing the ways of doing things and adopting new practices of knowledge sharing and codification; and (iii) the existence of different organizational arrangements which affected the learning process and pulled in different directions, and the need to articulate them.

The codification of the codifiable tacit knowledge is a key activity in building the minimum essential knowledge base, strengthening the process of knowledge creation and accelerating the build up of strategic capabilities. However much of the literature related to the nature of knowledge stresses the role of tacit knowledge in the accumulation of strategic capabilities. Tacit knowledge is conceived as a source of distinctiveness and competitiveness (see for instance Nelson and Winter, 1982; Winter, 1987; Teece, Pisano and Shuen, 1990; Teece and Pisano, 1994; and Nonaka and Takeuchi, 1995). The discussion about codification is basically located in relation to the degree of tacitness and codifiedness and the mechanisms used to convert tacit into codified knowledge, but not in terms of a potential lack of codification and the problems that this could bring. The description of VGC presented in the preceding chapters has revealed that even though tacit knowledge was crucial in the building up of both the minimum essential knowledge base and the embryonic strategic capabilities, one of the main stumbling blocks in this process was that this knowledge continued to be essentially tacit. To hold as tacit codifiable tacit knowledge has been the firm's weakness and not a strength. The codification of the codifiable tacit knowledge is a key to facilitate the conversion of individual into organizational learning, increase the knowledge accumulation process and to complete the Transition Process.

Different learning strategies and limited coordination of learning

Different organizational units pursued different learning strategies and learned at different speeds. Hence, they created and accumulated knowledge of a different nature and depth in each knowledge field, technical area and technical-function. The limited coordination of these different learning strategies affected the building of strategic capabilities.

According to the SML differences within a firm are purposely promoted and strategic capabilities have to be strengthened in relation to other non-strategic capabilities. However the problem of how to maintain an equilibrium between these areas of knowledge in order to be able to integrate knowledge and build strategic capabilities is not made clear. In addition the existence of distinct learning strategies within a firm is an issue that is barely touched on. The focus of this book has been on the problems of coordinating the learning when there are differences in learning strategies between organizational units.

The existence of different learning strategies between the organizational units in VGC was associated with the knowledge specialization process and the different business and technology strategies pursued by the divisions to which these units belonged. The limited coordination of learning left the learning strategies pursued by the units to be basically driven by the divisions. This weakened the efforts to build strategic capabilities which required coordination of the learning activities and integration of the knowledge across organizational boundaries.

Limited integration of knowledge across organizational boundaries

VGC experienced difficulties in integrating the knowledge internally across business-function, plant and department; it also found it difficult to integrate knowledge with other divisions of the Vitro-Group to look for potential synergy. There were some instances of knowledge integration but these were not sufficient to change practices. The limited knowledge integration was associated with the weak bridges between units, the minimal efforts made by the firm to build and strengthen these bridges, and the close relationship the firm established between knowledge integration and the creation of new knowledge at the international frontier.

The SML points out that the building of strategic capabilities is based on the ability to create new knowledge and integrate it with the existing knowledge base to develop strategic assets. The VGC reveals that knowledge integration processes are also required to utilize, adapt and change existing knowledge.

Instability of the knowledge creation process

VGC accumulated knowledge in certain areas and also built a number of embryonic strategic capabilities. However the directions of the knowledge accumulation and the intensity of the efforts to create knowledge in each area changed several times. This resulted in a highly unstable knowledge creation process in each area, which affected the accumulation in a specific direction and reduced the potentiality to build strategic capabilities.

The instability of the knowledge creation process in the main areas of accumulation was related to the lack of purpose to build strategic capabilities and the instability of the dual technology strategy pursued by the firm. The instability of the knowledge creation process was higher in glass composition and electronic control systems – two embryonic strategic capabilities closely related to more formal R&D activities. This instability also affected the accumulation in other more practically based embryonic strategic capabilities, which could have been nurtured as a by-product of that process.

11.3 FACTORS INFLUENCING THE KNOWLEDGE MANAGEMENT

This research looked at certain factors that influenced the features of knowledge management and contributed to their limited and unstable nature. This book has examined in detail two factors: the failure to consider the firm's knowledge as a system and the instability of the firm's dual technology strategy. As analyzed in Chapter 10, these factors furthered the difficulties to build strategic capabilities and complete the Transition Process.

The failure to consider the firm's knowledge as a system

VGC lacked a systemic view to articulate several aspects related to the knowledge system, such as learning mechanisms, a wide range of organizational arrangements, stocks of tacit and codified knowledge, and on-going learning processes within the firm. The lack of interrelatedness also occurred at the level of the organizational units, which operated quite independently of one another. Even at times when the firm made more consistent efforts to manage knowledge explicitly to build strategic capabilities, it encountered difficulties in achieving the expected results. Several isolated learning mechanisms, organizational arrangements and processes were established without being coordinated with one another. As a result the firm did not take into account either the differences between the individual and organizational dimensions of the learning processes or the differences in the knowledge depths and learning strategies of different organizational units. VGC did not recognize the importance of strong links between different organizational units and did not perceive the learning dimension of the R&D activities. All this weakened the knowledge creation process.

The SML introduced the idea of adopting a 'system thinking' for managing the knowledge. Several authors look at the firm as a knowledge system, which comprises a set of interdependent but interrelated dimensions (see for instance Senge, 1990; Leonard-Barton, 1992a, 1992b and 1995a; and Porter, 1996). Such a knowledge system constitutes the basis for a learning organization, developing competitive advantages or building strategic capabilities. This book adopted that idea and examined in detail certain problems that the firm faced in managing knowledge without that system thinking approach, for instance the contradictory effects of several learning mechanisms and organizational arrangements, and the failure to consider the learning dimension of several technology related activities.

That SML recognizes that mechanisms, activities, values and ways of doing things are interrelated and operate as a system so that isolated actions introduced in other knowledge systems may never produce the same result. However normative recommendations are derived from successful knowledge systems that operate in some companies and are suggested to be introduced in other companies. The VGC case illustrates that these normative recommendations are not necessarily adequate when applied to a different knowledge system. Problems emerged in VGC over establishing new ways of doing things brought from outside, and fitting in new mechanisms and practices with current ones. Other problems were generated from imbalances when introducing new organizational arrangements. Therefore the general issue of adopting a way of system thinking seems to be more relevant than normative recommendations related to specific mechanisms, activities, values and ways of doing things.

Instability of the firm's dual technology strategy

VGC pursued two technology strategies in parallel. It sought to rely on its innovative technological capabilities to be at the international technological frontier in certain areas and, at the same time, pursued a fast follower strategy. Both strategies were supported by decisions taken by the top management and received organizational support. However the organizational support for each strategy was unstable over the whole period, which affected the aims and efforts to manage the company's knowledge, furthering the difficulties to build strategic capabilities and complete the Transition Process.

The SML is centered on the experiences of the large and innovative firms and has analyzed technology strategies to build strategic capabilities. The DCL, concerned with the successful building of technological capabilities experienced by firms from catching up countries, has highlighted the consistent and persistent technology strategy pursued by those firms over a considerable period of time. Neither body of literature has considered the restrictions on developing strategic capabilities associated with having either a dual technology strategy or an unstable technology strategy, as was the case in VGC.

Several factors lay behind the duality and instability of the technology strategy. First, the Transition Process has two poles, keeping the minimum essential knowledge base and building strategic capabilities, and VGC took decisions directed towards these different poles. Second, there was the failure of top management to recognize the depth of knowledge reached in any area. This was exacerbated by the continuous comparison with the depth of knowledge, level of investment in R&D and number of patents of the technology source. Third, top management failed to identify the potential of certain embryonic strategic capabilities to develop to become strategic knowledge assets to distinguish the firm competitively, and the need to nurture them with R&D activities in order to reach that stage. This failure and the lack of a clear and persistent purpose contribute to explaining why the embryonic strategic capabilities did not progress to become strategic capabilities.

Laying behind the instability of the technology strategy there were other factors, such as power conflicts inside the Vitro-Group and a turbulent macroeconomics context, particularly during the Transition Process. These factors also contributed to explain the changes in the support of each strategy. In this book these factors were considered but not examined in detail.

All these issues reveal some of the types of problems that a firm in a Transition Process encounters in trying to build up the knowledge base to build strategic capabilities.

11.4 SUGGESTIONS FOR FUTURE RESEARCH

This book has argued that the Transition Process is complex. During this transition the firm has to build up deeper and broader stocks of knowledge and develop new types of knowledge management. The VGC case illustrates that the limited nature of several knowledge management processes constituted a major reason for its truncated Transition Process. The lack of recognition that knowledge was a system and the instability of the dual technology strategy added to this weakness.

The main strength of this book is the depth of the single-case study. However the single-case study prevent any broad generalizations for theory or policy. Nevertheless it does raise a large number of lines for further research, which are briefly outlined below.

Research issues

The problems VGC confronted in building strategic capabilities and making the Transition Process are certainly not exclusive to this firm. Some problems could be related to the culture of the firm, but many others are specific to the developing country context and can certainly be found in several Latin American firms that are world level players. Yet other problems can be extracted from the literature on knowledge management about the largest and most innovative companies in the world. Further research is required to discriminate the specific from the general problems.

This book analyzed in detail the internal knowledge management process which is derived from the literature on knowledge management, and related this process to the story of long-term accumulation, which characterizes the DCL. The knowledge management processes and other aspects of the Transition Process need to be much better understood if the insights of research on strategic management in advanced countries, or on technological learning in developing countries, are to be useful for firms in such a Transition Process and therefore in the late stages of 'catching up'. In particular the SML should bring light to the building of the primary strategic capabilities, along with the detailed description of how problems were overcome, including the failures during that process. DCL should relate deeply the technological and organizational dimensions of the capability building process, and analyze also firms that are in such a Transition Process.

The research has shed some light on the capabilities that matter when the firm is building the first strategic capabilities. The VGC case suggests that a firm's capability for learning at the organizational level, coordinating learning and integrating knowledge across organizational boundaries is a capability that matters in building the primary strategic capabilities and completing the Transition Process. However it was beyond the scope of this research to go into great depth in identifying the capabilities that are significant and how the firm might build them. Future research in this area could yield an important contribution to the long-term process of strategic capability building.

Unevenness in the depth of knowledge between technical-functions and organizational units was identified as a symptom of the Transition Process. It seems that uneven stocks of knowledge have contributed to making the coordination of the learning strategies and the knowledge integration process more difficult. Therefore lack of knowledge along with problems in the knowledge management would lie behind the difficulty to build strategic capabilities. This book on its own does not produce evidence about the relationship between unevenness, the features of the knowledge management and the Transition Process. Nonetheless interesting questions which might be pursued in future research are: (i) To what extent the uneven knowledge depth between technical-functions and organizational units makes it difficult to coordinate the learning and to integrate knowledge across different firm's boundaries, (ii) To what extent the lack of knowledge impedes the building of strategic capabilities, and (iii) What is the relationship between type of unevenness and the building of strategic capabilities.

The research identified certain difficulties the firm observed in changing the way of doing things and achieving a fit between old and new practices. This issue is behind the limited nature of the knowledge management features. However it was beyond the scope of this research to identify the specific conditions that hampered the introduction of new practices, and the problems associated with fitting what was learned with existing ways of doing things and the existing knowledge base. Research into these matters, possibly through in-depth cases studies, could contribute to the understandings of these issues.

The VGC case suggests that a system thinking approach to knowledge management could help to overcome several of its problems. Such an approach should tackle explicitly the uneven depths of knowledge within the firm, the existence of differences between learning strategies pursued by organizational units, and the contradictory impacts of different learning mechanisms and organizational arrangements. The knowledge management should consider different dimensions, such as the establishment of specific organizational arrangements, the articulation between different subsystems and the fit between the old and new ways of doing things. Even though the VGC case illustrates some of these issues, more research is needed to identify the key aspects of such a system, what are the different effects of certain actions and which aspects must be more closely related.

The small dimension and instability of the R&D activities were associated with the lack of recognition of their learning role and the instability of the technology strategy. This seems to be behind the difficulties the firm had in making efficient use of external sources of knowledge, learning from internal sources, systematically analyzing internal and external experiences and fitting them into its own routines and procedures, and codifying the codifiable tacit knowledge. However it is not clear to what extent the characteristics of the R&D activities affected those activities, and how much in-house R&D is required to acquire the learning capabilities of this activity. These issues require further research.

This book reveals that knowledge codification is a key issue in two stages, when building the minimum essential knowledge base and during the Transition Process. The VGC case suggests that firms during these stages have to: (i) distinguish between rigorously tacit knowledge and codifiable tacit knowledge, (ii) codify the codifiable tacit knowledge, and (iii) establish organizational arrangements to access to the organizational memory. The balance and combination of tacit and codified knowledge seems to be a more important issue than to stress only that tacit knowledge is the source of firm's distinctiveness, as the SML does. However it is not clear empirically either, What knowledge must be codified?, or What is the relationship between tacit and codified knowledge? Even though these questions emerge from the evidence presented so far, the answers require further research.

Research strategy

This book provides insights into the difficulties to access the actual ways of doing things in a firm and the differences between what managers say (and probably believe) happens, and the actual way that things are done. The mix of old and new practices in the firm made the evaluation of the firm's behavior difficult. As described in Chapter 9, although a short visit to the firm revealed the type of learning mechanisms formally used and the established organizational arrangements, a very detailed analysis was required to obtain an understanding of how they actually worked. This evidence has a methodological impact in terms of reliance on the information obtained from managers in the course of short visits. Therefore when defining the research strategy it is important to consider questions such as: (i) To what extent do interviews with managers or high level technical staff allow the researcher to identify how things are actually being done?, (ii) How long does a visit to a company need to be in order to understand what is really going on?, and (iii) How much narrower does the focus have to be if there is only a short time available?

Bibliography

Aboites, J. and M. Soria (1999), *Innovación: propiedad intelectual y estrategias tecnológicas*, México: Miguel Angel Porrúa/UAM-X.

Alchian, A. and H. Demsetz (1972), 'Production, Information Costs and Economic Organization', *American Economic Review*, no. 62, pp. 777–95.

Amsden, A.H. (1989), *Asia's Next Giant: South Korea and Late Industrialisation*, New York: Oxford University Press.

Aoki, M. (1986), 'Horizontal vs. Vertical Information Structure of the Firm', *American Economic Review*, Vol. 76, no. 5, pp. 971–83.

Argyris, C. and D.A. Schön (1978), *Organizational Learning: a Theory of Action Perspective*, Reading, MA: Addison-Wesley.

Arrow, K. (1962), 'The Economic Implications of Learning by Doing', *Review of Economic Studies*, Vol. 29, no. 80, pp. 155–73.

—— (1974), *The Limits of Organization*, New York: W.W. Norton & Co.

Arundel, A., Gert van de Paal and L. Soete (1995), 'Innovation Strategies of Europe's Largest Industrial Firms (PACE Report)', Maastricht: MERIT, University of Limburg.

Augsdorfer, P. (1996), 'Bootlegging', DPhil Thesis, SPRU, University of Sussex.

Bell, M. (1984), 'Learning' and the Accumulation of Industrial Technological Capacity in Developing Countries', in K. King and M. Fransman (eds), *Technological Capacity in the Third World*, London: Macmillan, pp. 187–209.

Bell, M., B. Ross-Larson and L.E. Westphal (1984), 'Assessing the Performance of Infant Industries', *Journal of Development Economics*, Vol. 16, nos. 1–2, pp. 101–28.

Bell, M. and K. Pavitt (1993), 'Technological Accumulation and Industrial Growth: Contrasts Between Developed and Developing Countries', *Industrial and Corporate Change*, Vol. 2, no. 2, pp. 157–210.

—— (1995), 'The Development of Technological Capabilities', in I.u. Haque (ed.), *Trade, Technology and International Competitiveness*, Washington: The World Bank, pp. 69–101.

Capdevielle, M., M. Cimoli and G. Dutrénit (1997), 'Specialization and Technology in Mexico: a Virtual Pattern of Development and Competitiveness?', Interim Report IR–97–016/May, Laxenburg: IIASA.

Casalet, M. (1994), 'La Formación Profesional y Técnica en México', *Comercio Exterior*, Vol. 44, no. 8, pp. 725–33.

Casar, J.I. (1989), *Transformación en el Patrón de Especialización y Comercio Exterior del Sector Manufacturero Mexicano. 1978–1987*, Ensayos e Investigaciones Sobre el Desarrollo Industrial de México, Mexico: Nacional Financiera/ILET.

—— (1994), 'El Sector Manufacturero y la Cuenta Corriente. Evolución Reciente y Perspectivas', in F. Clavijo and J.I. Casar (eds), *La Industria Mexicana en el Mercado Mundial*, Lecturas El Trimestre Económico no. 80, Mexico: FCE, pp. 309–83.

CATVE (1989), 'Documento Informativo: Proceso de Fabricación de Envases de Vidrio', Monterrey, Vitro Envases, Vitro S.A.

—— (1995), 'Documento Informativo: Máquinas Formadoras de Envases', Monterrey, Vitro Envases, Vitro S.A.

CEPAL (1995), 'Análisis de la Competitividad de las Naciones, Versión 2.0.', Manual de Uso, CEPAL, Santiago de Chile.

Chandler, A.D. (1990), *Scale and Scope: the Dynamics of Industrial Capitalism*, Cambridge, MA: Belknap Press.

Chudnovski, D. (1996) '¿Aprendizaje o Innovación?', Paper presented at the Aprendizaje Tecnológico, Innovación y Política Industrial: Experiencias Nacionales e Internacionales, Mexico City.

Clark, K.B. and T. Fujimoto (1991), *Product Development Performance*, Boston, Ma: Harvard Business School Press.

Clavijo, F. and J. Casar (eds) (1994), *La Industria Mexicana en el Mercado Mundial: Elementos para una Política Industrial*, 2 vols, Lecturas El Trimestre Económico no. 80, México: FCE.

Coase, R.H. (1937), 'The Nature of the Firm', *Economica*, no. 4, pp. 386–405.

Cohen, W.M. and D.A. Levinthal (1989), 'Innovation and Learning: the Two Faces of R&D', *The Economic Journal*, no. 99 (September), pp. 569–96.

—— (1990), 'Absorptive Capacity: a New Perspective on Learning and Innovation', *Administrative Sciences Quarterly*, Vol. 35, no. 1, pp. 128–52.

Cohen, M.D. and L.S. Sproull (eds) (1996), *Organizational Learning*, California: Sage Publications.

Coombs, R. (1996), 'Core Competencies and the Strategic Management of R&D', *R&D Management*, Vol. 26, no. 4, pp 345–55.

Cooper, R. (1988), 'The New Product Process: a Decision Guide for Management', *Journal of Marketing Management*, no.3 , pp. 238–55.

Corona, J.M., G. Dutrénit and C.A. Hernández (1994), 'La Interacción Productor-Usuario: una Síntesis del Debate Actual', *Comercio Exterior*, Vol. 44, no. 8, pp. 683–94.

Cowan, R. and D. Foray (1997), 'The Economics of Codification and the Diffusion of Knowledge', *Industrial and Corporate Change*, Vol. 6, no. 3, pp. 595–622.

Dahlman, C. and L.E. Westphal (1982), 'Technological Effort in Industrial Development. An Interpretative Survey of Recent Research', in F. Stewart and J. James (eds), *The Economics of New Technology in Developing Countries*, London: Frances Pinter, pp. 105–37.

Dahlman, C. and J. Fonseca (1987), 'From Technological Dependence to Technological Development: the Case of the USIMINAS Steel Plant in Brazil', in J. Katz (ed.), *Technology Generation in Latin American Manufacturing Industries*, London, Macmillan, pp. 154–82.

Dahlman, C., B. Ross-Larsen and L.E. Westphal (1987), 'Managing Technological Development', *World Development*, Vol. 15, no. 6, pp. 759–75.

Dahlman, C. and C. Frischtak (1993), 'National System Supporting Technical Advance in Industry: The Brazilian Experience', in R. Nelson (ed.), *National Innovation Systems*, New York: Oxford University Press, pp. 414–50.

David, P. and D. Foray (1994), 'Dynamics of Competitive Technology Diffusion through Local Network Structures', in L.A. Leydesdorff and P. Van den Besselaar (eds), *Evolutionary Economics and Chaos Theory: New Directions in Technology Studies*, London: Pinter Publishers, pp. 13–68.

Ditac (1995), 'Compendio de Tecnología sobre Fabricación de Envases de Vidrio a Través de Patentes Norteamericanas. 1970–1995', Monterrey, Vitro SA.

Dodgson, M. (1993), 'Organizational Learning: A Review of Some Literatures', *Organizational Studies*, Vol. 14, no. 3, pp. 375–94.

Donaldson Lufkin & Jenrette Securities (1995), 'Packaging-Industry Report', Sept. 13, Investment Reports Database.

Dosi, G. and L. Marengo (1993), 'Some Elements of an Evolutionary Theory of Organizational Competences', in R.W. England (ed.), *Evolutionary Concepts in Contemporary Economics*, Ann Arbor: University of Michigan Press.

Dosi, G. (1996), 'The Contribution of Economic Theory in the Understanding of a Knowledge-based Economy', in D. Foray and B.A. Lundvall (eds), *Employment and Growth in the Knowledge-based Economy*, Paris: OECD.

Dutrénit, G. and M. Capdevielle (1993), 'El Perfl Tecnológico de la Industria Mexicana y su Dinámica Innovadora en la Década de los Ochenta', *El Trimestre Económico*, Vol. LXI (3), no. 239 (Julio-Septiembre), pp. 643–74.

Enos, J.L. and W.H. Park (1988), _The Adoption and Diffusion of Imported Technology: The Case of Korea_, London: Croom Helm.

Enos, J.L. (1991), _The Creation of Technological Capability in Developing Countries_, London: Pinter Publishers.

Fajnzylber, F. (1990), _De la Caja Negra al Casillero Vacío_, Santiago de Chile: CEPAL.

——— (1991), 'Inserción Internacional e Innovación Institucional', _Revista de la CEPAL_, Vol. 44, no. Agosto, pp. 149–78.

Fama (1993), 'Cinco décadas desarrollando tecnología para la industria', Monterrey, Vitro-S.A.

Fernández, M.A. (1993), _El Vidrio en México_, Monterrey: Centro de Arte Vitro.

Fiol, C.M. and M.A. Lyles (1985), 'Organizational Learning', _Academy of Management Review_, no. 10, pp. 803–13.

Foray, D. and B.A. Lundvall (1996), 'From the Economics of Knowledge to the Learning Economy', in D. Foray and B.A. Lundvall (eds), _Employment and Growth in the Knowledge-based Economy_, Paris: OECD.

Fransman, M. and K. King (eds) (1984), _Indigenous Technological Capability in the Third World_, London: Macmillan.

Fransman, M. (1986), _Technology and Development_, Brighton: Wheatsheaf Books.

——— (1994), 'Information, Knowledge, Vision and Theories of the Firm', _Industrial and Corporate Change_, Vol. 3, no. 3, pp. 713–58.

Freeman, C. (1982), _The Economics of Industrial Innovation_, 2nd edn, London: Pinter Publishers.

Garrido, C. (1998), 'El Liderazgo de las Grandes Empresas Industriales Mexicanas', in W. Péres (ed.), _Grandes Empresas y Grupos Industriales Latinoamericanos_, Mexico: Siglo XXI, pp. 397–472.

Garrido, C. and W. Péres (1998), 'Las Grandes Empresas y Grupos Industriales Latinoamericanos en los años noventa', in W. Péres (ed.), _Grandes Empresas y Grupos Industriales Latinoamericanos_, Mexico: Siglo XXI, pp. 13–80.

Garvin, D.A. (1993), 'Building a Learning Organization', _Harvard Business Review_, Vol. 71, no. 4 (July-August), pp. 78–91.

'Glass: a Clear Vision for a Bright Future' (1996), Representatives of the American Glass Industry, January, US.

Glick, W.H., G.P. Huber, C.C. Miller, D.H. Doty and K.M. Sutcliffe (1995), 'Studying Changes in Organizational Design and Effectiveness: Retrospective Event Histories and Periodic Assessments', in _Longitudinal Field Research Methods_, California: Sage Publications, pp. 126–54.

Grupo Financiero Bancomer (1995), 'Industry Analysis: La Industria Mexicana de Envases de Vidrio', Análisis Sectorial, Mexico DF.

Hedberg, B. (1981), 'How Organizations Learn and Unlearn', in P. Nystrom and W.H. Starbuck (eds), _Handbook of Organizational Design_, New York: Oxford University Press, pp. 3–27.

Henderson, R.M. (1994), 'The Evolution of Integrative Capability: Innovation in Cardiovascular Drug Discovery', *Industrial and Corporate Change*, Vol. 3, no. 3, pp. 607–30.

Herbert-Copley, B. (1990), 'Technical Change in Latin American Manufacturing Firms: Review and Synthesis', *World Development*, Vol. 18, no. 11, pp. 1457–69.

Hobday, M. (1995), *Innovation in East Asia. The Challenge to Japan*, Aldershot, UK and Brookfield, US: Edward Elgar.

Huber, G.P. (1996), 'Organizational Learning: the Contributing Processes and the Literatures', in M.D. Cohen and L.S. Sproull (eds), *Organizational Learning*, California: Sage Publications, pp. 124–62.

Iansiti, M. and K. Clark (1994), 'Integration and Dynamic Capability: Evidence from Product Development in Automobiles and Mainframe Computers', *Industrial and Corporate Change*, Vol. 3, no. 3, pp. 557–605.

Iansiti, M. (1998), *Technology Integration*, Boston, MA: Harvard Business School Press.

Katz, J. (1984), 'Domestic Technological Innovations and Dynamic Comparative Advantage: Further Reflections on a Comparative Case-Study Program', *Journal of Development Studies*, Vol. 16, nos. 1–2, pp. 13–38.

—— (ed.) (1986), *Desarrollo y Crisis de la Capacidad Tecnológica Latinoamericana*, Buenos Aires: BID-CEPAL-CIID-PNUD.

—— (ed.) (1987), *Technology Generation in Latin American Manufacturing Industries*, London: Macmillan.

—— (1995) 'Technology and Industrial Restructuring in Latin America: the New Evidence', Paper presented at the Transfer of Technology, Trade and Development, University of Venice.

—— (ed.) (1996), *Estabilización Macroeconómica, Reforma Estructural y Comportamiento Industrial: Estructura y Funcionamiento del Sector Manufacturero Latinoamericano en los anos 90*, Buenos Aires: CEPAL/ IDRC/Alianza Editorial.

Katz, J. and E. Ablin (1978), 'From Infant Industry to Technology Exports: the Argentine Experience in the International Sale of Industrial Plants and Engineering Works', Working Paper 14, Buenos Aires: IDB-ECLA.

Katz, J. and N. Bercovich (1993), 'National System of Innovation Supporting Technical Advance in Industry: The Case of Argentina', in R. Nelson (ed.), *National Innovation Systems*, New York: Oxford University Press, pp. 451–75.

Kim, L., J. Lee and J. Lee (1987), 'Korea's Entry into the Computer Industry and its Acquisition of Technological Capability', *Technovation*, no. 6, pp. 277–93.

Kim, L. (1993), 'National System of Industrial Innovation: Dynamics of Capability Building in Korea', in R. Nelson (ed.), *National Innovation Systems*, New York: Oxford University Press, pp. 357–83.

—— (1995), 'Crisis Construction and Organizational Learning: Capability building in Catching-up at Hyundai Motor', Report, October, Seoul: College of Business Administration, Korea University.

—— (1997a), 'The Dynamics of Samsung's Technological Learning in Semiconductors', *California Management Review*, Vol. 39, no. 3 (Spring), pp. 86–100.

—— (1997b), *From Imitation to Innovation. The Dynamics of Korea's Technological Learning*, Boston, MA: Harvard Business School Press.

Lall, S. (1987), *Learning to Industrialize: The Acquisition of Technological Capability by India*, London: Macmillan Press.

—— (1992), 'Technological Capabilities and Industrialization', *World Development*, Vol. 20, no. 2, pp. 165–86.

—— (1993), 'Technological Capabilities', in J.J. Salomon (ed.), *The Uncertain Question: Science, Technology and Development*, pp. 264–301, Tokyo: United Nations University Press.

—— (1995), 'Developing Industrial Technology: Lessons for Policy and Practice', Washington: The World Bank.

Lara, A. (1994), 'Competitividad y Aprendizaje Tecnológico en el Sector de la Electrónica de Consumo', *Comercio Exterior*, Vol. 44, no. 9, pp. 770–79.

Lawrence, P.R. and J.W. Lorsch (1967), *Organization and Environment*, Boston, MA: Harvard Business School Press.

Leonard-Barton, D. (1992a), 'Core Capabilities and Core Rigidities: a Paradox in Managing New Product Development', *Strategic Management Journal*, no. 13, pp. 111–25.

—— (1992b), 'The Factory as a Learning Laboratory', *Sloan Management Review*, Vol. 34, no. 1 (Fall), pp. 23–38.

—— (1995a), *Wellsprings of Knowledge*, Boston, MA: Harvard Business School Press.

—— (1995b), 'A Dual Methodology for Cases Studies', in G. Huber and A.H. Van de Ven (eds), *Longitudinal Field Research Methods*, pp. 38–64, California: Sage Publications.

Leonard, D. and S. Sensiper (1998), 'The Role of Tacit Knowledge in Group Innovation', *California Management Review*, Vol. 40, no. 3 (Spring), pp. 112–32.

Levin, R., A. Klevorick, R. Nelson and S. Winter (1987), 'Appropriating the Returns from Industrial Research and Development', *Brookings Papers on Economic Activity*, Vol. 3, pp. 783–820.

Levitt, B. and J. March (1988), 'Organizational Learning', *Annual Review of Sociology*, Vol. 14, pp. 319–40.

Lundvall, B.A. (1988), 'Innovation as an Interactive Process: from User-Producer Interaction to the National System of Innovation', in G. Dosi, C.

Freeman, R. Nelson, G. Silverberg and L. Soete (eds), *Technical Change and Economic Theory*, New York: Columbia University Press.

—— (ed.) (1992), *National Systems of Innovation. Towards a Theory of Innovation and Interactive Learning*, London: Pinter Publishers.

March, J.G. and H. Simon (1958), *Organizations*, New York: Wiley.

Marengo, L. (1991), 'Knowledge, Coordination and Learning in an Adaptive Model of the Firm', DPhil Thesis, SPRU, University of Sussex.

—— (1992), 'Coordination and Organizational Learning in the Firm', *Journal of Evolutionary Economics*, no. 2, pp. 313–26.

Meigh, E. (1960), 'The Development of the Automatic Glass Bottle Machine', *Glass Technology*, Vol. 1, no. 1 (February), pp. 25–50.

—— (1972), *The Story of the Glass Bottle*, England: Ramsden & Co. Ltd.

Mitchell, G. (1986), 'New Approaches for the Strategic Management of Technology', in M. Horwitch (ed.), *Technology in the Modern Corporation, a Strategic Perspective*, New York: Pergamon, pp. 132–44.

Mitchell, G. and W. Hamilton (1988), 'Managing R&D as a Strategic Option', *Research Technology Management*, Vol. 31, no. 3 (May–June), pp. 15–22.

Miyazaki, K. (1993), 'The dynamics of competence building in European and Japanese firms: the case of optoelectronics', DPhil Thesis, SPRU, University of Sussex.

—— (1994), 'Search, Learning and Accumulation of Technological Competencies: the Case of Optoelectronics', *Industrial and Corporate Change*, Vol. 3, no. 3, pp. 631–54.

Morgan Stanley & Co. Inc. (1994), 'Vitro-Company Report', Nov. 22, Investment Reports Database.

Morgan Stanley & Co. Inc. (1995), 'Owens-Illinois-Company Report', Sept. 14, Investment Reports Database.

Nakaoka, T. (1993), 'Technological Capability Building in Developing Countries and Japan's Technological Cooperation', *Technology and Development*, Vol. 6.

Nelson, R. (1991), 'The Role of Firm Differences in an Evolutionary Theory of Technical Advance', *Science and Public Policy*, Vol. 18, no. 6, pp. 347–52.

—— 'Economic Growth via the Co-evolution of Technology and Institutions', in L.A. Leydesdorff and P. Van den Besselaar (eds), *Evolutionary Economics and Chaos Theory: New Directions in Technology Studies*, London: Pinter Publishers.

Nelson, R. and S. Winter (1982), *An Evolutionary Theory of Economic Change*, Cambridge, MA: Harvard University Press.

Nichols, N.A. (1993), 'From Complacency to Competitiveness: an Interview with Vitro's Ernesto Martens', *Harvard Business Review*, Vol. 71, no. 5 (September–October), pp. 163–68.

Nightingale, P. (1997), 'Knowledge and Technical Change: Computer Simulation and the Changing Innovation Process', DPhil Thesis, SPRU, University of Sussex.

Nonaka, I. (1994), 'A Dynamic Theory of Organizational Knowledge Creation', *Organization Science*, Vol. 5, no. 1, pp. 14–37.

Nonaka, I. and H. Takeuchi (1995), *The Knowledge-Creating Company*, New York: Oxford University Press.

Nonaka, I. and N. Konno (1998), 'The Concept of "Ba": Building a Foundation for Knowledge Creation', *California Management Review*, Vol. 40, no. 3 (Spring), pp. 40–54.

Pack, H. (1992), 'Learning and Productivity Change in Developing Countries', in G.K. Helleiner (ed.), *Trade Policy, Industrialization and Development: New Perspectives*, Oxford: Clarendon Press.

Papadopoulos, J.A. (1990), 'The European Glass Container Industry', Msc Thesis, The Management School, Imperial College of Science, Technology and Medicine.

Patel, P. and K. Pavitt (1994), 'Technological Competencies in the World's Largest Firms: Characteristics, Constraints and Scope for Managerial Choice', STEEP Discussion Paper no. 13, May, Brighton: SPRU.

Pavitt, K. (1984), 'Sectoral Patterns of Technical Change: Towards a Taxonomy and a Theory', *Research Policy*, Vol. 13, no. 9, pp. 343–73.

—— 'Key Characteristics of the Large Innovating Firms', *British Journal of Management*, Vol. 2, pp. 41–50.

—— 'Technologies, Products and Organisation in the Innovating Firms: What Adam Smith Tells Us and Joseph Schumpeter Doesn't', *Industrial and Corporate Change*, forthcoming.

Penrose, E. (1959), *The Theory of the Growth of the Firm*, Oxford: Basil Blackwell.

Péres, W. (ed.) (1997), *Políticas de Competitividad Industrial*, Mexico: Siglo XXI.

Pérez, C. (1992), 'Cambio Técnico, Restructuración Competitiva y Reforma Institucional en los Países en Desarrollo', *El Trimestre Económico*, Vol. LIX, no. 233 (enero-marzo), pp. 23–64.

—— 'La Modernización Industrial en América Latina y la Herencia de la Sustitución de Importaciones', *Comercio Exterior*, Vol. 46, no. 5, pp. 347–63.

Pirela, A., R. Rengifo, R. Arvanitis and A. Mercado (1991), *Conducta Empresarial y Cultura Tecnológica. Empresas y Centros de Investigación en Venezuela*, Caracas: Ediciones del CENDES.

—— (1993), 'Technological Learning and Entrepreneurial Behaviour: a Taxonomy of the Chemical Industry in Venezuela', *Research Policy*, Vol. 22, no. 5, pp. 431–53.

Pirela, A. (ed.) (1996), *Cultura Empresarial en Venezuela*, Caracas: Fundación Polar-CENDES.

Pisano, G.P. (1997), *The Development Factory*, Boston, MA: Harvard Business School Press.

Polanyi, M. (1962), *Personal Knowledge: Towards a Post-Critical Philosophy*, New York: Harper Torchbooks.

—— (1966), *The Tacit Dimension*, London: Routledge & Kegan Paul.

Porter, M.E. (1985), *Competitive Strategy: Techniques for Analyzing Industries and Competitors*, New York: The Free Press.

—— (1996), 'What is Strategy', *Harvard Business Review*, Vol. 74, no. 6 (November-December), pp. 61–78.

Pozas, M.A. (1993), *Industrial Restructuring in Mexico. Corporate Adaptation, Technological Innovation, and Changing Patterns of Industrial Relations in Monterrey*, Monograph Series no. 38, San Diego: Center for US–Mexican Studies (UCSD)/El Colegio de la Frontera Norte.

Prahalad, C.K. and G. Hamel (1990), 'The Core Competencies of the Corporation', *Harvard Business Review*, Vol. 68, no. 3 (May-June), pp. 79–91.

Rosenberg, N. (1976), *Perspectives on Technology*, Cambridge, UK: Cambridge University Press.

Rothwell, R. (1977), 'The Characteristics of Successful Innovators and Technically Progressive Firms', *R&D Management*, Vol. 7, pp. 191–206.

Sada, R.G. (1981), *Ensayos sobre la historia de una Industria*, Monterrey: Litográficos Monterrey S.A.

Scott-Kemmis, D. and M. Bell (1985), 'Technological Capacity and Technical Change: Case Studies', Report on a Study of Technology Transfer in Manufacturing Industry in Thailand, Working Paper, Brighton: SPRU.

Senge, P.M. (1990), *The Fifth Discipline*, New York: Doubleday.

Senker, J. (1995), 'Tacit Knowledge and Models of Innovation', *Industry and Corporate Change*, Vol. 4, no. 2, pp. 425–47.

—— (1959), 'Theories of Decision Making in Economics', *American Economic Review*, Vol. 49, pp. 253–83.

Simon, H.A. (1996), 'Bounded Rationality and Organizational Learning', in M.D. Cohen and L.S. Sproull (eds), *Organizational Learning*, California: Sage Publications, pp. 175–87.

Teece, D.J. (1976), 'Vertical Integration and Vertical Divestiture in the US Petroleum Industry', Stanford: Institute for Energy Studies.

—— (1986), 'Profiting from Technological Innovation: Implications for Integrating, Collaborating, Licensing, and Public Policy', *Research Policy*, Vol. 15, no. 6, pp. 285–305.

Teece, D., G. Pisano and A. Shuen (1990), 'Firm Capabilities, Resources and the Concept of Strategy', Working Paper 90–8, Berkeley: Consortium on

Competitiveness and Cooperation, University of California, Center for Research in Management.

Teece, D. and G. Pisano (1994), 'The Dynamic Capabilities of Firms: an Introduction', *Industrial and Corporate Change*, Vol. 3, no. 3, pp. 537–56.

Teece, D., R. Rumelt, G. Dosi and S. Winter (1994), 'Understanding Corporate Coherence: Theory and Evidence', *Journal of Economic Behavior and Organization*, Vol. 23, pp. 1–30.

'The future Lies in Quality Management Systems' (1991), *Glass Industry*, Vol. November, no. 27, p. 16.

Tidd, J., J. Bessant and K. Pavitt (1997), *Managing Innovation: Integrating Technological, Market and Organisational Change*, Chichester: Wiley. (The references are based on the draft version).

Tirado, R. (1994), 'La Innovación Tecnológica en la Industria Informática y las Telecomunicaciones en México', *Comercio Exterior*, Vol. 44, no. 8, pp. 716–24.

Tremblay, P. (1994), 'Comparative Analysis of Technological Capability and Productivity Growth in the Pulp and Paper Industry in Industrialised and Industrialising Countries', DPhil Thesis, SPRU, University of Sussex.

Unger, K. (1985), *Competencia Monopólica y Tecnología en la Industria Mexicana*, Mexico: El Colegio de México.

—— *Ajuste Estructural y Estrategias Empresariales en México. Las Industrias Petroquímica y de Máquinas Herramientas*, Mexico: CIDE.

USITC (1993), 'Industry & Trade Summary: Glass Containers', June, Washington: US International Trade Commission.

Van de Ven, A.H. and G. Huber (1995), 'Introduction', in A.H. Van de Ven and G. Huber (eds), *Longitudinal Field Research Methods*, California: Sage Publications, pp. VII–XIV.

Vera-Cruz, A., J.C. Villa Soto and A. Villegas de Gante (1994), 'El Subsistema Nacional de Innovación en Biotecnología: el Papel de los Centros de Investigación en México', *Comercio Exterior*, Vol. 44, no. 8, pp. 705–15.

Villavicencio, D. (1990), 'La Transferencia de Tecnología: un Problema de Aprendizaje Colectivo', *Argumentos*, no. 10–11, pp. 7–18.

Villavicencio, D. and R. Arvanitis (1994), 'Transferencia de Tecnología y Aprendizaje Tecnológico. Reflexiones Basadas en Trabajos Empíricos', *El Trimestre Económico*, Vol. LXI(2), no. 242 (abril-junio), pp. 257–79.

Vitro S.A. (1981), 'Annual Report', Monterrey: Vitro S.A.

Vitro S.A. (1984), 'Annual Report', Monterrey: Vitro S.A.

Vitro S.A. (1985), 'Annual Report', Monterrey: Vitro S.A.

Vitro S.A. (1986), 'Annual Report', Monterrey: Vitro S.A.

Vitro S.A. (1987), 'Annual Report', Monterrey: Vitro S.A.

Vitro S.A. (1989), 'Annual Report', Monterrey: Vitro S.A.

Vitro S.A. (1990), 'Annual Report', Monterrey: Vitro S.A.

Vitro S.A. (1991), 'Annual Report', Monterrey: Vitro S.A.

Vitro S.A. (1992), 'Annual Report', Monterrey: Vitro S.A.

Vitro S.A. (1993a), 'Annual Report', Monterrey: Vitro S.A.

Vitro S.A. (1993b), 'Employee Annual Report', Monterrey: Vitro S.A.

Vitro S.A. (1993c), 'Folleto de Inducción', Monterrey: Vitro S.A.

Vitro S.A. (1994), 'Annual Report', Monterrey: Vitro S.A.

Vitro S.A. (1995), 'Annual Report', Monterrey: Vitro S.A.

Vitro S.A. (1996a), 'Annual Report', Monterrey: Vitro S.A.

Vitro S.A. (1996b), 'Description of the job positions', edited by Vitro Envases.

Vitro S.A. (1997), 'Annual Report', Monterrey: Vitro S.A.

Vitro S.A. (1998), 'Annual Report', Monterrey: Vitro S.A.

Von Hippel, E. (1988), *The Sources of Innovation*, New York: Oxford University Press.

—— 'Sticky Information and the Locus of Problem Solving: Implications for Innovation', *Management Science*, Vol. 40, no. 4 (April), pp. 429–30.

Von Tunzelmann, G.N. (1995), *Technology and Industrial Progress: the Foundations of Economic Growth*, Aldershot, UK and Brookfield, US: Edward Elgar.

Westphal, L., L. Kim and C. Dahlman (1985), 'Reflections on the Republic of Korea's Acquisition of Technological Capability', in N. Rosenberg and C. Frischtak (eds), *International Technology Transfer*, New York: Praeger Publishers.

Williamson, O. (1975), *Markets and Hierarchies: Analysis and Antitrust Implications*, New York: The Free Press.

—— *The Economic Institutions of Capitalism*, New York: The Free Press.

Winter, S. (1987), 'Knowledge and Competence as Strategic Assets', in D.J. Teece (ed.), *The Competitive Challenge: Strategies for Industrial Innovation and Renewal*, Cambridge, MA: Ballinger, pp. 159–83.

Yin, R.K. (1994), *Case Study Research. Design and Methods*, Second edn, *Applied Social Research Methods Series*, California: Sage Publications.

Index